"This is truly an amazing compilation of inform   ... in New Mexico should be without this book."

—Thomas E. Chavez, PhD
Director of the Palace of the Governors
Author of *An Illustrated History of New Mexico, Quest for Quivera: Spanish Exploration on the Plains 1540–1821,* and *Manuel Álvarez (1794–1856): A Southwestern Biography*

"Enchanted Lifeways tells it all—in a precise way. For the reader who . . . wants to know where the action is."

—Joe Sando
Indian Pueblo Cultural Center
Author of *Pueblo Nations: Eight Centuries of Pueblo History*

"A comprehensive guide for the casual traveler or dedicated sightseer interested in learning about the many cultural resources New Mexico has to offer. This book may also . . . open the eyes of New Mexico residents to what their own neighborhood has to offer."

—Robert J. Torrez
State Historian

"If you want to get a fuller experience of New Mexico—or if you just want to get your bearings—here's the place to start. Think of *Enchanted Lifeways* as a navigational guide to the spirit of the state. Keep it in the glove box for those quick, necessary departures to places you can never know too well or honor too much."

—William de Buys
Author of *Enchantment and Exploitation* and *River of Traps*

ENCHANTED LIFEWAYS

THE HISTORY, MUSEUMS, ARTS & FESTIVALS OF NEW MEXICO

Compiled by the New Mexico Office of Cultural Affairs

FOREWORD BY JOHN NICHOLS

New Mexico Magazine • Santa Fe, New Mexico

Governor of New Mexico: Gary Johnson
Cultural Affairs Director: Gary Morton

Project Director: Doug Svetnicka
Editor: Ellen Kleiner
Section Profiles and Photo Research: Richard Harris
Design: Jim Wood
Cover: John Sloan. "Music on the Plaza." 1920. Oil on canvas. Collection of the Museum of Fine Arts, Museum of New Mexico, gift of Mrs. Cyrus McCormick.

With special thanks to: Janette DeBaca, Student Intern, Office of Cultural Affairs; Mary Ann Anders, Historic Preservation Division; Anne Green and Tamara Goodman, New Mexico Arts Division.

Photographer Credits:
Facing page 1 © Jack Parsons; page 6 © Jonathan A. Meyers; page 24 © Miguel Gandert; page 78 © Mark Kane; page 134 © Pamela Porter; page 166 © Charles Mann; page 12 courtesy Farmington Convention and Visitors Bureau; pages 11, 16, 18, 20, 22, 26, 30, 42, 49, 52, 55, 57, 62, 65, 80, 86, 91, 100, 102, 105, 112, 115, 136, 140, 144, 156, 159, 160, 175, 191, 196, and 200 by Mark Nohl, courtesy of New Mexico Economic & Tourism Department; pages 8, 14, 29, 36, 40, 44, 51, 70, 75, 88, 108, 152, 169, and 187 courtesy of the Museum of New Mexico.

ISBN 0-937206-39-3
Manufactured in Korea
Library of Congress Catalog Card Number 95-070213

10 9 8 7 6 5 4 3 2 1

This publication is one of several ongoing efforts by the New Mexico Office of Cultural Affairs to develop and promote New Mexico's cultural treasures. For information about the agency and its programs, please contact the New Mexico Office of Cultural Affairs, 228 East Palace Avenue, Santa Fe, NM 87501; 505-827-6364.

Published and distributed by: New Mexico Magazine
                                   Lew Wallace Building
                                   495 Old Santa Fe Trail
                                   Santa Fe, NM 87503
                                   505-827-7447

THE REGIONS OF NEW MEXICO

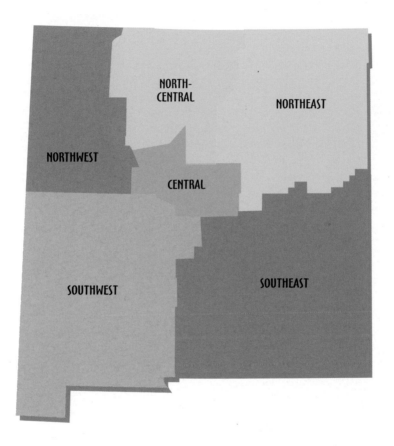

Many sites listed throughout these regions appear on state, national, and world registers. These place designations have been coded as follows:

⊚   State Register of Cultural Properties

☐   National Register of Historic Places

△   National Historic Landmark

⊕   World Heritage Site

T he power of New Mexico is, and has always been, her people, living together in a lovely, yet challenging environment complicated by a heady blend of languages, traditions, and lifestyles. Indeed, the beauty of New Mexico—emerging from her history, architecture, art forms, and community festivals—is unlike any other in the world. We who are fortunate to know New Mexico realize that the state's greatest strength lies in this unique spirit of diversity.

I am reminded of a story that my predecessor in the Office of Cultural Affairs, the late Helmuth J. Naumer, used to tell. As a boy, Helmuth was helping old man Isidro build an adobe wall at the Naumer home in the foothills of Santa Fe. "Don't make it straight," instructed Isidro, "because if you do, it will have no character. A wall should be like life—*full* of character. Life without character is boring." That is New Mexico: never straight, never boring, and full of character and vibrancy.

We celebrate the distinction of our New Mexico with this guide to her cultural wealth, in the hope that it offers fitting tribute to the spirit and creativity of her people.

Gary Morton
Cultural Affairs Director
State of New Mexico

CONTENTS

FOREWORD

by John Nichols

arrived in New Mexico dog dirty and loaded for bear in the summer of 1957: I was 16 years old. I got off a Greyhound bus in Albuquerque, bought myself a pair of knee-high purple mule-ear boots, then went up to Taos. I spent my first night there in the La Fonda Hotel on the Plaza, where I lay in bed and listened to a honky-tonk piano player downstairs. That's when my infatuation with New Mexico began.

During that visit, I never took coup on the D. H. Lawrence paintings in the La Fonda office of owner Saki Karavas, but I did see women replastering the beautiful Ranchos de Taos church. I also viewed the world-renowned "Shadow of the Cross" painting inside that church, spent an afternoon at historic Taos Pueblo, met Dorothy Brett and Frank Waters at an art opening of Brett's work, and witnessed Indians dancing by firelight outside Jack Denver's—*Whoa, you missed it!*—motel on the main drag.

Then I headed way down south to Rodeo, which is a flyspeck located about 40 miles below Lordsburg. From Rodeo, I tried hitch-hiking west to Portal, Arizona, just across the border. Walking for seven hours in the desert before catching a ride, I almost died of thirst. But I lived, and for the next five weeks fought forest fires in the Chiricahua Mountains with local Chicanos and Mexican nationals. At the end of that magic summer, on my way home to the East Coast, I got trapped in Lordsburg in a flash flood that delayed me for a day. While

waiting, I earned big bucks shoveling mud out of several restaurants and saddle shops, and received a kiss in gratitude from a local beauty queen who said her name was María.

Talk about magnificent introductions to a mighty rich territory! That winter I read a captivating book about the Southwest, Tom Lea's novel *The Wonderful Country* . . . and I was hooked. Soon as I could—12 years later—I returned to New Mexico, and have barely set foot outside her borders since. The state is too big to be a grain of sand, though it sure encompasses infinity big-time. People ask me how come I never fish in Colorado or Montana? I reply: Why should I waste gas traveling all over kingdom come when there are about 6 billion trout in scenic rivers both calm and vociferous within a half hour of my own back door?

That, and countless other fascinations, abound, which is what this book is all about. I don't know if culture includes breathtaking landscapes and hungry fish, but I figure ultimately *every*thing goes into the same mix: history, language, architecture, Christmas *luminarias,* and the kind of food we eat, whether it is chile, bread pudding, or meatloaf with wax beans and stale gravy. The kaleidoscope of flavor is what makes us each unique: it can include Anasazi rock art, or an old-time fiddler playing a *varsoviana,* or a dinosaur bone (in an Albuquerque museum) being ogled by a class of fifth graders.

I live in Taos, *donc* I have been inundated with so much culture over the past 25 years I'm almost punchy from it. I have danced at the Taos Pueblo Powwow; I've almost been thrown into the Río Pueblo by Indian clowns on San Gerónimo Day; I've had picnics on

Colorful cliffs form the backdrop for Christ-in-the-Desert Monastery near Abiquiú. Photograph by Jack Parsons

Mabel Dodge Luhan's grave (while taking cheap shots at Kit Carson's venerated memory); and I have saluted Padre Martínez from the courtyard of what used to be his very own *hacienda* on Ranchitos Road.

But if you really want to know what Taos is about, let me tell you this: recently, I saw a traveling exhibition of Goya etchings at our Millicent Rogers Museum—that's right, *Goya* etchings… right here in River City! As if that weren't enough, I've had a large gas balloon fall in my backyard; I was fired at by angry *acequia parciantes* years ago, when I was a commissioner on the Pacheco Ditch (and the treasurer to boot!); and I have written chapters of my books at the Harwood Library in full view of its intriguing Patrocinio Barela woodcarving collection. Barela's unique *santos* would send *escalofrios* up the spine of the most hardened aesthetic voyeur.

Shoot, would you believe that I've also inspected an archaeological dig out at Fort Burgwin south of town? Or that I have recited prose riffs from Vivaldi's *Four Seasons* on stage at the Taos Community Auditorium during the Summer Chamber Music Festival? To boot, I have lustily cheered a number of courageous poets at the annual Taos World Heavyweight Poetry Bout, and the experience was every bit as much fun as rooting for Mike Tyson or Muhammed Ali.

Long ago I even went up to the D. H. Lawrence shrine near San Cristóbal and penciled an appropriately smarmy bit of doggerel in the guest book there. Taos gets as much fanfare mileage out of old D. H. as Lincoln County derives from Billy the Kid. You want my opinion, I wish the two of them could've met in a High Noon sort of showdown at a neutral site, say Ojo Sarco or Alamogordo. I figure they would have blasted each other full of nonfatal

holes, and then crawled off to write a best-selling book about it: *Billy and Dave's Excellent Gunfight (as told to Pat Garrett and Lew Wallace!)*.

Do you think it's the altitude that makes me silly?

Yessir, I've been all over New Mexico, seen things, done stuff, had a ball. Hey, I've watched Zozobra burn in Santa Fe… then I almost expired in the human crush trampling toward an exit! I also attended Indian Market—once—and figured that that once was enough. Beautiful crafts, jewelry, artwork, you bet, but a little bit of that histrionic k-fuffle goes a right long way with me. Personally, I had more fun getting drenched in rain at the Santa Fe Opera during a performance of *Salome*. Or, if you truly like an edge to your culture, you can do as I did one evening long ago after an opening of Jerry West's latest works, and drive the wrong way down Canyon Road at night. Moral—? It's pretty easy to wind up confused in The City Different.

But I also saw Galway Kinnell read poetry in that town. And some years back I attended the greatest lowrider show *ever,* right on the Santa Fe Plaza. So, just when you think you have Santa Fe pigeonholed as a kind of Californicated artsy-totsy Shangri-la full of New Age space cadets being chased around by Robin Leach and his camera crew, the city turns around and backhands you with a kind of down-home authenticity you'd never find in New York.

I suffer from heart disease. Naturally, then, I've paid many visits to the world-famous *santuario* in Chimayó, and I have partaken of the magic healing dirt scooped from a hole in its floor. The dirt works fine, although some of my friends insist I defeat the purpose by washing that true grit down shortly thereafter with a pitcher of margaritas at the fabled Rancho de Chimayó restaurant nearby. Many ways there are, however, to skin a cat. Hence, I've also taken a few salutory plunges at the hot springs near Jémez Pueblo; and last summer I lay down in the ruins atop the Puyé Cliffs during a fantastic sunset, trying to get right with God. Who knows if my heart beats stronger because of these experiences... but you oughtta take a gander at my *soul!*

Then again, I suppose 25 years of New Mexico living will put a radiant (though hopefully not a *radiated!*) shine on even the most tarnished spirit.

Speaking of radiated, on countless occasions, while pondering the pros and cons of human evolution, I have stared at replicas of the atomic bombs Fat Man and Little Boy at the Los Alamos Bradbury Science Museum. In my younger days I played hockey with bloodthirsty physicists on a rink at the bottom of Omega Canyon, right near the Los Alamos Medical Center (which saved my daughter's life when, as an infant, she contracted pneumonia). The most fun I ever had in that town, though, was when a group of theoretical and experimental physicists guided me through the fusion facilities. I don't suppose these facilities are on any tourist agenda, but they should be. It's a fascinating and thought-provoking journey into the future, and into the moral and ethical dialogues that define our times.

No, I am not a proponent of nuclear war, nuclear energy, or even the nuclear family. But when you live in a place as downright explosive as our state, you do tend to think that even the most trite, everyday revelation is pure... dynamite.

I suppose I should own up to cashing in on the culture-for-hire craze currently sweeping New Mexico. Yes, I admit, every July I take

money from defenseless shutterbugs during a photographic workshop in Taos. And last August I went through the hell of teaching a writing workshop in Santa Fe (which was actually a lot of fun despite the paucity of pecuniary recompense), and I survived to tell the tale. But I have never taught anyone how to ski, paint, or carve a roadrunner out of piñon wood, so I may yet get my three days in heaven before the devil knows I'm dead.

The astute observer has probably guessed by now that I like the contrasts and contradictions of New Mexico. For example, I have derived as much pleasure from snapping pictures of the mysterious Very Large Array antennae just west of Socorro as I have from taking photographs of the cliff dwellings at Bandelier. In that vein, my trip to Mogollón was doubly exciting; it's a fascinating old mining town . . . and I kept wondering if some shady local ghost inhabiting a cave down in that weird cul-de-sac was gonna take a potshot at me.

Brrr... gives me the willies. But I'd go back in a hot second.

The litany never ends. I have attended deer dances at Taos Pueblo; I *almost* made it to a White Zombie concert at the Albuquerque Convention Center (*they* cancelled, not me); I've also disco danced surrounded by transvestites at Route 66 on Central Avenue, 'Burque; and not too long ago I shared a podium with Ed Abbey at the venerable KiMo Theater, also in downtown Duke City. We—Ed and I—were doing a Sierra Club benefit in praise of mountain lions.

The Gerónimo Surrender Monument southwest of Rodeo is a lonely place, out in the stinging hot flats between two mystical mountain ranges—the Chiricahuas of Arizona and the Peloncillos of New Mexico. Just as lonely are the ruins of an old hotel in Elizabethtown, north of Eagle Nest in the Moreno Valley. Not much remains of that once gold-crazy village except a fascinating cemetery and a colorful hunting guide named Zeus who lives, surrounded by baying hounds, in the canyon below. Closer to Angel Fire, at the other end of that valley, is the DAV Vietnam Veterans National Memorial Chapel constructed on a pretty hill by Dr. Victor Westphall, a chapel every bit as powerful as that long black wall in Washington, DC. It, too, is a lonely place, and one that seems to have a direct historical connection hundreds of miles—and over a century of years—down south to that desolate piece of earth where Gerónimo turned himself in and the Apache nation was forever changed.

Back up in the Chama country, I have often visited Abiquiú, Ghost Ranch, and the Echo Amphitheater. That area still has a strong memory for another rebel, land grant activist Reies Tijerina. This gives the countryside a nice depth of feeling. Fact is, not much is *neutral* in New Mexico, which is what makes us especially interesting. My favorite town in that neighborhood is Los Ojos, home of Tierra Wools, a wonderful wool-producing cooperative . . . plus there's a trout hatchery nearby.

Like I said, I dunno if fish count as culture on the official ballots, but they sure do in my book. Furthermore, although I truly understand why some folks get major aesthetic jollies from antique churches (such as the exquisite one in Trampas), I'll trade you an 18th-century altar screen for a Fenwick 3-ounce, 8½-foot, 6-weight graphite rod on the Río Grande Wild and Scenic River section near Big Arsenic any day, and you can keep the change.

Traveling most anywhere in New Mexico is worth double the price of admission. Snowcapped mountains, scenic orchard valleys, land so wide it could be the ocean. With its space and spectacular light, this state is so crawling in artists that if you suddenly froze them all into a frieze, they'd probably look like a diorama of a diamondback den at the American International Rattlesnake Museum in Albuquerque! All kidding aside, if you live here you can't help but see a lot of wonderful painting, whether it be by Raymond Jonson or Helen Hardin or Maya Torres, or by that uppity Hurd/Wyeth bunch from down south.

We've got major league poets, too, like Luci Tapahanso, Demetria Martínez, John Brandi, and Harold Littlebird. Yes, we have writers, painters, and actors up the gazot. And flamenco dancers, to boot. Know what—? You can actually get a degree in flamenco at the University of New Mexico; my wife Miel Castagna can attest to that. Hey, María Benítez has been good so long the state should make her *governor.* I saw María 20 years ago and was awed; then I caught her act again just the other day—same effect. She keeps on getting better.

Truth to tell, I've never had a dull moment in New Mexico. I once fished the Los Lunas drain in a snowstorm while migrating sandhill cranes cavorted in the fields all around me. I guess they were headed for the Bosque del Apache, one of the great wildlife refuges in North America. Too, I've attended the Apple Festival in Hillsboro—its museum is the greatest. And speaking of that area of the state, years ago I gave a speech about racism in America to a large crowd in Silver City; I fully expected to be stoned to death afterward. Instead, I received a standing ovation! Years later, however, I was not so lucky at Albuquerque's Río Grande Zoo. An orangutan, who took umbrage at my comments, threw a rock at me . . . but missed by at least six inches.

Land, culture, history—you name it, we possess it in plethoras, droves, monumental helpings. One of my favorite haunts in Albuquerque is the Río Grande Nature Center. Why? Well, I can rollerblade along the walkway there while casting for trout in the ditch that runs parallel. Now if *that* ain't culture with a capital *T,* I don't know what is.

Here comes the sad part, though. New Mexico has so many places I consider must-see locations, yet I have never seen them. One is Trinity Site in White Sands, where they first set off The Bomb. And the day after I take coup on *that* disturbing monument, I plan to walk along the main street of Columbus reliving the moment in 1916 when Pancho Villa's troops invaded the good old USA.

Then, too, I admit to a decades-long jonesing for a Bat Flight Breakfast at Carlsbad Caverns, during which I will be able to watch all those *murciélagos* returning from their night on the town.

Plainly, I love bats.

Even more plainly, I also love New Mexico. Meaning I could go on forever prattling about this hallowed land. I could tell you about wheat in Tucumcari, or about the gunslingers' graves in Cimarrón, or about the Jack Dempsey museum in Manassa—whoops, that's just over the border in Colorado! Bottom line, of course, is that this foreword should simply whet your appetite, goading you to study this book, make up an itinerary, then see it all for yourself. If you'll pardon the extended angling metaphor, please take my words *in toto* as nothing more than a clever artificial fly dropped onto the surface water just above where you—oh, patient *lecteur*—may be tailing, waiting for a bit of nourishment to float by . . .

Presto! Here it is; and you better strike *now,* while the iron is hot . . . then fire up the old Ford and hit the road, Jack or Jackie. It's a great, big, wonderful state we live in.

John Nichols is the author of six works of nonfiction, screenplays, and nine novels, including The Sterile Cuckoo, The Milagro Beanfield War, The Magic Journey, An Elegy in September, *and* Keep It Simple.

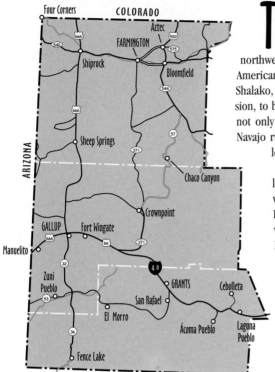

The New Mexican notion of culture takes in more than opera, art galleries, and trout fishing. In no part of the state is this more evident than the northwestern, home to nearly 80 percent of the state's American Indian population. Cultural events range from Shalako, the solemn and mysterious Zuni kachina procession, to boisterous rodeos and powwows. Fine arts include not only contemporary paintings and sculptures but also Navajo rugs that each take more than a year to weave on looms fashioned of cedar branches.

Here, shards of 800-year-old Anasazi pottery litter the ruins of cities such as Chaco and Aztec, where the art, architecture, and astronomy rivaled Europe's despite the lack of metal tools. Both sites were abandoned long before ancestors of the Navajo first set foot in this land. Here, too, the still inhabited pueblos of Acoma and Zuni form living links to the distant past.

As hundreds of prehistoric Indian petroglyphs and inscriptions by Spanish conquistadores and Anglo explorers at El Morro attest, the region has been a cultural crossroads for centuries. As modern visitors invariably discover, it still is.

ACOMA PUEBLO

NM 23, 12 miles from exit off I-40
PO Box 309, 87034
800-747-0181
Acoma (People of the White Rock), inhabited since before the 12th century, is one of the two oldest continuously occupied towns in the nation. Often called Sky City, the pueblo is situated on top of a mesa, about 430 feet above the valley floor. The Acoma people are known for their delicately decorated black-on-white pottery. ☉☐

Buffalo dancer takes part in a ceremony at Zuni Pueblo. Photograph by Jonathan A. Meyers

MUSEUMS AND EXHIBIT SPACES
Acoma Pueblo Museum
PO Box 309, 87034
505-252-1139
A pueblo-operated museum featuring Indian pottery and history exhibits from the 15th century to the present. Fee.

HISTORIC BUILDINGS AND SITES
San Estévan del Rey Mission Church
505-252-1139
Built from 1629 to 1642 and repaired in 1799, this is one of the oldest churches in the United States and among the finest Spanish Colonial mission churches in New Mexico. An intriguing blend of Indian and Spanish influences. ☉☐

COMMUNITY EVENTS

Acoma Pueblo Christmas Festivals
San Estévan del Rey Mission Church
Three days of tradi-
tional costumed
dances celebrating
the birth of Jesus,
beginning
December 25th.

**Arts and Crafts
Festivities**
Tourist Visitor Center
505-252-1139
Held in late July.

**Governor's Feast
Day**
Held at Old Acoma
Pueblo in February.

**San Estévan Feast
Day**
Popular festival held September 2nd at Old
Acoma Pueblo. Includes a midmorning Mass
and procession as well as an afternoon
Harvest Dance, food booths, and a large arts
and crafts fair.

San Juan Feast Day
Rooster pull at Old Acoma Pueblo on June
24th.

San Lorenzo Feast Day
Fiesta Day in the neighboring settlement of
Acomita on August 10th.

San Pedro and San Pablo Feast Days
Rooster pull at Old Acoma Pueblo on June
29th.

Santa María Feast Day
Held the first Sunday in May at the neighboring settlement of McCarty's.

Santiago Feast Day
Rooster pull at Old Acoma Pueblo on July
25th.

LIBRARIES
Acoma Community Library Resource Center
PO Box 469, 87034
505-552-6604

Acoma residents ascend the foot trail to Sky City in this rare 1882 photograph. Photograph by Ben Wittick, courtesy Museum of New Mexico, neg. 16039

AZTEC

US 550 at NM 544
The town was founded near a prehistoric
Indian ruin on the east side of the Animas River
in 1876, when portions of the Jicarilla Apache
Reservation were opened for non-Indian settlement. Aztec is now the seat of San Juan County,
developed in 1887 in response to residents'
desires to free themselves from the powerful
political forces of Río Arriba County.

MUSEUMS AND EXHIBIT SPACES
Aztec Museum and Pioneer Village
125 North Main Street, 87410
505-334-9829

Displays at the museum feature clocks, dolls, quilts, cameras, oil-field equipment, farm equipment, china, pioneer rooms, office equipment, and other early pioneer artifacts. Also included are rocks, minerals, and Indian relics from prehistoric times. The village encompasses a sheriff's office, jail, law office, doctor's office, 1880 log cabin, and blacksmith shop. Fee.

Aztec Ruins National Monument
US 550 to Ruins Road
PO Box 640, 87410
505-334-6174
A large, early-12th-century pueblo built by the Anasazi people, mistakenly identified as Aztecs by nearby settlers. On the grounds is a restored Great Kiva. The visitor center contains exhibits of pottery, basketry, and other items made by the early pueblo inhabitants. Fee. ◉□

HISTORIC BUILDINGS AND SITES
Aztec Main Street Historic District
Downtown area
505-334-9829
A well-preserved segment of commercial street development dating back to 1900 through 1915. Various architectural styles. ◉□

Lovers Lane Historic District
Downtown area
An eight-block residential area developed between 1887 and World War I. Architectural styles include Queen Anne, Colonial Revival, hipped cottage, and bungalow. ◉□

LIBRARIES
Aztec Public Library
201 West Chaco Street, 87410
505-334-9456

COMMUNITY EVENTS
Aztec Fiesta Days
505-334-9551
A carnival, regional tug-of-war competition, barbecue, parades, booths, and entertainment on the first weekend in June.

Aztec Founders' Day
Aztec Museum
505-334-9829
Music and special exhibits as well as a parade, horseshoe tournament, and costume contest to celebrate Aztec's founding in 1876. Held the second Saturday in September.

Festival de los Farolitos
Aztec Ruins National Monument
505-334-9551
A pre-Christmas *farolito* display. The walls of the ruins as well as many homes and businesses are lit with thousands of "little fires."

BLOOMFIELD

US 64 at NM 44
The town just east of Salmon Ruins was first named Porter, for a general who established trading posts in the region. Later renamed after one of its early settlers, Bloomfield quickly became known for its cattle rustling, stagecoach robberies, and general outlaw activity. In the 1880s, noted gunman Port Stockton, an outlaw from the Lincoln County War, moved to town and was made a peace officer. He was unable to part with his violent ways, and gunplay continued in Bloomfield.

MUSEUMS AND EXHIBIT SPACES
Bloomfield Cultural Complex
333 South First Street, 87413
505-632-2840
Featuring changing exhibits and events related to
regional history as well as arts and crafts. Dedicated
to the diverse cultures of the Four Corners area.

Salmon Ruins and Heritage Park
US 64, 2 miles west of Bloomfield
PO Box 125, 87413
505-632-2013
Named after homesteader George Salmon, the
600- to 750-room pueblo was one of many settlements founded by 11th-century Chacoan
Indians. Newly opened Heritage Park encompasses the dwelling sites of eight cultures. San
Juan Archaeological Research Center, located
within the park, houses a library as well as artifacts from the ruins, photographs, and Salmon
Brothers' manuscripts. Guided tours, films, and
lectures are available to the public. An ongoing
archaeological excavation site. ❑

LIBRARIES
Bloomfield Community Library
333 South First Street
PO Box 1839, 87413
505-632-8315

PUBLIC ART
Bloomfield Cultural Complex
333 South First Street
Estéban Harris
"Reflections of a Tin Warrior, #12"—acrylic-
and-tin on wood
Robin Ryder Knight
"Desert Landscape"—wool tapestry
Fabian De Vallenti Noberto
Pottery
Nelson Tsosie
"Shy Maiden"—black soapstone sculpture

CEBOLLETA

NM 279, 8 miles north of Laguna Pueblo
A Navajo mission established here in the mid-
18th century was later invaded by Albuquerque-
area cattlemen who, in the early 1800s, built a
fortified town. Seeking refuge from the warfare,
the Spanish settlers fled to nearby Los Portales
Cave. The cave was later converted to a shrine
with an altar carved from the rock.

CHACO CULTURE NATIONAL HISTORICAL PARK

NM 57, 63 miles south of Bloomfield
Star Route 4, Box 6500
Bloomfield, 87413
505-786-7014
Chaco Canyon, as it is known, flourished as a
major Anasazi cultural center during the 9th
and 10th centuries. Pueblo Bonito, the most
magnificent of the stone-masonry dwellings,
contained more than 600 rooms in addition to
numerous kivas, and stood four stories high.
The current site, referred to as the Stonehenge
of the West, includes 13 major Great House
Indian ruins along with a museum, library, and

Kivas fill the central plaza of Pueblo Bonito ruins at Chaco Culture National Historical Park. Photograph by Mark Nohl

campground. Self-guided tours are available. Fee. ◉□⊖

EL MORRO
NATIONAL MONUMENT

NM 53, 43 miles southwest of Grants
505-783-4226
Amid grasslands and pine trees stands Inscription Rock, a 200-foot cliff into which bands of Indians, Spanish conquistadores, Franciscan missionaries, and westbound gold-seekers and outlaws carved their initials, poetry, and trail messages. The markings in soft sandstone bear testimony to 300 years of exploration in the Southwest. Interspersed among these historic records are pre-Columbian pet-

roglyphs. On the mesatop lie the ruins of two 13th- to 14th-century Indian pueblos with about 250 rooms each. ◉□

FARMINGTON

US 64, at US 550 and NM 371
Once part of the Jicarilla Apache Reservation, the area was established as an Anglo town in 1876. Settlement began in the agriculturally fertile region at the confluence of the San Juan, Animas, and La Plata Rivers. Known by the Navajo people as Totah (Among the Rivers), Farmington rapidly became a center for farming and ranching, and later, the production of oil, gas, coal, and uranium.

MUSEUMS AND EXHIBIT SPACES

Bolack Electrical/Mechanical Museum
3901 Bloomfield Highway, 87401
505-325-7873
Featuring former New Mexico Governor Tommy Bolack's collection of items depicting the early development of electrical power, telephone, radio, communication systems, oil-field equipment, and the farming industry. Tours by appointment.

Bolack Game Reserve and Wildlife Museum
3901 Bloomfield Highway, 87401
505-325-4275
Wildlife reserve and museum owned and operated by 1962 governor Tommy Bolack. Tours by appointment.

Kids play on a downtown Farmington "beach" during a Freedom Days Fourth of July celebration. Photograph courtesy Farmington Convention and Visitors Bureau

COMMUNITY EVENTS

Farmington Freedom Days
Downtown area, 800-448-1240
An auction, food fair, street dance, ice cream social, parade, concert, Western-style contests, and fireworks on the Fourth of July weekend.

Farmington Museum
302 North Orchard Avenue, 87401
505-599-1174
Exhibits include pioneer and Indian trading post artifacts, San Juan Basin environmental displays, New Mexico's first children's experience center, and a historic Farmington frontier town. A museum store offers items for sale.

HISTORIC BUILDINGS AND SITES

Fruitland Trading Post
US 64, 11 miles west of Farmington
Established in 1886 by the Fruitland Trading Company, this trading post provided necessities for Navajo Indians living on the reservation. It also served as an outlet for locally produced rugs, jewelry, and baskets. ◉

Palmer House
210 North Allen Avenue
This two-room adobe-and-log house, completed in 1878, is the oldest standing building in Farmington. In the backyard is a Canadian

Farmington International Balloon Festival
Farmington Lake, 800-448-1240
Hot-air balloon launches and races on Memorial Day weekend.

Farmington Trade Days/SummerFun Showcase
Farmington Civic Center, 203 West Main Street, 87401, 505-325-0279
A retail trade show for Four Corners merchants, featuring food, entertainment, fashion shows, artists, and craftmakers on the first weekend in June.

Holiday Arts and Crafts Fair
Garden Room at the Best Western Inn
505-632-2013
A benefit arts and crafts fair for the San Juan

white birch tree shipped by train from Canada at the turn of the 20th century.

Thomas Jefferson Arrington House
506 West Arrington Street
Built in 1887 for a prominent Farmington pioneer, the adobe home is one of the few examples of prerailroad Territorial-style architecture in San Juan County.

PERFORMING ARTS
Anasazi: The Ancient Ones Pageant
Lion's Wilderness Park Amphitheater
800-448-1240
An outdoor musical drama about the area's Navajo and Mormon pioneer heritage. The pageant runs Wednesdays through Saturdays, from mid-June through late August.

San Juan Stage Company, Inc.
PO Box 3226, 87401
505-632-3668
This community theater group presents six different productions from late August through mid-June.

San Juan Symphony
3101 Centenary Avenue, 87402
505-326-4969
Blending musical talent from both Farmington and Durango, Colorado, the symphony presents concerts October through April at the San Juan Community College Theater and the Farmington Civic Center, as well as in Durango.

CULTURAL ORGANIZATIONS
Northwest New Mexico Arts Council
PO Box 2777, 87499
505-599-1150
Provides information and technical assistance to regional visual and performing artists. Also sponsors a summer showcase of local artists and their work.

Archaeological Research Center and Library at Salmon Ruins. Held in late November or early December.
Native American Days
Animas Valley Mall, 505-326-5465
Native American dancing, choral music, traveling exhibits, and an arts and crafts fair in mid-September.
Riverfest
Berg Park/Animas Parkland, 800-448-1240
A celebration of the rivers, with music, food, entertainment, riverside trail walks, raft rides, and a juried fine arts fair. Held on Memorial Day weekend.

San Juan College Apple Blossom Festival
San Juan College, 505-326-7602
An Indian powwow, dance, parade, barbecue, and 10-K run held in April or early May.
San Juan County Fair
McGee Park on US 64, 800-448-1240
The largest county fair in New Mexico, this week-long event features a live concert, livestock shows, exhibits, a fiddling contest, parade, arts and crafts show, and carnival. Held in late August.
Totah Festival
Farmington Civic Center, 800-448-1240
An Indian-juried fine arts and crafts show and marketplace, including an Indian rug auction. Held on Labor Day weekend.

LIBRARIES
Farmington Public Library
100 West Broadway, 87401
505-599-1270
Presents arts and crafts exhibitions.

PUBLIC ART
Farmington Special Preschool
Stuart Ashman
"The Orchestra"—sculpture

Harriet B. Sammons Building
Animas Street
Cynthia Barber
"Cañon de Maravillas"—sculpture
Rod S. Hubble
"Legacy of Day"—acrylic painting
Frank McGuire
"Song of Welcome"—sculpture

Francis Rivera
"Rites of Passage"—pastel painting
Glen Strock
"El Valle"—gouache

San Juan College
College Boulevard
Joe Orlando
"A Song of Harmony"—limestone sculpture
Dee Tosiano
"Shepherd Girl"—bronze sculpture

FORT WINGATE

NM 400, 16 miles southeast of Gallup
Established in 1860, Fort Wingate was used to
contain Navajo Indians until 1925, when it was
turned over to the Bureau of Indian Affairs
(BIA). The BIA used the fort as a vocational

Navajo rugs hang from the exhibit hall ceiling at Gallup's Inter-Tribal Indian Ceremonial in this 1940 photograph. Photograph by Wyatt Davis, courtesy Museum of New Mexico, neg. 29215

boarding school. One of eight such facilities in the area during the 1930s, Fort Wingate became the showcase boarding school for the Navajo Nation. The school closed in 1968. ◉□

FOUR CORNERS NATIONAL MONUMENT

Intersection of New Mexico, Arizona, Utah, and Colorado
The only place in the United States where a person can stand in four states at once. A marble platform displays each of the four state seals.

GALLUP

I-40, at US 666 and NM 602
A longtime major trading center for the Navajo and Zuni communities to the north and south, Gallup emerged in 1881 from a railroad construction camp. Named after David Gallup, paymaster for the Atlantic & Pacific (now Santa Fe) Railroad, the town currently serves as a colorful hub of activity for visitors to the most ancient continuously inhabited pueblos in the state and to the Navajo Reservation. The area remains a prominent trading center for Indian arts and crafts, especially jewelry and rugs.

MUSEUMS AND EXHIBIT SPACES
Red Mesa Arts Center
105 West Hill Avenue, 87301
505-722-4209
Presents monthly thematic shows featuring the work of 40 to 60 local artists.

Red Rock Museum
Red Rock State Park, 4 miles east of Gallup
PO Box 328, Church Rock, 87311
505-863-1337

COMMUNITY EVENTS
Inter-Tribal Indian Ceremonial
Red Rock State Park, 4 miles east of Gallup
PO Box 1, Church Rock, 87311
800-233-4528
New Mexico's oldest all-Indian exhibition, featuring tribes from the United States, Canada, and Mexico. A powwow, rodeo, Indian arts and crafts, performing arts, food booths, and a parade. Sponsored by the Inter-Tribal Indian Ceremonial Association in August.
Winter Market
Red Mesa Arts Center, 105 West Hill Avenue, 87301, 505-722-4209
An arts and crafts show sponsored by the Gallup Area Arts Council in early December.

Displays the material culture of the Anasazi as well as modern arts and crafts of the Zuni, Hopi, and Navajo tribes. Temporary exhibits feature the work of local artists. Fee.

HISTORIC BUILDINGS AND SITES
Atchison, Topeka & Santa Fe Railway Depot
201 East 66th Avenue
A reminder of the railroad's importance in the settlement of Gallup. Built in 1923, the depot blends Mission-style architecture with Spanish-Pueblo Revival style in tribute to local Indian cultures. Developed by Mary Colter, chief designer for the Fred Harvey Company. ◉

El Morro Theater
207 West Coal Avenue
505-722-SHOW
Completed in 1928, the theater has been a mainstay of entertainment in the area. ◉□

Dancers' headdresses rest outside a tepee at the Inter-Tribal Indian Ceremonial in Gallup. Photograph by Mark Nohl

El Rancho Hotel
1000 East 66th Avenue
An excellent example of rustic-style architecture, typified by a "picturesque Western" appearance. Built in 1936 by "Griff" Griffith, brother of film producer D. W. Griffith, the hotel served as an outpost for the Western movie industry. Much of this history is recorded in a photo "museum" on the balcony of the lobby. ☉□

Grand Hotel (Ricca's Mercantile)
306 West Coal Avenue
Erected around 1925 as a dry goods store with a bus depot downstairs and a hotel upstairs, the building epitomizes the plain decorative brick commercial style of architecture popular in the 1920s and 1930s. The exterior has remained unaltered. ☉□

Harvey Hotel
408 West Coal Avenue
Constructed of sandstone and other local building materials in 1928, this decorative brick commercial-style hotel (not a Fred Harvey hotel) competed with the nearby Grand Hotel for business. ☉□

McKinley County Courthouse
201 West Hill Avenue
Designed by the architectural firm Trost and Trost of El Paso, Texas, the building was completed in 1938 in "picturesque" Spanish-Pueblo Revival style. Details include a bell tower with battered walls and *vigas*; wood beams and corbels; and Indian-motif reliefs. The courtroom wall murals, painted by Lloyd Moylan, depict the history of McKinley County. ☉□

Palace Hotel
236 West 66th Avenue
Built on a prominent corner in 1912 as a
hipped-roof, two-story structure in modified
Richardsonian Romanesque style. A grand representation of locally quarried sandstone. ⊚◻

Rex Hotel
300 West 66th Avenue
Constructed in 1910 of locally quarried sandstone, this commercial-style building stands as
a reminder of Gallup's early-19th-century coal
boom. ⊚◻

Vásquez de Coronado's Route
I-40, west of Gallup
The trail taken by Francisco Vásquez de
Coronado, leader of an army of Spaniards
and Indians, when he entered New Mexico
from Arizona in July 1540. His hope was to
find the Seven Cities of Cíbola, which proved
to be six Zuni villages situated near the present pueblo. During his attack on the village
of Hawikuh, Vásquez de Coronado was nearly
killed.

PERFORMING ARTS
Gallup Film Festival
El Morro Theater
505-722-4209
An October celebration of Western and
American Indian films. Sponsored by the Gallup
Area Arts Council.

Gallup Gallery Concert Series
108 West Coal Avenue, 87301
505-863-4563
An evening adult concert series and daytime
children's music theater series in a season running September to May.

Gallup Summer Indian Dance Program
Red Rock State Park, 4 miles east of Gallup
PO Box 1, Church Rock, 87311
505-863-3896
Each evening, Memorial Day through Labor Day,
one of seven dance groups from the Navajo,
Zuni, and Acoma tribes is spotlighted in a display of traditional Indian dances. Discussions
follow on tribal and regional histories, traditions, arts and crafts, and native foods.

Square Dance Fest-i-gal
Red Rock State Park
800-242-4282
More than 600 dancers from the United States
and Canada meet to square dance under the
direction of professional callers in mid-April.

CULTURAL ORGANIZATIONS
Gallup Area Arts Council
105 West Hill Avenue, 87301
505-722-4209
Produces a performing arts series for adults
and children from September through May, featuring music, dance, and theater. Sponsors a
four-week Performing Arts Academy in July and
August for youth and adults interested in
drama, dance, music, storytelling, script writing, video production, and visual arts and set
design. Also operates the Red Mesa Arts Center.

Gallup Historical Society
PO Box 502, 87301
505-863-5663
Owns several historic properties, including the
Southwestern Mine Office, Gamerco Mine Hoist
House, Gamerco Smoke Stack, and an Atchison,
Topeka & Santa Fe caboose and boxcar, as well
as memorabilia from a variety of area coal
mines. Offers periodic tours of the properties

and surrounding area. Also conducts a Downtown Walking Tour during New Mexico Heritage Preservation Week in May. The tour includes visits to regional interest areas, speakers, audio and visual presentations, and a picnic.

Inter-Tribal Indian Ceremonial Association
PO Box 1, Church Rock, 87311
505-863-3896
Sponsors the annual Inter-Tribal Indian Ceremonial, Gallup Summer Indian Dance Program, Indian Country Guide Service, and an Indian artist referral service. A state agency responsible for preserving and promoting New Mexico's Indian heritage.

LIBRARIES
Octavia Fellin Public Library
115 West Hill Avenue, 87301
505-863-1291

PUBLIC ART
Gallup National Guard Armory
Country Road 43
Nelson Tsosie
"Navajo Codetalker"—black soapstone sculpture

McKinley County Courthouse
201 West Hill Avenue
Carol Milligan, William Mitchell, and *Jacque Xavier*
"Saltillo Rug"—steel sculpture

A sculpture made from miners' drill bits adorns the entrance to the New Mexico Museum of Mining in Grants. Photograph by Mark Nohl

Lloyd Moylan
History of New Mexico mural
New Deal Art

Miyamura Park
701 Montoya Boulevard
Armando Alvarez
"We the People"—sculpture

GRANTS

I-40 at NM 53
Located just north of the great lava bed known
as El Malpais (The Badlands), the town began
as a coaling station for the Santa Fe Railway.
Around 1880, it was dubbed Grant's Camp,
after Canadian bridge contractor Angus A.
Grant. In 1950, Navajo sheep rancher Paddy
Martínez found a strange-looking yellow rock
and, turning it in to authorities, sparked the
discovery of a vast number of uranium deposits
in the area. Until the 1970s, when the mines
closed, Grants was considered the uranium
capital of the United States.

MUSEUMS AND EXHIBIT SPACES
New Mexico Museum of Mining
100 Iron Street, 87020
505-287-4802
Highlights the history of the area found to contain a mother lode of uranium. Offerings
include a guided tour into a simulated uranium
mine, displays of Indian artifacts, and geology
exhibits. Fee.

HISTORIC BUILDINGS AND SITES
Pueblo Revolt Site
I-40, east of Grants
Region in which the western pueblos of Acoma
and Zuni revolted against Spanish rule during
the Pueblo uprising that began August 10,
1680. Also the area in which refugees from the
Río Grande pueblos, escaping from the reconquest of their lands the following decade,
joined with local Keres-speaking Indians to
form Laguna Pueblo.

CULTURAL ORGANIZATIONS
Cíbola Arts Council
1501 Estancia Avenue, 87020
505-287-7311
Presents a performing arts season of concerts,
theater, and film from September through May.

LIBRARIES
Mother Whiteside Memorial Library
525 West High Street
PO Box 96, 87020
505-287-7927

PUBLIC ART
First Presbyterian Church
400 Nimitz Drive
Ron Powell and *Arthur Tatkoski*
Stained glass windows

Grants National Guard Armory
2001 East Santa Fe Avenue
Carlos Callejo
"Grants"—mural

Grants State Bank
824 West Santa Fe Avenue
Robert Kie
Desert scene mural

New Mexico Museum of Mining
100 Iron Street
Cynthia Barber
Wall sculpture

Old Laguna Village as seen from Interstate 40. Photograph by Mark Nohl

New Mexico State University–Grants Campus
1500 North Third Street
Bob Peters
Steel sculpture

St. Theresa's Catholic Church
500 East High Street
Father Howard Meyer, OFM
Virgin Mary—lava rock
Jerry Montoya
Desert and sky painting

LAGUNA PUEBLO

Off I-40, 45 miles west of Albuquerque
PO Box 194, 87026
505-552-6654

Originally established around 1450, this is the largest Keres-speaking pueblo, with about 8,000 members of Shoshone, Tanoan, Keresan, Zuni, and Plains Indian ancestry. The Laguna people live in six major settlements centered politically at Old Laguna Village, and are known for their distinctive pottery, paintings, and jewelry, and for their love of baseball. The pueblo has eight semipro teams and hosts an all-Indian tournament each September.

HISTORIC BUILDINGS AND SITES
San José de la Laguna Mission Church and Convent
505-552-9330
Unlike most early Franciscan churches in New Mexico, this stark whitewashed adobe complex survived the Pueblo uprising of 1680. It retains

COMMUNITY EVENTS

Feast Day at Encinal
A Mass, procession, and ceremonial dances celebrating the Nativity of the Blessed Mother. Held September 8th.

Feast Day at Mesita
A Mass, procession, and dances honoring the feast day of San Antonio on August 15th.

Feast Day at Paguate
A Mass, procession, and dances in commemoration of Santa Elisabet on September 25th.

Feast Day at Paraje
Celebration of the Feast Day of Santa Margarita-María. A Mass, procession, and ceremonial dances on October 17th.

New Year's Day Celebration at Old Laguna Village
A Mass, procession, and traditional dances.

San José Feast Day at Old Laguna Village
A Mass, procession, Harvest Dance, carnival, sporting events, and arts and crafts exhibits attracting visitors from other tribes. Laguna's largest public event, held on September 19th. A more traditional San José Feast Day is observed in Old Laguna Village on March 19th.

San Juan Feast Day
All villages
Grab Day celebrated on June 24th.

San Lorenzo Feast Day at Acomita
Grab Day celebrated on August 10th.

San Pedro and San Pablo Feast Days
All villages
Grab Day celebrated on June 29th.

Santa Ana Feast Day at Seama
A Mass, procession, and dances on July 26th.

Santiago Feast Day
All villages
Grab Day celebrated on July 25th.

Three Kings Day
Old Laguna Village
New tribal officers honored through the transfer of the Canes of Authority on January 6th.

most of the structures and artifacts placed in the mission almost 300 years ago. ☉▢

LIBRARIES
Laguna Pueblo Library
PO Box 194, 87026
505-552-6280

MANUELITO

I-40, near the Arizona border
The site of numerous Indian pueblos dating from about AD 500 to 1325, when the area was abandoned. Resettled around 1800 by Navajos, the region became home to Manuelito, one of the last chiefs to surrender for confinement at the Bosque Redondo Reservation near Fort Sumner in 1864. Navajo survivors returned to Manuelito in 1868.

SAN RAFAEL

NM 53, 4 miles south of Grants
Formerly known as El Gallo (The Rooster) and located at a spring just west of the great lava flow El Malpais, the area was visited by members of Francisco Vásquez de Coronado's expedition in 1540. In 1862, it became the site for the second Fort Wingate, focus of the US Army's campaign against the Navajos. The settlement of Spanish colonists that grew up near the fort stayed on after the army's evacuation in 1869.

SHIPROCK

US 64 at US 666
Named for the imposing volcanic peak nearby,
which figures prominently in Navajo legends,
this area has for centuries been part of the
Navajo homeland. Early in the 20th century,
Shiprock became headquarters of the Northern
Navajo Agency. Today, the town remains a cen-
ter for business, trading, and health care.

HISTORIC BUILDINGS AND SITES
Navajo Nation
Northwestern New Mexico and northeastern
Arizona
602-871-6436
Navajo country, spanning nearly 16 million acres,
is home to the largest Indian group in the United
States, about one-third of whom live in New
Mexico. The center of Navajo business and govern-
ment is in Window Rock, Arizona, west of Gallup.
The Navajo people, who traditionally live in octago-
nal homes called *hooghans,* are known for their
fine blankets, silverwork, and sandpaintings.

Shiprock Pinnacle
12 miles southwest of Shiprock
This solidified lava-and-igneous-rock formation
rising 1,700 feet from the desert floor is known
in Navajo as Tse be dahi (Rock with Wings).
According to legend, this rock was once the

The pinnacle of Shiprock towers above the Navajo Reservation.
Photograph by Mark Nohl

great bird that brought the Navajo people here
from the North.

CULTURAL ORGANIZATIONS
Navajo Arts and Humanities Council
PO Box 1979, 87420
505-368-5291

LIBRARIES
Shiprock Cultural Media Center
PO Box 6002, 87420
505-368-5181

ZUNI PUEBLO

NM 602 at NM 53
PO Box 339, 87327
505-782-4481
Inhabited 1,700 years ago and continuously
occupied for the past 700 years, this settlement
marks the site of first contact between the
Indians of the Southwest and an armed
European expedition: in 1540, Francisco
Vásquez de Coronado arrived at the Zuni village

COMMUNITY EVENTS
Northern Navajo Fair
Shiprock Fairgrounds, 800-448-1240
Arts and crafts, a parade, rodeo, pow-
wow, traditional songs, and Yeibichei
dances held in early October.

of Hawikuh, mistaking it for one of the seven fabled Golden Cities of Cíbola. Formerly known as Halona, this isolated pueblo was one of the last to be converted to Catholicism by the Franciscans. Today, it is the largest pueblo in New Mexico. The Zuni people, who speak a language unrelated to other tribal dialects, are known for their intricate beadwork, animal fetish carvings, and silver and turquoise jewelry. ☺□

MUSEUMS AND EXHIBIT SPACES
A:Shiwi A:Wan Museum and Heritage Center
Building 1220, NM 53
PO Box 1009, 87327
505-782-4403
Displays historic photos as well as arts and history exhibitions.

Zuni Arts and Crafts Center
1222 NM 53
PO Box 425, 87327
505-782-5531
Offers jewelry, pottery, fetishes, and paintings for sale.

HISTORIC BUILDINGS AND SITES
La Nuestra Señora de Guadalupe de Halona
The original mission church constructed in the pueblo plaza between 1633 and 1666 was destroyed in the Pueblo Revolt of 1680, reconstructed by Franciscans, and again restored in 1969. Today's church, decorated with weavings and Zuni-painted murals depicting the pueblo's cultural life, portrays a unique combination of Indian and Spanish decor. Considered one of the

COMMUNITY EVENTS
Shalako Ceremony and Dance
A night-long house-blessing ceremony held in early December to celebrate the end of the old year and the beginning of the new one. The dancers—10-foot-tall masked Shalakos—wear colorful costumes of intricate design. The ceremony begins with a ritual crossing of the small river that runs through the pueblo, and attracts visitors from around the world.
Zuni Fair
Zuni Pueblo Fairgrounds
A parade, rodeo, dances, games, food booths, and the Miss Zuni competition. Held in early September.
Zuni Rain Dance
Held in June.

most beautiful mission churches in New Mexico.

Zuni-Cíbola Complex
Four archaeological sites illustrating the development of Zuni culture: Village of the Great Kivas, Yellow House, Kechipbowa, and Hawikuh. Village of the Great Kivas, the settlement most often visited, is prized for its impressive array of petroglyphs and pictographs. □△

LIBRARIES
Zuni Public Library
PO Box 339, 87327
505-782-5630

There is magic in the sunshine that colors the high mesas, mountains, and valleys of north-central New Mexico. Filtered through the thinnest mountain-high, desert-dry air, it throws crisp-edged shadows. It paints the seasons, dancing low off snow-crested adobe walls, shimmering in autumn aspen leaves like a golden mirage, and setting indigo summer storm clouds aflame at day's end.

Some say it was the unique quality of light that lured the finest painters from the East Coast and Europe to this southwestern land at the dawn of the 20th century. By the time New Mexico became a state in 1912, Taos was well on its way to becoming a world-renowned artists' colony, with Santa Fe hot on its heels. Since then, the arts have spilled over into many small villages—Dixon, El Rito, Abiquiú, Galisteo, and a dozen others—touching and being touched by centuries-old American Indian and Hispanic folk traditions, and weaving a unique cultural tapestry.

Today, north-central New Mexico boasts more artists per capita than any other region of comparable size in the United States—and still, painters, sculptors, poets, musicians, dancers, and filmmakers keep coming. Few can say exactly why. In this land of many languages, the reason reaches beyond the realm of words. It's... uh... something about the light.

ABIQUIÚ

US 84, 18 miles north of Española
Once the site of a Tewa pueblo, Abiquiú was settled in the mid-18th century by a group of Spaniards and *genízaros* (Hispanicized Indians). Years later, explorers Fray Francisco Atanasio Domínguez and Fray Silvestre Vélez de Escalante visited the settlement. In 1778, it became one of the stops along the Spanish Trail

Baile de los Matachines lights the darkness on Christmas Eve at Picurís Pueblo. Photograph by Miguel Gandert

linking Santa Fe with Southern California. Today, the town in the bend of the Río Chama, nestled within the pastel-colored sandstone cliffs of the Gallina Fault zone, is perhaps best known as Georgia O'Keeffe country.

MUSEUMS AND EXHIBIT SPACES
Florence Hawley Ellis Museum of Anthropology
Ghost Ranch Conference Center
US 84, 14 miles north of Abiquiú
HC 77, Box 11, 87510
505-685-4333
Spotlights cultures within a 60-mile radius: prehistoric Gallina and Chama Valley, historic

Navajo, Pueblo Indian, early Spanish-American, and Anglo. The museum houses a library and hosts a two-week archaeology seminar in August.

Ghost Ranch Living Museum
Ghost Ranch Conference Center
US 84, 14 miles north of Abiquiú
505-685-4312
Dedicated to the conservation of native botanical specimens, animals, and geologic records. Paintings and prints pertaining to natural resources are on display. Lectures, films, and self-guided and guided tours are available.

Ruth Hall Museum of Paleontology
Ghost Ranch Conference Center
US 84, 14 miles north of Abiquiú
HC 77, Box 11, 87510
505-685-4333

Exhibits fossil plants and animals from northern New Mexico. Summer events include a fossil preparator uncovering the bones of Coelophysis, the New Mexico state fossil dating back 225 million years, as well as a week-long paleontology seminar.

HISTORIC BUILDINGS AND SITES
Christ-in-the-Desert Monastery
Forest Road 151, 13 miles west of US 84
A secluded Benedictine settlement on the banks of the Chama River. The monastery—noted for its architectural excellence—is composed of adobe, stone, glass, and wood, reminiscent of the religious architecture of early New Mexico. ◉

Domínguez-Vélez de Escalante Trail
US 84, north of Española

Hot-air balloons brighten the sky over Angel Fire. Photograph by Mark Nohl

A route blazed north from Santa Fe in 1776 by Fray Francisco Atanasio Domínguez and Fray Silvestre Vélez de Escalante, Franciscans determined to spread Christianity among the Indians. Abiquiú was the last Spanish settlement the missionaries saw in their five-month journey. Forced by inclement conditions to turn back from central Utah before reaching their destination—the new missions at Monterey, California—the friars opened what was to become the Spanish Trail leading from Santa Fe to Los Angeles.

Old Spanish Trail
US 84, north of Abiquiú
A trail blazed by mule-trader Antonio Armijo while wending his way from Abiquiú to California in 1829 to 1830. Turning west near present-day Abiquiú Dam to Largo Canyon and the San Juan River, he forged the blueprint for a trade route between Santa Fe and Los Angeles.

ANGEL FIRE

US 64 to NM 434
Having originated as a ski resort in 1968, the town now serves as a year-round retreat for enthusiasts of a variety of winter sports as well as fishing, boating, golfing, hiking, and chamber music.

MUSEUMS AND EXHIBIT SPACES
DAV Vietnam Veterans National Memorial Chapel
US 64, 6 miles north of Angel Fire
PO Box 608, 87710
505-377-6900
A chapel erected in 1968 by Dr. Victor Westphall in memory of his son and other United States personnel killed in the Vietnam War. First dedicated as the Vietnam Veterans

COMMUNITY EVENTS
Angel Fire Artsfest
PO Box 547, 87710
505-377-6934
A display and sale of fine arts and traditional crafts. Event includes a juried show with cash awards in several categories, a food bazaar, and children's activities. Held in early October.
Balloons over Angel Fire
PO Box 547, 87710
505-377-6661
A hot-air balloon glow, arts and crafts, food booths, street dance, and auto show in mid-July.
Labor Day in the Pines
Olympic Park
PO Box 547, 87710
505-377-6661
Music, food booths, and arts and crafts on Labor Day weekend.
Memorial Day Activities
DAV Vietnam Veterans National Memorial Chapel
US 64, 6 miles north of town
505-377-6900
Events include a bike tour and fitness walks.

Peace and Brotherhood Chapel, it was rededicated on May 30, 1983.

PERFORMING ARTS
Angel Fire Repertory Theater Society
PO Box 547, 87710
505-377-6724
Presents light comedy, melodrama, and revues on summer weekends.

Music from Angel Fire
DAV Vietnam Veterans National Memorial
Chapel
PO Box 502, 87710
505-377-3233
Offers a classical and jazz music series featuring
internationally renowned artists in a season run-
ning from late August through early September.
Concerts are broadcast by National Public Radio
to a listening audience of about 6 million people.

CULTURAL ORGANIZATIONS
Moreno Valley Arts Council
PO Box 355, 87710
505-377-6401

LIBRARIES
Angel Fire Community Library
1 North Angel Fire Road
PO Box 298, 87710
505-377-3511

PUBLIC ART
Public Sculpture Garden
Inn at Angel Fire, NM 434
Bill Shanehouse
Sculpture

CERRILLOS

NM 14, 23 miles south of Santa Fe
The area just east of San Marcos, a large
pueblo abandoned during the Pueblo Revolt of
1680, evolved into an important stop on the
Santa Fe Railway in the 1880s: a shipping point
for area mines of silver, gold, turquoise, lead,
zinc, and coal. After the mines closed, the
region was deserted. Today, Cerrillos is a small-
town haven for antique dealers, artists, and
mining-town restoration buffs. ◉

HISTORIC BUILDINGS AND SITES
Gold and Turquoise Mines
Scene of the first gold placer mining west of the
Mississippi River. The discovery of precious
metal in the rugged Ortiz Mountains south of
Cerrillos occurred in 1828—21 years before
the California gold rush—after which the district produced more than 99,000 ounces of
placer gold. Nearby is the notable Los Cerrillos
(Little Hills) region, containing the remains of
ancient turquoise mines worked by the Indians
centuries before the Spanish arrived. Los
Cerrillos is considered the oldest mining district in the United States.

CHAMA

US 84, 9 miles from the Colorado border
What began in 1865 as a small crossroads community accommodating wagon traffic between
Santa Fe and Colorado sprang into an important
supply center with the coming of the Denver &
Rio Grande Western Railroad in the 1880s. At its
elevation of nearly 8,000 feet, Chama figured
prominently in the transport of lumber, precious
ore, and crude oil. The present town of Chama,

COMMUNITY EVENTS
Chama Days
Rodeo Grounds
505-477-0149
A parade, rodeo, arts and crafts, and
dances in early August.
Chama Winter Carnival
505-756-2306
Dances, a hot-air balloon rally, and
cross-country ski competitions in
February and early March.

Wagon loads of ore are being hauled to the train depot in Cerrillos for shipment in 1884. Photograph by J. R. Riddle, courtesy Museum of New Mexico, neg. 76055

still dappled with log buildings, serves as an outdoor recreation center replete with facilities for trout fishing, hunting, camping, picnicking, hiking, boating, snowmobiling, and cross-country skiing.

HISTORIC BUILDINGS AND SITES
Burns-Kelly Store
Terrace Avenue and Fifth Street
A regional landmark for more than a century, this once-bustling general store was built in 1886 by T. D. Burns and later owned by Pat Kelly. ◉

Chama Jailhouse
2074 NM 17
The original log jailhouse, built in 1879. ◉

Cumbres & Toltec Scenic Railroad Depot
500 South Terrace Avenue
PO Box 789, 87520
505-756-2151

In 1880, the Denver & Rio Grande Western Railroad built a narrow-gauge stretch of rail, known as the San Juan Extension, to serve the mines of southwestern Colorado. Currently, the Cumbres & Toltec Scenic Railroad operates 64 miles of that narrow-gauge system, running between Chama and Antonito, Colorado. Jointly owned by New Mexico and Colorado, its restored rolling stock constitutes America's longest and highest-running steam railroad—a "living museum" of railway history. A Moonlight Ride, sponsored by Friends of the Railroad, is offered in mid-June. ◉☐

Foster Hotel (formerly Chama Hotel)
Terrace Avenue and Fourth Street
Built in 1881 to support the Denver & Rio Grande Western Railroad's entry into the area, this hotel was one of the first community buildings in Chama and the only one to survive several disastrous fires that blazed through the town. ◉☐

A gateway of adobe and hand-hewn wood welcomes visitors to the Santuario de Chimayó. Photograph by Mark Nohl

LIBRARIES
Eleanor Daggett Memorial Library
Fourth and Maple Streets
PO Box 795, 87520
505-756-2388

CHIMAYÓ

NM 76, 10 miles east of Española
Occupied for centuries by Tewa Indians, this tract of land near the confluence of three streams was established as a Spanish provincial village shortly after the reconquest of New Mexico in 1693. Since 1817, it has served as a holy site for religious pilgrims. The present-day village retains both the historical pattern of settlement around a defensible plaza and the community's importance as a center of northern New Mexico Spanish tradition. Chimayó is known worldwide for its textile weavers.

HISTORIC BUILDINGS AND SITES
Plaza del Cerro
Chimayó's old plaza epitomizes a fortified colonial plaza better than any other location in New Mexico. The old town square, with its surrounding low adobe structures, is thought to date back to the 1740s. The original *torreón* (defensive watchtower), still in good condition, overlooks the plaza. ◉□

Santuario de Chimayó
NM 520
PO Box 235, 87522
505-351-4889
Since its construction in 1817, this church has been the destination of countless pilgrims and visitors drawn by testimonies about the curative power of the earth from the anteroom beside the altar. As many as 30,000 people participate in an annual Good Friday pilgrimage to the historic sanctuary. ◉□△

LIBRARIES
Chimayó Community Library
PO Box 537, 87522
505-351-4881

CÓRDOVA

NM 76, 3 miles east of Chimayó
Formerly called Pueblo Quemado (Burned Pueblo), the village was renamed after a family who settled in the region following the Spanish reconquest of 1693. This small, hillside community high in the Sangre de Cristo Mountains went on to develop a long tradition in woodcarving. Today, skilled artisans can be seen transforming the native aspen and cedar into *santos* (carved images of the saints) as well as

decorative items. Near the center of town is the church of San Antonio de Padua, built in 1831.

DIXON

NM 75 at NM 68
Set between the hills and canyons of the Embudo River, this village is rich with apple orchards and humming with artists. Many of the buildings were constructed of local stone.

COMMUNITY EVENTS
Open Studio Tours
Many artists and craftmakers open their doors to the public on this autumn weekend in early November. Sponsored by the Dixon Arts Association.

LIBRARIES
Embudo Valley Library
2 NM 75
PO Box 310, 87527
505-579-9181

EAGLE NEST

US 64 and NM 38, 16 miles south of Red River
This small Moreno Valley resort community is situated along the edge of Eagle Nest Lake. Founded in 1920 near a newly completed dam, the village was called Therma; however, the spotting of golden eagles in the nearby mountains in 1935 prompted the townspeople to rename their hamlet. Eagle Nest is a center for trading, sailing, surfing, fishing, and other forms of recreation.

COMMUNITY EVENTS
High Country Arts Festival
PO Box 44, 87718
505-377-2567
An arts and crafts festival in late July.

HISTORIC BUILDINGS AND SITES
Wheeler Peak
West of Eagle Nest
Visible across the Moreno Valley and soaring 13,161 feet above sea level is the highest peak in New Mexico. Wheeler Peak is composed of resistant granites and gneisses formed in the Precambrian age. The valley is underlain by soft sandstone and shale covered by stream and glacial deposits. Placer gold was mined just north of Wheeler Peak during the 1860s.

LIBRARIES
Eagle Nest Public Library
Willow Creek Drive
PO Box 168, 87718
505-377-2486

ELIZABETHTOWN

NM 38, 5 miles north of Eagle Nest
This gold-mining town boasted more than 7,000 residents during its heyday in the 1860s. In 1870, E-town became the seat of newly formed Colfax County. By the beginning of the 20th century, most of the mines were played out, then fire destroyed the business district in 1903. All that remains are a few foundations, ruins, and a cemetery.

EL RITO

NM 554, 12 miles north of US 84 junction
Settled in the 1830s by Abiquiú-area residents,
El Rito was selected as a teacher-training site
by the Territorial Legislature of 1909. Soon
afterward, the Spanish-American Normal School
was established to train teachers for northern
New Mexico schools. Now, after several changes
in name and purpose, the institution is
Northern New Mexico Community College.

LIBRARIES
El Rito Public Library
PO Box 5, 87530
505-581-4789

PUBLIC ART
**Northern New Mexico Community College
Administration Building**
US 84
D. Paul Jones
"The Founding of San Juan, The First Capital of
New Spain"—oil triptych
New Deal Art

EMBUDO

NM 68 at NM 75
This stretch of land in a narrow canyon of the
Río Grande was named Embudo (Funnel) by
17th-century Spanish settlers. Later, it became a
service stop on the Denver & Rio Grande
Railway. Then, in 1888, the nation's first
stream-gaging station was erected along the
town's riverbank. The railroad station is now a
restaurant, and many structures built in 1880
are still standing. ◉☐

HISTORIC BUILDINGS AND SITES
Embudo Stream-Gaging Station
NM 68
The station was established in 1888 as the first
United States Geological Survey training center
for hydrographers. Those who trained here
conducted some of the earliest hydrological
studies known, setting the stage for later evalua-
tions of the nation's surface-water resources. ◉

PERFORMING ARTS
Música y Danza Folklorica del Norte
PO Box 61, 87531
505-579-4300
Devoted to the research and performance of
traditional New Mexican music and dance,
including *Penitente alabado, corrido,* and *ballet folklorico.* A forum, as well, for New
Mexican composers.

ESPAÑOLA

US 84-285, 24 miles north of Santa Fe
Just north of this longtime heart of Pueblo
Indian culture was the site of the first Spanish
colony in New Mexico, established in 1598
when Juan de Oñate, under contract with the
Spanish crown to colonize the area, placed a
cross in pueblo soil. The colony, called San
Gabriel de los Caballeros, remained for nearly a
century the northern frontier of Spanish settlement in the United States. Española itself was
formed in the late 19th century as a railroad
stop. Fed by the Río Grande, it is now, as it was
then, a major nucleus for farming and ranching. Española continues to reflect its Indian and
Spanish heritage.

MUSEUMS AND EXHIBIT SPACES
Bond House Museum
710 Bond Street, 87532
505-753-8172
A Victorian-trimmed and -decorated home constructed in 1887 by Franklin Bond, a Canadian-born pioneer in the mercantile and ranching history of northern New Mexico. Donated to the city after Bond's death, the building is now a repository for the artistic and cultural heritage of the Española Valley. ⊚☐

Oñate Center
NM 68 at Alcalde
PO Box 1256, 87532
505-852-4639
Offers local arts and crafts exhibits as well as weekend cultural events and performing arts presentations.

HISTORIC BUILDINGS AND SITES
Chimayó Trading Post
205 Sandia Drive, 87532
505-753-9414
Established between World Wars I and II by E. D. Trujillo, one of northern New Mexico's most prolific entrepreneurs, in response to the tourist demand for Hispanic crafts, especially weaving. ⊚

San Gabriel—on the Camino Real
NM 68, 15 miles north of Española
The seat of the Spanish Colonial government in New Mexico from 1601 to 1610. Governor Juan de Oñate, having set up headquarters in what he called San Juan Pueblo in 1598, three years later moved his place of command across the Río Grande to Yunque-Ouinge (Mockingbird Place) Pueblo. Christened San Gabriel, it served as the Spanish capital until Oñate's successor founded a new capital at Santa Fe nine years afterward.

COMMUNITY EVENTS
Española Valley Arts Festival
Northern New Mexico Community College
505-753-2831
Arts and crafts, food booths, and entertainment in early October.

Oñate Fiesta
Valdez Park
505-753-2831
A parade, food, and entertainment in commemoration of the first governor of New Mexico. Held the second week in July.

CULTURAL ORGANIZATIONS
Española Valley Arts Council
PO Box 3997, 87533
505-747-1171

LIBRARIES
Española Public Library
314-A Oñate Street NW, 87532
505-753-3860

PUBLIC ART
Española National Guard Armory
US 84 at Fairview Drive
Sam Leyba
Ceramic tile mural

Northern New Mexico Community College Administration Building
US 84
Frederico Vigil
"1680 Pueblo Revolt"—frescoes

GALISTEO

NM 41, 21 miles southeast of Santa Fe
Spanish families settled this Tanoan Pueblo site
in the late 1700s. Today's village features a
restored Spanish *hacienda,* an old church, and
other adobe structures. Numerous petroglyphs
can be found in the area. ☉

HISTORIC BUILDINGS AND SITES
Galisteo Pueblo
NM 14 and 41, near Galisteo
From these four large Tano-speaking pueblos in
the Galisteo Basin came the chief leaders of the
Pueblo Revolt of 1680. Twenty-six years after
the uprising, 150 Tano families resettled in
Galisteo Pueblo. Droughts, famine, Comanche
raids, and disease led to its abandonment by
1788, at which point most survivors had moved
west to Santo Domingo Pueblo. ☉

JICARILLA APACHE RESERVATION

US 64, 25 miles west of Chama
PO Box 507, Dulce, 87528
505-759-3242
Mountainous, forested homestead to the Jicarilla
people who, until settling on the 742,000-acre
reservation in 1887, were traditionally nomadic.
Jicarilla, Spanish for "wicker basket," was the
name given to these Athabascan descendants in
acknowledgment of their basketry skills. Today,
the Jicarilla people are known not only for their
basket making but also for their beadwork and
cattle and sheep ranching. The reservation land
is open to fishing and hunting by permit, as well
as camping, cross-country skiing, boating, and
other outdoor activities. ☉▢

COMMUNITY EVENTS
Gojiiya Feast Day
Stone Lake
NM 537, 21 miles south of Dulce
505-759-3242
Blending religion and revelry, Gojiiya
celebrates a variety of important events,
including thanksgiving for a bountiful
harvest. Gojiiya also commemorates the
tribe's move to a homeland in northern
New Mexico from ancestral habitats in
the plains and mountains of southeastern Colorado, northeastern New Mexico,
western Texas, Oklahoma, and Kansas.
The mid-September observance includes
ceremonial dances and rituals, footraces
of the Ollero (White) and Llanero (Red)
clans, a powwow, and a trading bazaar.

Jicarilla Apache Day
505-759-3242
A founding observance held on February
11th.

Little Beaver Roundup
Community Center, Hawks Drive
PO Box 507, Dulce, 87528
505-759-3242
A parade, powwow, rodeo, dances, and
arts and crafts in mid-July.

MUSEUMS AND EXHIBIT SPACES
Jicarilla Museum
PO Box 507, Dulce, 87528
505-759-3242
Exhibits of basketry, beadwork, paintings, and
other arts and crafts.

LIBRARIES
Jicarilla Apache Community Library
Hawks Drive
PO Box 306, 87528
505-759-3616

LAMY

US 285, 15 miles south of Santa Fe
The closest the Santa Fe Railway came to providing
transcontinental passenger service to Santa Fe.
Railroad builders, following the Santa Fe Trail from
Kansas City, decided that the south rim of the Santa
Fe basin was too steep for the main line. Laying
rail for a shuttle into Santa Fe, they continued the
main line southwest into the Río Grande Valley and
Albuquerque. The result: the Santa Fe rail station
was constructed 15 miles south of town in Lamy!
The village was named for Archbishop Jean
Baptiste Lamy, a French clergyman who was sent
from Ohio, to restore Catholicism to Santa Fe. An
old-time saloon has been refurbished as a restaurant, and Amtrak still runs one train a day in each
direction through the village.

LAS TRAMPAS

NM 76, 25 miles north of Española
Settled around 1751 as a walled adobe village in
beaver-trapping country, Las Trampas (The Traps)
remains one of the finest examples of early
Spanish-American agricultural communities in the
United States. For villagers living in this secluded
valley, tradition guides the way of life. ◉□△

HISTORIC BUILDINGS AND SITES
San José de Gracia Church
Las Trampas Plaza
Built over a 20-year period beginning in 1760,
subsidized by the tithing of villagers' crops, ded-

icated to the 12 apostles, and adorned with
tower bells of silver and gold, this is one of the
best preserved and least altered Spanish
Colonial churches in New Mexico. It is also one
of the most significant 18th-century Spanish
churches in the United States, replete with
wooden *reredos* (sculpted religious panels) on
side walls and under the balcony. ◉□△

LOS ALAMOS

NM 502, 18 miles west of US 84-285
Located near ancient Indian ruins dotting the
Pajarito Plateau, Los Alamos (The Cottonwoods)
began in 1918 as a ranch school founded by
Detroit native Ashley Pond. By 1942, the school's
log buildings had given way to facilities for the Los
Alamos National Laboratory. Officials in
Washington, DC, had chosen this eastern slope of
the Jémez Mountains for the highly secretive
Manhattan Project which, under the direction of
physicist Robert Oppenheimer, was to develop an
atom bomb. Following the explosions at Hiroshima
and Nagasaki, scientific pursuits at Los Alamos
expanded into the areas of metallurgy, geothermal
and solar investigations, and genetic research.

MUSEUMS AND EXHIBIT SPACES
Bandelier National Monument
NM 4, 12 miles south of Los Alamos
HCR 1, Box 1, Suite 15, 87544
505-672-3861
Set within this spectacular canyon cut deep into
the slopes of the Jémez Volcano are 12th-centu-
ry Indian cliff dwellings and surface villages.
The monument encompasses waterfalls and
wilderness area for backcountry hiking as well
as an extensive visitor center with explanatory
exhibits, artifacts, and a library. Fee. ◉□△

Officials announce the establishment of New Mexico's newest, smallest county in 1950. Photograph by Harold D. Walter, courtesy Museum of New Mexico, neg. 53110

Bradbury Science Museum
15th Street and Central Avenue
Los Alamos National Laboratory
Mail Stop C-330, 87545
505-667-4444
Displays interpret Project Y—development of the atom bomb—as well as the defense, energy, and basic science research undertaken at Los Alamos National Laboratory. Offerings include self-guiding interactive exhibits, computer programs, and films.

Fuller Lodge Art Center and Gallery
2132 Central Avenue
PO Box 790, 87544
505-662-9331
The center conducts arts and crafts classes and sponsors two fairs, one in August and the other in October. The gallery presents invitational and juried exhibits of artwork from New Mexico and around the world. Exhibits change monthly.

Los Alamos County Historical Museum
1921 Juniper Street
PO Box 43, 87544
505-662-6272
On display in the former Ranch School Guest House, built in 1922, are Laura Gilpin's and T. Harmon Parkhurst's photographs of the school; memorabilia from the school and the Manhattan Project; a collection of Indian pottery and 1940s pottery; and prehistoric Indian artifacts. Also available are slides, photo archives, and oral history tapes. The museum grounds encompass prehistoric Indian ruins as well as a relocated and restored Hispanic homesteader's cabin. ☺

Los Alamos National Laboratory (formerly Los Alamos Ranch School for Boys)
Diamond Drive at West Jémez Road
PO Box 1663, 87545
505-667-5061
Headquarters of the Manhattan Project which, beginning in 1942, led to the development of the atom bomb. The lab remains a center for nuclear and other scientific research. ⊚□△

PERFORMING ARTS
Bridge the Gap
Downtown area
505-662-0013
A communitywide music festival held in June.

Los Alamos Concert Series
PO Box 572, 87544
505-662-2936
An October-to-April season of five concerts featuring internationally known soloists and ensembles such as the Martha Graham Dance Company, Yo-Yo Ma, the Canadian Brass, and Fredrica von Stade. Sponsored by the Los Alamos Concert Association.

Los Alamos Light Opera
PO Box 353, 87544
505-662-4739
Local talent productions held at the Civic Auditorium the last two weekends in February.

Los Alamos Little Theater
1670 Nectar, 87544
505-662-8105
Classic and contemporary plays on weekends in January, March, and May.

CULTURAL ORGANIZATIONS
Los Alamos Arts Council
3514 Arizona Avenue, 87544
505-667-5329

Los Alamos Historical Society
PO Box 43, 87544
505-662-6272
Operates the Los Alamos County Historical Museum, sponsors a year-round lecture series, and conducts an award-winning publishing program, conferences, workshops, tours to historic sites, and educational outreach in schools.

Los Alamos Recorder Society
324 Andanada Avenue, 87544
505-662-7382
The local chapter of the American Recorder Society.

LIBRARIES
Los Alamos County Library
1742 Central Avenue, 87544
505-662-8240

COMMUNITY EVENTS
Early Christmas Arts and Crafts Fair
Los Alamos Middle School
505-662-9331
Sponsored by the Fuller Lodge Art Center on the last Saturday in October.

Los Alamos Arts and Crafts Fair
Fuller Lodge Lawn
2132 Central Avenue
505-662-8105
Sponsored by the Fuller Lodge Art Center in mid-May, and again in mid-November.

PUBLIC ART

Ashley Pond
Trinity Drive
Craig Dan Goseyun
"Apache Harvest"—bronze sculpture
Thomas Hicks
"Strange Trio"—steel sculpture
Jinkie Hughes
"Who Me?"—steel sculpture
Madeleine McAlpin Vanderpool
"Corky"—bronze sculpture

Bradbury Science Museum
15th Street and Central Avenue
Frank Morbillo
"Entropy Column"—steel and concrete fountain

University of New Mexico-Los Alamos
Mesa Gymnasium
Diamond Drive
Janet Maher
Ceramic tile mural

LOS OJOS

US 84, 10 miles south of Chama
In this historic district, founded around 1860,
villagers raise nearly extinct churro sheep and
weave wool in the same ways as before, carrying
forward an old Río Grande tradition. Many of the
original village houses are still standing. ⊚▢

HISTORIC BUILDINGS AND SITES

T. D. Burns Store
US 84
A large, pitched-roof adobe building constructed around 1875 by local merchant and politician Thomas D. Burns. The first major public
building in Los Ojos, the store served as a community center; an arena for political, social,

---

COMMUNITY EVENTS
Fiesta de Santiago
505-558-7231
A religious procession and community
celebration in late July.

and cultural activities; and headquarters for *El
Nuevo Mundo,* a Tierra Amarilla-area newspaper published around 1907 to 1908. ⊚▢

La Gruta: Shrine of Our Lady of Lourdes
Old Highway
This shrine was constructed in 1919 by Señora
Josefa Gallegos Burns following her miraculous
escape from injury when she lost control of her
buggy while traveling to church in Los Ojos. ⊚▢

Los Ojos Fish Hatchery and Burns Lake
Bungalow
Hatchery Road
A complex constructed in 1932 to 1933 as a
WPA project devised to breed fish in the southern part of the Chama River Valley. Designed in
decorative Beaux Arts style, the hatchery currently produces about 7 million rainbow trout
eggs annually, as well as brown trout and koka-
nee and coho salmon. Self-guided tours. ⊚▢

San José Church
Completed in 1936, the church houses a magnificent altar imported in 1919 to commemorate the area's World War I veterans.

MADRID

NM 14, 27 miles south of Santa Fe
A coal-mining town in the 1880s, Madrid, with
its rows of wood-frame company houses, was
abandoned as the demand for coal diminished

COMMUNITY EVENTS

Christmas in Madrid
505-471-3450
Gallery open houses and refreshments
amid giant nursery rhyme and Christmas
figures from seasons past. Held in early
December.

Madrid Blues Festival
Madrid Ballpark
PO Box 1925, 87103
A Memorial Day weekend event spon-
sored by the New Mexico Jazz Workshop.

soon after World War II. Although still billed as
a ghost town, it has been resurrected. In 1975,
many of the old houses were sold to artists and
historic-district renovators, who restored the
dwellings. Partly unoccupied and dilapidated,
and partly repopulated, Madrid is now a thriving arts and crafts center. ☉☐

MUSEUMS AND EXHIBIT SPACES

Old Coal Mine Museum
Main Street, 87010
505-473-0743
On display are a coal mine shaft and railroad,
as well as such mining artifacts as antique cars
and Engine 769, a 1900 Atchison, Topeka &
Santa Fe steam locomotive. Fee.

PERFORMING ARTS

Engine House Theatre
Main Street, 87010
505-473-0743
A converted locomotive repair building featuring Victorian melodrama with local actors on

Saturdays, Sundays, and holidays from
Memorial Day weekend through Labor Day.

Madrid Music in the Open Air
Madrid Park
505-989-9662
Summertime jazz, bluegrass, and chamber
music concerts on Sundays.

Mine Shaft Tavern Dinner Theatre
Main Street, 87010
505-473-0743
Original mysteries and classic stage plays with
local actors, presented October through mid-
January.

NAMBÉ PUEBLO

**US 285 to NM 503, 21 miles northeast of
Santa Fe**
Route 1, Box 117-BB, Santa Fe, 87501
505-455-2036
The pueblo of Nambé (Mound of Earth in the
Corner), inhabited since approximately 1300,
is now a shadow of its former self. Less than
two dozen of its 200 precolonial structures
remain. Extensive intermarriage during the
colonial years led to a blending of beliefs and
ceremonies. Although residents of this once
largely agricultural pueblo now work in nearby
Española or Los Alamos, due to a recent resur-
gence of interest in the traditional rituals and
crafts, weaving and the making of black-on-
black and white-on-red pottery are being revived. The pueblo is set amid spectacular beauty—with breathtaking views of the Sangre de
Cristo Mountains and within walking distance of
Nambé Falls and Nambé Lake. ☉☐

COMMUNITY EVENTS

Dances to Commemorate the Christmas Season
Traditional dances during Christmas week.

Easter Celebration
A Mass, procession, and traditional dances.

Nambé Pueblo Feast Day
A morning Mass and procession, followed by traditional Indian dances, in honor of the pueblo's patron saint, San Francisco de Asís. Held on October 4th.

Nambé Pueblo Waterfall Ceremony
Nambé Falls Recreation Area
Dance teams present the Buffalo, Corn, Deer, Comanche, and Spear Dances on the Fourth of July.

Three Kings Day
Transfer of the Canes of Authority honoring new tribal officials on January 6th.

Sheep graze on the stubble of harvested fields at Picurís Pueblo, around 1940. Photograph by T. Harmon Parkhurst, courtesy Museum of New Mexico, neg. 68820

PICURÍS PUEBLO

NM 68, 20 miles south of Taos
PO Box 127, Peñasco, 87553
505-587-2519

Settled between 1250 and 1300 by Tiwa-speaking residents of a large pueblo near Taos, Picurís (Those Who Paint) was described by Spanish explorers as the site of a six-story building and one of the largest of the northern pueblos. Today it is one of the smallest. During the Pueblo

COMMUNITY EVENTS

Candlemas Day
Traditional observances on February 2nd.

Dances to Commemorate the Christmas Season
A sundown torchlight procession of the Virgin, Vespers, and a Matachines Dance.

Easter Celebration
A Mass, procession, and dances, including the Corn Dance.

High Country Arts and Crafts Festival
A large tricultural arts and crafts exhibit, dances, and a fishing contest to benefit the pueblo's San Lorenzo mission church. Held in early July.

New Year's Day Celebration
A Mass, procession, and traditional dances, including the Turtle and Matachines Dances, on January 1st.

San Lorenzo Feast Day
Sunset dances followed by a morning Mass and procession and afternoon Buffalo, Comanche, or Corn Dances; ceremonial footraces; a pole climb; and an arts and crafts fair. Held on August 9th and 10th.

Three Kings Day
Transfer of the Canes of Authority to honor new tribal officers on January 6th.

Revolt of 1680, the village was abandoned; in 1706, it was repopulated. Beneath today's village lie the ruins of a much larger community with three now-restored underground kivas. The Picurís people, secluded deep within the Sangre de Cristo Mountains, have clung to their customs, including the making of iridescent, bronzelike, unornamented cookware. ☺□

MUSEUMS AND EXHIBIT SPACES

Picurís Pueblo Museum Center
PO Box 228, Peñasco, 87533
505-587-2519
Displays include prehistoric artifacts, photos and text of local history, and the work of regional contemporary artists. The museum also maintains the historic pueblo ruins, mission church, scalp house, and several restored kivas.

POJOAQUE PUEBLO

US 84-285, 16 miles northwest of Santa Fe
Route 11, Box 71, Santa Fe, 87501
505-455-2278
Centrally located among the six Tewa-speaking tribes, Pojoaque is the smallest pueblo in New Mexico. True to its original name, Po suwae geh (Water Drinking Place), the settlement was a place at which travelers stopped to drink water at the confluence of three rivers. On the grounds of the original pueblo are structures predating the invasion of the Spanish in the 16th century. Although the present-day pueblo is without a definable village and its population has twice dwindled to near extinction, the Pojoaque people have reestablished their traditional crafts of pottery making, embroidery, crochet work, and beading on leather. Pojoaque was the first pueblo to elect a woman governor.

MUSEUMS AND EXHIBIT SPACES

Poeh Center
US 84-285, 12 miles north of Santa Fe
Route 11, Box 71, Santa Fe, 87501
505-455-3334

COMMUNITY EVENTS

Our Lady of Guadalupe Feast Day
A midmorning Mass and procession followed by Buffalo, Butterfly, Bow and Arrow, and Comanche Dances on December 12th.

An arts and crafts complex celebrating the Tewa-speaking pueblos of Pojoaque, Tesuque, Nambé, San Juan, San Ildefonso, and Santa Clara. The center includes a museum, a gallery offering one of the largest selections of Indian pottery in northern New Mexico, art studios around a working plaza, as well as a resource center, traditional cooking area, presentation plaza, and cultural training center.

CULTURAL ORGANIZATIONS

Northern Pueblos Arts Council
Poeh Center
Route 11, Box 27E, Santa Fe, 87501
505-455-0224

LIBRARIES

Pojoaque Pueblo Community Library
Route 11, Box 71, Santa Fe, 87501
505-455-7511

RANCHOS DE TAOS

NM 68, 3 miles south of Taos
Once a farming center for local Indians, the village was settled by the Spanish in 1716. Its original two-story adobe buildings and much celebrated church are still clustered around the old plaza.

The graceful curves of San Francisco de Asís Church at Ranchos de Taos have captivated generations of painters and photographers. Photograph by Mark Nohl

MUSEUMS AND EXHIBIT SPACES

Fort Burgwin Research Center
NM 518, 6 miles south of Ranchos de Taos
PO Box 300, 87557
505-758-8322
Fort Burgwin was built in the 1850s to protect
Taos from the displaced Ute and Jicarilla
Apache Indians. Abandoned in 1860, the fort
was converted into an academic campus for
Southern Methodist University. The center offers
public lectures every Tuesday night in June,
July, and August; archaeological excavation
tours by advance arrangement; and a museum
in the summer months.

HISTORIC BUILDINGS AND SITES

Ranchos de Taos Plaza
Established in 1779, the Plaza is enclosed by
about 20 buildings of frame and adobe, including the historic mission church of San
Francisco de Asís, built in 1803. ◎□

San Francisco de Asís Church
Ranchos de Taos Plaza
505-758-2754
Built in the early 19th century by Franciscans,
this is the most frequently painted and pho-
tographed church in the United States and an
outstanding example of adobe mission architecture. Replete with *reredos* (sculpted religious
panels), *retablos* (altar screens), *santos*
(painted or carved wooden images of the
saints), and religious paintings, the church
continues as a place of worship and an integral
part of the community. ◎△

CULTURAL ORGANIZATIONS

Taos Hispanic Arts Council
5273 NDCBU, 87571
505-758-1773

RED RIVER

NM 38, 12 miles east of Questa
Soon after gold was discovered in the surrounding Rocky Mountains, Red River was established
as a pioneer mining settlement. By 1905, the
town boasted a population of 3,000. Twenty
years later, the mines—and for the most part,
the town—were abandoned. Today, the village
serves as a year-round mountain resort devoted
to cross-country and downhill skiing, snowmobiling, biking, hiking, fishing, and horseback riding. Structures dating from the 1880s and 1890s
remain, along with the Red River Schoolhouse
and Miners Hospital, buildings constructed
between 1914 and 1915, during the final stage of
mining prosperity in Red River City. ◎□

MUSEUMS AND EXHIBIT SPACES

Tall Pines Museum
Tall Pine Resort
PO Box 567, 87558
505-754-2241
Local history and mining exhibits housed in a
cabin built during the region's early mining days.

COMMUNITY EVENTS

Aspencade Celebration
Brandenburg Park
800-348-6444
An art show, square dance, and German
wurstfest in late September.
Mardi Gras in the Mountains
Ski Basin
800-348-6444
A "Fat Tuesday" celebration with parades
on the ski slopes and balls in the lodges
in late February to early March.

PERFORMING ARTS
Red River Summer Melodrama Season
Mine Shaft Theater, Red River Inn
505-754-2930
Performances on Tuesdays and Fridays, June through Labor Day.

LIBRARIES
Red River Public Library
High Street
PO Box 1020, 87558
505-754-6564

A San Ildefonso Pueblo woman bakes bread in a traditional horno around 1940. Photograph by Wyatt Davis, courtesy Museum of New Mexico, neg. 3712

SAN ILDEFONSO PUEBLO

US 84-285 to NM 502, 24 miles north of Santa Fe
Route 5, Box 315A
Santa Fe, 87501
505-455-3549
Nestled in the Río Grande Valley between two mountain ranges, this pueblo has been continuously occupied by the San Ildefonso people since before 1300. During the Spanish reconquest, following the Pueblo Revolt of 1680, villagers retreated to the top of

COMMUNITY EVENTS
Dances to Commemorate the Christmas Season
A Matachines Dance.

Easter Celebration
A Mass, procession, and dances.

Eight Northern Indian Pueblos Artist and Craftsman Show
Featuring the work of more than 600 North American Indians; traditional Pueblo and Plains dances between 11 am and 4 pm; and food booths. Scheduled for the third weekend in July.

New Year's Day Celebration
A Mass, procession, and traditional dances.

San Antonio Feast Day
A Corn Dance on June 13th.

San Ildefonso Pueblo Feast Day
Firelight Buffalo and Deer Dances and a church procession in the plaza, followed by a midmorning Mass the next day. Held on January 22nd and 23rd.

Three Kings Day
Transfer of the Canes of Authority to new tribal officers on January 6th.

Black Mesa, where they lived for four years. In August 1694, San Ildefonso became the last of the pueblos to submit to the reconquest. Today the pueblo is known worldwide for its black-on-black pottery, revived in the 1920s by María Martínez, and for its watercolor artists. About 20,000 visitors traverse San Ildefonso's large central plaza each year. ◎☐

MUSEUMS AND EXHIBIT SPACES
San Ildefonso Pueblo Museum
Route 5, Box 315-A, Santa Fe, 87501
505-455-2424
Exhibits contemporary and traditional pottery, paintings, and other artifacts depicting the rich history of the San Ildefonso people.

HISTORIC BUILDINGS AND SITES
Black Mesa
From atop this 1,000-foot volcanic butte, visible from miles around, San Ildefonso warriors held off Don Diego de Vargas in 1694. In one of many myths about Black Mesa, the giant Tsah-ve-voh comes down from his home on the mesatop each fall to punish those who have misbehaved during the year. The top of the mesa is covered with ruins of pit houses and villages. This landmark is sacred to the San Ildefonso people and not open to the public. ◎

LIBRARIES
San Ildefonso Pueblo Community Library
Route 5, Box 315A, Santa Fe, 87501
505-455-2424

SAN JUAN PUEBLO

NM 68 at US 285
PO Box 1099, 87566
505-852-4400

Twenty-two years before the Pilgrims landed at Plymouth Rock, San Juan Pueblo was proclaimed the first capital of New Mexico by conquistador Juan de Oñate. At the time, the pueblo, consisting of two Tewa-speaking villages on facing banks of the Río Grande, was an intertribal meeting ground. Eighty-two years later, San Juan religious leader Popé launched the Pueblo Revolt of 1680. Present-day San Juan ceremonies take place under the auspices of a two-part social system composed of the Winter People and the Summer People. ◎☐

MUSEUMS AND EXHIBIT SPACES
Oke Oweenge Arts & Crafts Cooperative
San Juan Pueblo Village
PO Box 1095, 87544
505-852-2372
Here, visitors may watch artisans at work on a variety of art forms. Jewelry, carvings, redware and micaceous pottery, and other arts and crafts are available for purchase.

COMMUNITY EVENTS
Dances to Commemorate the Christmas Season
A sundown torchlight procession of the Virgin, Vespers, and a Matachines Dance on December 24th. A Turtle Dance on December 26th.

San Juan Pueblo Feast Day
A midmorning Mass and procession, followed by Comanche and Buffalo Dances, on June 24th.

Three Kings Day
Transfer of the Canes of Authority to new tribal officers on January 6th.

HISTORIC BUILDINGS AND SITES
San Gabriel de Yunque-Ouinge
US 285, .75 miles west of San Juan Pueblo
Site of an early Tewa pueblo and, later, the sec-
ond European settlement established in New
Mexico. The community was the seat of the
Spanish Colonial government from 1601 to
1610, when the capital was moved south to
Santa Fe. ⊘□△

CULTURAL ORGANIZATIONS
Eight Northern Pueblos Arts Council
Route 11, Box 27E, 87501
505-455-0224

LIBRARIES
San Juan Pueblo Community Library
PO Box 1099, 87566
505-852-2588

SANTA CLARA PUEBLO

NM 30, 2 miles southwest of Española
Box 580, Española, 87532
505-753-7330
Around the 13th century, nearly 1,500
Puebloans migrated from drought-ridden
Pajarito Plateau in the Jémez Mountains to the
Río Grande's fertile "Valley of the Wild Roses,"
as they called their new homeland. Each year in
July, the residents of Santa Clara leave the now
prosperous valley village for their ancestral
mesatop dwellings at Puyé Cliffs. Today's pueblo
is home to many noted sculptors, painters, and
potters distinguished for their often intricately
carved, highly polished redware and blackware.
Developed campsites and fishing ponds are
available to visitors. ⊘□

COMMUNITY EVENTS
Holy Innocents Day
Children's dances on December 28th.

San Antonio Feast Day
A Corn Dance on June 13th.

Santa Clara Pueblo Feast Day
A midmorning Mass and procession, fol-
lowed by afternoon Corn and Harvest
Dances, on August 12th.

Three Kings Day
Honoring of the new tribal leaders on
January 6th.

HISTORIC BUILDINGS AND SITES
Puyé Cliff Dwellings
1.3 miles west of Santa Clara Pueblo
505-753-7326
The prehistoric ruins of a 740-room pueblo
carved from volcanic tufa include a ceremonial
chamber, a Great Community House, and petroglyphs. Self-guided tours as well as guided tours
followed by a Pueblo feast are available with
advance reservations during the summer. ⊘□△

LIBRARIES
Santa Clara Pueblo Community Library
PO Box 580, Española, 87532
505-753-7326

SANTA CRUZ

NM 76, 8 miles east of Española
The village of Santa Cruz was settled on the south
side of the Río Santa Cruz in 1598 by Spanish
colonists who arrived with Juan de Oñate.

Abandoned during the Pueblo Revolt, the village was subsequently occupied by Indians from nearby Tano pueblos, who remained until Don Diego de Vargas ordered them out during the Spanish reconquest. A new village, built in 1695 on the north side of the Río Santa Cruz, became the second official "royal villa" in Spanish New Mexico. For more than 300 years, Santa Cruz remained an important stop on the Camino Real between Santa Fe—the first "royal city"—and Taos.

HISTORIC BUILDINGS AND SITES
La Iglesia de Santa Cruz de la Cañada
Dominating the plaza at Santa Cruz is an extraordinary church constructed in the shape of a cross, with three-foot-thick adobe walls, corbeled *vigas* (log roof beams), a restored *reredos* (sculpted religious panel), and a *retablo* (painted wooden altar screen). Built in 1733, the mission is one of the largest in New Mexico and holds a treasury of Spanish-Mexican art. ☉□

Santa Cruz Dam
NM 76, 14 miles east of Española
The dam was created between 1926 and 1929 by the Santa Cruz Irrigation District to provide irrigation water to about 5,000 acres of land along the Río Santa Cruz. ☉

SANTA FE

I-25 at US 84-285
Founded by Don Pedro de Peralta near the site of an ancient Tanoan Indian village in 1607, La Villa de Santa Fe in 1610 became the oldest capital city in the United States. Over its Palace of the Governors have flown the flags of four nations: Spain, Mexico, the Confederacy, and the United States. Throughout nearly four centuries of history, Santa Fe has been a prominent center for the

arts, religion, and commerce. In the 1800s, the town's muddy, open Plaza was the energetic terminus to the much-traveled Santa Fe Trail. As the railroad found its way west, the town continued its role as an important cultural center. Due to its fascinating diversity of buildings and people, combined with its 7,000-foot altitude and delightful climate, Santa Fe has been a popular destination for nearly all of its prolific history.

MUSEUMS AND EXHIBIT SPACES
El Rancho de las Golondrinas
La Cienega—I-25, 15 miles southwest of Santa Fe
334 Los Piños Road, 87505
505-471-2261
A living-history museum featuring the original complex of one of the Southwest's most historic Spanish Colonial ranches. El Rancho de las Golondrinas (The Ranch of the Swallows) has been restored with replicas of structures built on the original foundations in the early 1700s. The grounds also include an old mountain village, working water mills, wheelwright and blacksmith shops, a schoolhouse, threshing grounds, and a Penitente meetinghouse. Costumed docents answer questions about the ranch, and local craftworkers demonstrate their skills. Las Golondrinas, open April through October, offers special festivals throughout the summer. Fee.

Governor's Gallery
State Capitol
505-827-3017
Presents temporary art exhibits, an annual Governor's Award for Achievement in the Arts, and public openings.

Institute of American Indian Arts Museum
108 Cathedral Place, 87501
505-988-6281
Features exhibits from the National Collection
(continued on page 50)

MUSEUM OF NEW MEXICO
113 Lincoln Avenue
PO Box 2087, 87504
505-827-6451
An 80-year-old state-operated system of four museums in Santa Fe, five historic site monuments around the state, four research libraries, an artifact conservation laboratory, an archaeological research section, a statewide programs and education unit, an award-winning museum press, and an exhibitions design and fabrication workshop. The museums are the Laboratory of Anthropology/Museum of Indian Arts and Culture, the Museum of Fine Arts, the Museum of International Folk Art, and the Palace of the Governors. The monuments are Fort Selden, Fort Sumner, Jémez, Coronado, and Lincoln. A part of the New Mexico Office of Cultural Affairs. ◉

Laboratory of Anthropology
708 Camino Lejo
PO Box 2087, 87504
505-827-6344
An anthropological and archaeological research facility that maintains a collection of more than 50,000 Indian artifacts as well as a comprehensive selection of books on the Southwest and a consulting staff of experts in archaeology and ethnology. Small exhibits are periodically displayed in this gracious structure designed in Spanish-Pueblo Revival style by local architect John Gaw Meem. The lab's prestigious collections are showcased in the nearby Museum of Indian Arts and Culture. ◉▢

Museum of Indian Arts and Culture
710 Camino Lejo
PO Box 2087, 87504
505-827-8000
The exhibits and programs focusing on Pueblo, Navajo, and Apache peoples of the Southwest communicate the message that Indian culture in this region is strong, vibrant, and growing. A Living Traditions program spotlights Indian artisans working in such traditional and contemporary art forms as basketry, pottery, jewelry, weaving, and beadwork.

Museum of Fine Arts
107 East Palace Avenue
PO Box 2087, 87504
505-827-4471
Exhibits include works by outstanding artists of the Southwest, including Georgia O'Keeffe, Andrew Dasburg, Laura Gilpin, Ernest Blumenschein, Marsden Hartley, and Eliot Porter, as well as contemporary artists. The building's 1917 Pueblo Revival style of construction—complete with split-cedar *latillas* (roof supports) and hand-hewn *vigas* (log roof beams)—has become synonymous with "Santa Fe style." The world-famous Santa Fe Chamber Music Festival makes its home in the museum's St. Francis Auditorium in the summer months.

Museum of International Folk Art
706 Camino Lejo
PO Box 2087, 87504
505-827-6350
Repository for the world's largest collection of international folk art and the nation's most important collection of Hispanic folk art. The

Palace of the Governors. Photograph by Mark Nohl

world-class Girard Collection occupies an entire wing of the museum. A newly opened Hispanic Heritage Wing offers permanent exhibition space to an outstanding collection of Hispanic folk art from around the world.

Palace of the Governors
Santa Fe Plaza
PO Box 2087, 87504
505-827-6474
This one-time adobe fortress and government center is the oldest continuously occupied public building in the United States.

Constructed in 1610 by the Spanish government, the Palace has served as headquarters for Colonial Spain, Mexico, Pueblo Indians, the US Army, and the Confederacy. Bordering the Plaza—the center of life in Santa Fe—the Palace chronicles nearly 450 years of European presence in the Southwest. In addition to a variety of permanent exhibits, including a full-scale reproduction of a mountain village chapel, are a photo archive, history library, and, outdoors under the portico, Indian artisans selling jewelry and pottery. Also on the premises is the Palace Press, a living exhibit of antique, hand-operated letterpresses. ◉□△

of Contemporary Indian Art as well as works by nationally recognized contemporary American Indian artists, educational programming, and extensive photography collections. Museum facilities include five galleries, education and performance space, the Allan Houser Art Park, and a book and gift shop. Fee.

Santa Fe Children's Museum
1050 Old Pecos Trail, 87501
505-989-8359
Offers hands-on exhibits, arts and science programs, monthly family performances, parent education, and other special events. Fee.

Wheelwright Museum of the American Indian
704 Camino Lejo
PO Box 5153, 87502
505-982-4636
A privately operated museum built, under the guidance of Navajo shaman Hastiin Klah, in the shape of an eight-sided Navajo *hooghan* in 1937. Changing exhibits feature contemporary and historic Indian art and culture. Special events include storytelling by Joe Hayes in July and August, and a children's powwow in the fall. Case Trading Post, on the lower level, sells Indian arts and crafts as well as books and handmade cards.

HISTORIC BUILDINGS AND SITES
Acequia Madre
Garcia and Acequia Madre Streets
Acequias (ditches) played a critical role in the early history of Santa Fe. By cutting off the water supply from the Acequia de la Muralla, which ran along the north wall of the city, Pueblo Indians forced the Spanish colonists to evacuate the Palace of the Governors in 1680. Using a similar strategy 13 years later, Vargas regained control of the city. Although little remains of that

main ditch, the Acequia Madre, on the south side of the Río de Santa Fe, still flows when the irrigation gates are opened. ☉

Archbishop Lamy's Chapel
Bishop's Lodge Resort
Bishop's Lodge Road
505-983-6377
A modest structure built in the foothills north of Santa Fe in the late 1860s to serve as the private retreat of the first bishop of New Mexico, Jean Baptiste Lamy. ☉

Atchison, Topeka & Santa Fe Railway Depot
Garfield Street
Constructed in 1909 in the California Mission style adapted by the Santa Fe Railway to introduce its passengers to regional architecture. ☉

Barrio de Analco
Old Santa Fe Trail and De Vargas Street area
A working-class neighborhood of Spanish Colonial heritage. *Analco* is said to be Nahuatl for "on the other side of the water"— the other side of the Río de Santa Fe. The *barrio* contains numerous examples of Spanish-Pueblo architecture characterized by adobe construction. ☉□△

Borrego House
724 Canyon Road
Although named for the socially and politically prominent Borrego family, who owned it from 1839 to 1906, the house was built by Gerónimo López sometime before 1769, when his will was filed. His will specified that the property consisted of "an orchard of fourteen trees and farming land" as well as the house. The rooms at the rear are the most ancient; the large room across the front, along with the portal supported by tapered, handmade columns, was added in the 19th century. ☉

Camino del Monte Sol Historic District
Camino del Monte Sol and vicinity
From the time of New Mexico's entrance into
the Union in 1912 until World War II, this area
of Santa Fe was the center of a nationally
known colony of artists. The artists led efforts
to re-create the city's historic adobe architecture while preserving and building their own
Pueblo Revival adobe homes. The district contains some of the first houses designed by John
Gaw Meem, the premier professional architect
of Revival styles. ☉☐

Canyon Road
In pre-Spanish times, this narrow, two-mile-
long street was an old Indian trail leading up
through Santa Fe Canyon and the mountains to
Pecos Pueblo. Later, it was the conduit the
Indians came down through to initiate the
bloody revolt against Spanish colonists in 1680.
The road is now lined with art galleries, shops,
and restaurants.

Cristo Rey Church
1107 Cristo Rey at Upper Canyon Road
505-983-8528
This church was built between 1939 and 1940
to provide a fitting sanctuary for the 18- by 40-
foot painted stone *reredos* (sculpted religious
panel) commissioned by Governor Marín del
Valle in 1760 for La Castrense, a military chapel
situated near the Plaza. After the chapel was
demolished, the plaque of Our Lady of Light
was stored for nearly 100 years before coming
out of the dark. The panel was sculpted by
Mexican carvers and imported to New Mexico
in the mid-18th century. Christo Rey Church is
one of the largest buildings of its kind ever
made of adobe.

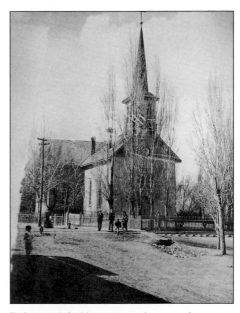

The Santuario de Guadalupe in 1900, nearly 130 years after it was
built. Courtesy Museum of New Mexico, neg. 10032

Cross of the Martyrs and Commemorative Walkway
Paseo de Peralta and Otero Street
The winding brick walkway leads to a huge white
cross dedicated, during La Fiesta de Santa Fe of
September 1920, to the Franciscans killed in the
Pueblo Revolt of 1680. Erected by the local
Knights of Columbus and the Historical Society of
New Mexico, the cross has played a central role
in religious processions ever since. An earlier
Cross of the Martyrs stands on a hill near the
Hayt-Wientge House, a familiar Victorian land-
mark at the north edge of the downtown area.

Don Gaspar Historic District
Don Gaspar Avenue, between Paseo de Peralta
and Coronado Road
Located south of the State Capitol Building, this
area reflects all three primary phases of New

Mexican architecture: traditional adobes, Territorial designs that came in with the railroad, and Revival styles. The majority of the structures were built between 1912 and 1945. ☺☐

Donaciano Vigil House
518 Alto Street
This house—probably half of a larger one—was bequeathed to Donaciano Vigil by his parents in the 1830s. Vigil served as secretary to Governor Manuel Armijo under the Mexican regime; secretary of New Mexico, as appointed by General Stephen Watts Kearny in 1846; civil governor after the assassination of Governor Bent in 1847; and secretary of the territory and register of land titles from 1848 to 1850. Visitors are welcome to tour the house when the Open sign is displayed.

El Zaguán
545 Canyon Road
The old *hacienda* and garden bought in 1849 by James L. Johnson, prominent Santa Fe merchant, was named El Zaguán (The Passageway) because of the long hall running from the patio to the garden. At one time, the property consisted of a 24-room house with servants' quarters across the street. The addition of a garden, reportedly laid out by Adolph Bandelier, brought peony bushes, imported from China over 100 years ago, and two large horse-chestnut trees—all of which are still flourishing. In 1962, the property was purchased for preservation by El Zaguán, Inc., and today, one of the apartments is an office for the Historic Santa Fe Foundation, Old Santa Fe Association, and Spanish Colonial Arts Society. ☺

Felipe B. Delgado House
124 West Palace Avenue
An excellent example of local adobe construction modified by late-19th-century architectural

Legends surround the spiral staircase in Loretto Chapel.
Photograph by Mark Nohl

details, this house was built in 1890 by Felipe B. Delgado, a socially prominent Santa Fe merchant. Delgado—a principle owner of mule and ox trains operating to and from Independence, Missouri, and Chihuahua—was a descendant of Captain Manuel Delgado, who came here in 1778 with the Spanish Royal Army. ☺

La Bajada
I-25, between Albuquerque and Santa Fe
"The Descent" marks the division between the Río Arriba (Upper River) and the Río Abajo (Lower River) sections of New Mexico. This steep, dangerous grade was for decades an obstacle to caravan traffic from the Río Grande Valley to Santa Fe on the Camino Real (Royal Road).

La Fonda
100 East San Francisco Street
505-982-5511
Located on Santa Fe's historic Plaza, this is one of New Mexico's premier—and still operating—Fred Harvey hotels.

**Lamy Building
(formerly St. Michael's Dormitory)**
Old Santa Fe Trail and De Vargas Street area
Erected in 1878, the building was three stories high, with classrooms and a community room on the first two floors and a dormitory on the third. Typical of many 19th-century structures, this college facility had a tower, porticos, galleries, a veranda, and a mansard roof. In 1926, the building was nearly destroyed by fire and was saved from complete devastation by the students. The structure now houses the New Mexico Department of Tourism and Santa Fe Visitors Welcome Center. Its graceful two-story portal is one of the few remaining in Santa Fe.

Loretto Chapel
Old Santa Fe Trail and Water Street
505-984-7971
The Chapel of Our Lady of Light was built for the Sisters of Loretto, the first nuns to come to New Mexico. The sisters, who had arrived in 1852 at the request of Archbishop Lamy, had established a school for young ladies in downtown Santa Fe. Patterned after the Parisian Sainte Chapelle, the Loretto Chapel was begun on the grounds of the academy in 1873. It was nearly completed when workers discovered insufficient room for building a safe staircase from the main floor to the choir loft upstairs. According to legend, the sisters' prayers for assistance were answered when a master carpenter appeared, built a remarkable staircase, and left without waiting to be paid. The chapel's staircase winds around two 360-degree turns, with no visible means of support. ◉

National Park Service Southwest Regional Office
1100 Old Santa Fe Trail, 87501
505-988-6100
This masterpiece of Spanish-Pueblo Revival-style architecture is the largest known adobe office building in the United States, and perhaps the largest secular adobe building as well. It houses an outstanding art collection ranging from 1930s works by members of Santa Fe's art colony to Pueblo pottery and Navajo rugs. ◉□△

Old Federal Building
108 Cathedral Place
A large structure built in Pueblo Revival style by the US Treasury Department in 1920. The former federal office building currently houses the Institute of American Indian Arts Museum. ◉□

Oldest House
215 East De Vargas Street
This house of unknown origin was labeled the "oldest building in Santa Fe" on the Stoner map of 1882—and indeed, a building in its approximate location appears on the Urrutia map of about 1760. Tree-ring specimens from some of the *vigas* indicate that the building is more than 300 years old. Its two lower-story rooms were constructed in pre-Spanish Pueblo Indian style, with thick adobe walls and a dirt floor. The Oldest House may be the last standing remnant of an ancient pueblo, dating back to about 1100. ◉

Padre Gallegos House
227–237 Washington Avenue
Both parts of this two-section house were built soon after 1857 for Padre José Manuel Gallegos—a colorful, controversial priest

defrocked by Archbishop Lamy in 1852. One of the most important political figures in 19th-century New Mexico, Padre Gallegos served two terms in the Mexican Departmental Assembly before being elected senator to the First Legislative Assembly in 1851. During and after the US Civil War, the building was used as a rooming house. In 1872, it housed the office of the secretary of the territory.

Pueblo Revolt Site
US 84-285, north of Santa Fe
Region from which the Tewa-speaking pueblos of San Juan, San Ildefonso, Santa Clara, Pojoaque, Nambé, and Tesuque directed the Pueblo Revolt. After Spaniards had captured two Indian runners at Tesuque on August 9, 1680, the Tewa warriors, joined by Taos and Picurís residents, formed two divisions and days later laid siege to Santa Fe.

Randall Davey Audubon Center
Upper Canyon Road
PO Box 9314, 87504
505-983-4609
The site of New Mexico's first sawmill, built in 1847. This Territorial-style building, constructed of stone, is now a National Audubon Society-owned museum displaying the furnishings and paintings of Randall Davey, who arrived in Santa Fe in 1919. Fee. ◉☐

Rio Grande Depot
Guadalupe and Garfield Streets
Built in 1903 at a cost of $4,497 for the Santa Fe Central Railway, a predecessor of the New Mexico Central Railway. The depot was also used by the Denver & Rio Grande and the Atchison, Topeka & Santa Fe Railway until 1941. The building is now a restaurant.

San Miguel Mission
401 Old Santa Fe Trail, 87501
505-983-3974
San Miguel, one of the oldest mission churches in the United States, was constructed in 1625 by the Tlaxcala Indians who came to New Mexico as servants of the Spanish soldiers and missionaries. The area surrounding the church had been part of an abandoned pueblo dating back to about 1100, portions of which were built into the chapel. The church was so severely damaged in the 1680 rebellion that when it was rebuilt in 1710, new foundations had to be laid. The mission offers permanent exhibits of 18th-century artifacts and taped tours. ◉

Santa Fe Historic District
Areas adjacent to Santa Fe Plaza
The buildings bordering the Plaza represent three and a half centuries of civilization, beginning with the 1610 establishment of the city as the seat of government for the northern frontier of the Viceroyalty of New Mexico (Mexico), a major division of the Spanish Colonial empire. Architectural styles run the gamut from Spanish-Pueblo to Territorial to nonindigenous European. ◉☐

Santa Fe Indian School
1501 Cerrillos Road, 87505
505-989-6300
The extensive campus was built primarily between 1890 and 1920, then remodeled in Spanish-Pueblo Revival style by Santa Fe architect John Gaw Meem as a Public Works Administration project in the 1930s. The atmosphere of the complex reflects early federal policies on Indian education.

Santa Fe Plaza
Heart of the city since 1607, the Plaza has witnessed countless historical, cultural, and social events. In the Plaza, the Pueblo Indians revolted

The interior of the Santuario de Guadalupe looks much as it did 200 years ago. Photograph by Mark Nohl

against Spanish rule in 1680; here, too, they capitulated to General Don Diego de Vargas in 1693. Marking the end of the Santa Fe Trail from Missouri, as well as the end of the Camino Real (Royal Road) from Chihuahua, Mexico, the dirt of the central square was stirred up continuously by freight wagons and burros laden with goods. Over the centuries, the Plaza has been transformed from the utilitarian meeting place it was in early days to a tree-shaded park encircled by a white picket fence, to an expanse of lawn crowned by a crenelated gazebo, to the lively, shaded pulse of activity it is today. ☉□△

Santa Fe Trail
Southeast of the Santa Fe Plaza
This stretch of land, known as the road to Independence (Missouri), was one of the most dramatic trade routes in the history of Western civilization. For more than two centuries after the colonization of New Mexico in 1598, the territory's only communication with the outside world was through Mexico. In 1805, Zebulon Pike, while exploring the Louisiana Purchase, crossed out of United States territory and into New Mexico, where he was escorted to Santa Fe and ultimately imprisoned in Chihuahua for trespassing. His reports inspired other Anglo pioneers to follow in his footsteps. James Purcell rode across the prairies from Missouri in 1805; and in 1821, Captain William Becknell, called the Father of the Santa Fe Trail, blazed the route that was to remain in use for the next 59 years. After Mexico's independence from Spain in 1822, traders and trappers from the East were welcome in New Mexico. Stagecoaches followed, with passengers headed west to make their fortunes or to find a home. Wagon loads of goods passed between the United

States and the "city of desire" at the end of the road. The arrival of the railroad in 1880 signaled an end to travel on the Santa Fe Trail. ◎

Santuario de Guadalupe

100 Guadalupe Street, 87501
505-988-2027
Built in 1781 west of Santa Fe Plaza, the historic Nuestra Señora de Guadalupe church is now an art and history museum. The *santuario* contains the Archdiocese of Santa Fe collection of New Mexican *santos* (carved images of the saints), Italian Renaissance paintings, and Mexican baroque paintings. Among the treasured works is "Our Lady of Guadalupe"—one of the largest and finest oil paintings of the Spanish Southwest—dated 1783 and signed by José de Alzibar, one of Mexico's most renowned painters. Events in music, drama, art, education, and religion are held at the *santuario*. Administered by the nonprofit Guadalupe Historic Foundation.

Scottish Rite Temple

463 Paseo de Peralta, 87501
505-982-4414
A brilliant pink Masonic temple built in 1910 to 1911 from designs based on the Alhambra, a Moorish building in Granada, Spain. *Alhambra* is Arabic for "red castle." ◎□

Sena Plaza

100 block of East Palace Avenue
One of Santa Fe's most popular courtyards was originally part of a land grant from Don Diego de Vargas to Captain Arias de Quiros. In 1844, the property, with its small house and patio, was bequeathed to the mother of Don José D. Sena, a major in the US Civil War, who later inherited it. Sena expanded the living quarters into a 33-room house, which he eventually occupied with his family. By 1864, the Sena

family was living along three sides of the large central patio, facing a coach house, stable, chicken house, and servants' quarters on the north. A second story was added on to the east and north portions of the estate in 1927, when the building was sold and remodeled into offices and shops. ◎

Seton Village

I-25, 6 miles southeast of Santa Fe
This village grew up around a 45-room house called The Castle, built by conservationist Ernest Seton, founder of the Boy Scout movement in the United States. Other buildings he constructed in the area were used for nature studies and training programs by the Boy Scouts, Campfire Girls, and Woodcraft League. Seton died in 1948. □△

St. Francis Cathedral

131 Cathedral Place
505-982-5619
Built from 1869 to 1884 under the direction of Santa Fe's first archbishop, Frenchman Jean Baptiste Lamy, this Romanesque cathedral, with its stained-glass windows, was an architectural anomaly in Santa Fe—so much so that the cathedral and the archbishop figured prominently in Willa Cather's 1929 novel *Death Comes for the Archbishop*. Nestled in a chapel within the cathedral is a small wooden statue known as La Conquistadora, the oldest representation of the Madonna in the United States. This image of the Blessed Mother was brought from Mexico City to Santa Fe by Fray Alonso de Benavides; carried to El Paso, Texas, during the Pueblo Revolt of 1680; and returned to Santa Fe with Vargas and his troops in 1693.

The Santa Fe Chamber Music Festival hosts some of the world's finest musicians. Photograph by Mark Nohl

PERFORMING ARTS

Estampa Flamenca
Picacho Plaza Hotel
750 North St. Francis Drive, 87501
505-982-1237
Summer performances by the María Benítez Spanish Dance Company, beginning in mid-June and continuing through mid-September.

Greer Garson Theater
College of Santa Fe
St. Michael's Drive, 87501
505-473-6511
The College of Santa Fe's Department of Performing Arts stages at least four productions a year, in a season running from September through May.

Railyard Performance Center
430 West Manhattan Avenue
505-982-8309
A performance space used for theater, dance, and music productions as well as classes and workshops for adults and children.

Sangre de Cristo Chorale
PO Box 4462, 87502-4462
505-662-9717
A 32-member group offering a repertoire of classical, baroque, Renaissance, and folk-spiritual music, both a cappella and with instrumental accompaniment. Fall and spring concerts are performed at the Santuario de Guadalupe or St. Francis Auditorium; a Christmas Dinner Concert is performed at the El Dorado Hotel. Concerts are also given in Los Alamos and Albuquerque.

Santa Fe Banjo and Fiddle Contest
Santa Fe Rodeo Grounds
PO Box 6523, 87502
505-471-3462
A showcase for rural string band tunes, northern New Mexican Hispano music, bluegrass, Mexican music, Texas-style fiddling, and a variety of traditional folk and acoustic music. The event features concerts, crafts exhibits, and workshops. Sponsored by the Southwest Traditional and Bluegrass Music Association on Labor Day weekend.

Santa Fe Chamber Music Festival
239 Johnson Street
PO Box 853, 87504
505-983-2075
A summer festival of international renown, drawing on talent from around the world. Each season features new works by composers in residence, chamber music masterpieces, jazz concerts, free performances for children, and

COMMUNITY EVENTS

Christmas at the Palace
Palace of the Governors
Santa Fe Plaza
505-827-6474
The traditional New Mexico holiday festivities include *farolitos* and *luminarias* lighting the Palace's portal and courtyard; servings of *bizcochitos,* coffee, and cider; and storytelling and music in the rooms of the historic building. The "true saint" (Santa Claus) and his elves arrive in the courtyard to chase away evil. Held in mid-December.

Civil War Weekend at El Rancho de las Golondrinas
La Cienega—I-25, 15 miles southwest of Santa Fe
334 Los Piños Road, 87505
505-471-2261
Reenactments of battles that occurred in nearby Apache Canyon and Glorieta Pass. Held in mid-May. Fee.

Contemporary Spanish Market
Lincoln Street
PO Box 6863, 87502
505-988-1878
First held in 1988, the event features contemporary Hispanic artists on the last full weekend in July, coinciding with Traditional Spanish Market.

La Fiesta de Santa Fe
Plaza and vicinity
PO Box 4516, 87501
505-988-7575
Established in 1712 to commemorate the 1692 peaceful reconnaissance of Santa Fe

daily open rehearsals. Organized in 1973, the event takes place in historic St. Francis Auditorium. Performances are taped for a nationally syndicated radio series.

Santa Fe Community Orchestra
2336 Camino Carlos Rey, 87505
505-473-2688
Formed in 1982, this orchestra of energetic and accomplished amateurs presents three or four concerts a year, featuring original pieces by local composers. The group performs at St. Francis Auditorium.

Santa Fe Community Theatre
142 East De Vargas Street, 87501
505-988-4262
Founded in the 1920s, the Santa Fe Community Theatre is the oldest theater group in the state. Approximately 8,000 people attend the group's regular shows, Fiesta Melodrama, and one-act series. The productions include a mix of avant-garde, established drama, and musical comedy.

Santa Fe Concert Association
PO Box 4626, 87502
505-984-8759
The oldest musical organization in Santa Fe, founded in 1936, presents a September-through-May season featuring international soloists and ensembles, youth concerts, Christmas Eve specials by the Música de Camara Ensemble, and other events by local performers. Concerts are held at the historic St. Francis Auditorium.

Santa Fe Dance Foundation
1504 Cerrillos Road, 87501
505-983-5591
A professional dance school specializing in ballet, modern, and creative movement classes for

ages three and up. Presentations include recitals, a choreographers' showcase, lecture demonstrations, and a full-length original ballet.

Santa Fe Desert Chorale
219 Shelby Street
PO Box 2813, 87504-2813
505-988-7505
New Mexico's only professional singing ensemble is composed of 20 to 30 vocalists selected during a national recruiting tour. Summer and Christmas-season concerts focus on seldom-performed contemporary works and music that celebrates the multicultural heritage of New Mexico and the Southwest.

Santa Fe Opera
US 84-285, 7 miles north of Santa Fe
PO Box 2408, 87504-2408
505-986-5900
Each summer, the Opera's outdoor amphitheater is backdrop to a varied selection of classics and rarely heard works, as well as an American premiere, that draws opera lovers from around the world. Since its inception in 1957, under the leadership of founder and general director John Crosby, the Santa Fe Opera has received international acclaim for its productions.

Santa Fe Performing Arts Company and School
2009 Pacheco Street
PO Box 22372, 87502
505-473-2240
Offers classes in acting, voice, music, and dance for children ages 3 to 18. The students present three productions yearly. Outreach services include an artists-in-residence program in the schools, teacher training workshops, and touring productions.

by Don Diego de Vargas, La Fiesta de Santa Fe is the oldest community festival in the nation. The pageantry includes the Fiesta Queen and her Court, a reenactment of the entry of Don Diego de Vargas and his 17-member retinue, two parades, dancing, singing, arts and crafts, and religious processions. La Fiesta begins the Friday after Labor Day, highlighted by the burning of Zozobra (Old Man Gloom), the most distinctively Anglo contribution to the nearly 285-year-old celebration. Festivities continue throughout the weekend, with a children's pet parade, a historical/hysterical parade, regional food, and much more.

Footsteps across New Mexico
Inn at Loretto
211 Old Santa Fe Trail, 87501
505-982-9297
A high-tech, 30-minute multimedia presentation on New Mexico and its prolific past. Fee.

Guadalupe Feast Day at the Santuario
100 Guadalupe Street, 87501
505-988-2027
A Mass and other celebratory events on December 12th.

Harvest Festival at El Rancho de las Golondrinas
La Cienega—I-25, 15 miles southwest of Santa Fe
334 Los Piños Road, 87505
505-471-2261
Costumed villagers portray life at harvest time on the Spanish Colonial El Rancho de las Golondrinas (The Ranch of the Swallows), dating from the early 1700s.

Events include Spanish singing, dancing, plays, food, and arts and crafts. Held the first weekend in October. Fee.

Las Posadas
Palace of the Governors
Santa Fe Plaza
505-827-6463
A traditional reenactment of Mary and Joseph's search for shelter before the birth of Jesus. Joseph, on foot, and Mary, astride a donkey, circle the Plaza, singing for entrance at several doors. The devil makes an appearance, and all doors remain closed until at last the holy ones are admitted to the Palace of the Governors courtyard. Held in mid-December.

Mountain Man Rendezvous and Buffalo Roast
Palace of the Governors
Santa Fe Plaza
505-827-6473
A trade fair featuring rows of blankets displayed with old-style beadwork, wearing apparel, guns, knives, and other artifacts. Rendezvous Day highlights mountain man music, black powder shooting, blacksmith forging, knife and tomahawk throwing, lectures on the Old Santa Fe Trail, slide presentations, films, and other activities. A Mountain Man's Dinner caps off the late August event.

Santa Fe Community College Arts and Crafts Shows
South Richards Avenue
PO Box 4187, 87502-4187
505-471-8200
Frequent and varied arts and crafts exhibits featuring the work of students and faculty,

Santa Fe Pro Música
329 Galisteo Street, Suite 502
PO Box 2091, 87504
505-988-4640
A music education and music performance organization with a season running from September to May.

Santa Fe Recorder Society
PO Box 8390, 87504
505-988-1076
Presents concerts in December and March, as well as demonstrations in local schools.

Santa Fe Symphony
200 West Marcy Street, Suite 147
PO Box 9692, 87504
505-983-1414
Founded in 1984, this full symphony orchestra performs in a September-through-May season at Sweeney Center.

Santa Fe Women's Ensemble
424 Kathryn Place, 87501
505-982-4075
This group of 12 semiprofessional local singers presents classical music from all periods, with occasional instrumental accompaniment. Spring concerts are held at the Loretto Chapel, as are five traditional Christmas performances.

Shakespeare in Santa Fe
369 Montezuma Avenue
PO Box 111, 87501
505-982-2910
A theater organization presenting Shakespearean plays and other works of literary and theatrical value to the Santa Fe community. Summer performances take place outdoors at St. John's College, and a winter Shakespeare-in-the-schools program brings shortened versions of

plays to public and private schools throughout the state. This company combines the talents of resident and guest artists and is the only Shakespearean theater group in New Mexico.

Something in the Air
Cathy Roe Productions
332 Camino del Monte Sol, 87501
505-988-3597
This spring dance concert is performed in the James A. Little Theater at the New Mexico School for the Deaf. Directed and choreographed by Cathy Roe, the performance integrates sign language into a variety of jazz and modern dance styles.

Southwest Children's Theatre Productions
Santa Fe Community Theatre
2537 Camino Estrido, 87505
505-984-3055
Offers children's plays and theater education. Spring and fall productions are performed at the Community Theatre and tour to northern New Mexico schools.

Southwest Repertory Theatre
PO Box 9932, 87501
505-982-1336
A regional, semiprofessional theater group staging three plays and a musical in late July through mid-August.

Theater of Music
535 Cordova Road, Suite 195, 87501
505-982-2221
Presents a winter and spring season of Broadway musicals.

including a Christmas Arts and Crafts Fair in early December.

Santa Fe Indian Market
Santa Fe Plaza
320 Galisteo Street, Suite 600, 87501
505-983-5220
More than 800 first-rate Indian artisans participate in this juried competition which, first held in 1922, is the oldest and largest exhibition of Indian art in the world. Displays include handmade baskets, pottery, rugs, jewelry, drums, kachinas, sandpaintings, and much more. All objects presented at Indian Market are for sale and must be handcrafted by Indians. Exhibit pieces are judged in advance; and at dawn on the first market day, collectors compete for award-winning items. Held in August.

Santa Fe Powwow
509 Camino de los Márquez, 87501
505-983-5220
Sponsored by the Southwestern Association on Indian Affairs, this traditional powwow (no contests) includes social dancing, exhibition dancing, food, and Indian Market artists' sale booths. Held in May.

Santa Fe Summerscene
Santa Fe Plaza
PO Box 1808, 87504
505-438-8834
A free music-and-dance concert series featuring local, regional, and national talent and sponsored by the Santa Fe Arts Commission and local businesses. Concerts are presented on Tuesdays and Thursdays, from late June through August.

A woman in Spanish Colonial dress demonstrates wool carding at El Rancho de las Golondrinas. Photograph by Mark Nohl

Santa Fe Wine Festival at El Rancho de las Golondrinas
La Cienega—I-25, 15 miles southwest of Santa Fe
334 Los Piños Road, 87505, 505-471-2261
Wine tasting, food, and entertainment sponsored by the New Mexico Vine and Wine Society in early July.

Spring Festival at El Rancho de las Golondrinas
La Cienega—I-25,
15 miles southwest of Santa Fe
334 Los Piños Road, 87505
505-471-2261
Costumed villagers portray life at spring planting time on the Spanish Colonial El Rancho de las Golondrinas (The Ranch of the Swallows), which dates back to the early 1700s. Events include Spanish singing, dancing, plays, food, and arts and crafts. Held the first weekend in June. Fee.

CULTURAL ORGANIZATIONS

Caballeros de Vargas
460 West San Francisco Street, 87501
505-982-8611
A group of men who for more than 30 years have brought historical accuracy and pageantry to many community celebrations. During La Fiesta de Santa Fe, the Caballeros stage a dramatic reenactment of General Don Diego de Vargas's reconquest of Santa Fe.

Center for Contemporary Arts
291 East Barcelona Road
PO Box 148, 87504
505-982-1338
Nationally recognized for its excellent programming, the CCA presents the work of international, national, and regional contemporary artists in visual arts exhibitions, nightly film screenings, dance concerts, new music concerts, performance art events, poetry readings, and video screenings. Also sponsors year-round programs for teenagers.

Chefs of Santa Fe
PO Box 8520, 87504
505-983-3518
The Santa Fe chapter of the American Culinary Federation consists of chefs and cooks dedicated to serving the culinary community, culinary arts students, and the community in general. Presents the Santa Fe Chile & Wine Festival, the Mayor's Chile Challenge, and a chefs' awards banquet. Also raises scholarships for young culinarians.

Guadalupe Historic Foundation
Santuario de Guadalupe
100 Guadalupe Street, 87501
505-988-2027
Administers the Santuario de Guadalupe as a

"living preservation" and a center for music, drama, art, education, and religion.

Hispanic Cultural Division
La Villa Rivera Building
228 East Palace Avenue, 87501
505-827-6364
Collects, preserves, and presents all aspects of Hispanic culture, and is currently developing a world-class Hispanic Cultural Center in Albuquerque. Expected to open in early 1998, the center will include gallery exhibition space, a theater for performance arts, a historical and genealogical research library, seminar and workshop facilities, and an outdoor amphitheater. A part of the New Mexico Office of Cultural Affairs.

Historic Preservation Division
La Villa Rivera Building
228 East Palace Avenue, 87501
505-827-6320
Identifies, preserves, and protects New Mexico's archaeological, architectural, and historic resources. The organization places significant cultural resources on state and national registers, administers federal and state tax incentive programs, and manages development grants for the preservation of historic structures. A part of the New Mexico Office of Cultural Affairs.

Historic Santa Fe Foundation
El Zaguán
545 Canyon Road
PO Box 2535, 87501
505-983-2567
Formed in 1961 to complement the Old Santa Fe Association, the foundation's primary purpose is to help preserve Santa Fe's unique historic buildings.

Summer Festival & Frontier Market at El Rancho de las Golondrinas
La Cienega—I-25,
15 miles southwest of Santa Fe
334 Los Piños Road, 87505
505-471-2261
An event featuring mountain men and traders in early August. Fee.

Taste of Santa Fe
Inn at Loretto
211 Old Santa Fe Trail
505-983-4823
More than 20 Santa Fe-area restaurants offer tastes of their fare to benefit community nonprofit organizations. Held in May.

Traditional Spanish Market
Palace of the Governors
Santa Fe Plaza
PO Box 1611, 87504
505-983-4038
First organized in 1925, this is the oldest and largest market in the United States for Hispanic artists working in traditional arts and crafts. Music, colonial folk dancing, a Matachines pageant, religious services, and artists' demonstrations create the ambiance of a village celebration. Held the last full weekend in July.

Winter Market
La Fonda Hotel
PO Box 1611, 87504
505-983-4038
Created in 1989, Winter Market features storytelling, traditional winter activities, as well as Spanish Colonial arts and crafts. Held the first full weekend in December.

Historical Society of New Mexico
PO Box 1912, 87504-1912
505-827-7332
Founded in 1859, the society encourages a
greater appreciation and knowledge of New
Mexico's architectural and cultural heritage;
presents educational, publicity, and preservation programs; publishes a newsletter and
books; and hosts special events. Advisory services are available upon request.

Institute for Spanish Arts
PO Box 8418, 87504-8418
505-983-8477
Presents María Benítez Estampa Flamenca in a
traditional tablao venue at the Picacho Plaza
Hotel from mid-July through mid-September.
The Institute also offers an International
Spanish Dance Workshop each summer.

New Mexico Arts Division
La Villa Rivera Building
228 East Palace Avenue, 87501
505-827-6490
Supports programs of artistic excellence
throughout the state. The division operates four
major programs: Arts in Education, to promote
the teaching of art disciplines in schools; Arts
Services, to foster the growth and development
of artists and arts groups; Art in Public Places,
to encourage a 1 percent allocation of funds for
public art in state buildings; and Field Services,
to provide technical assistance to constituents.
A part of the New Mexico Office of Cultural
Affairs.

New Mexico Community Foundation
PO Box 149, 87504
505-982-9521
The foundation's Churches: Symbols of
Community program provides technical assis-

tance to communities wishing to preserve their
historic churches.

New Mexico Council on Photography
119 East Marcy Street, 87501
505-984-1669
Supports photographers and museum photography collections throughout the state. The group
presents annual awards, including the Eliot
Porter Award and the Willard Van Dyke Award,
and conducts a Portfolio Review critique session.

New Mexico Music Educators Association
1150 Don Gaspar Avenue, 87501
505-982-1091
Promotes the advancement of music education
in public, private, and parochial schools and
other learning institutions.

New Mexico Office of Cultural Affairs
La Villa Rivera Building
228 East Palace Avenue, 87501
505-827-6364
A state agency charged with administering the
Museum of New Mexico, the Space Center, the
Museum of Natural History and Science, the
Farm/Ranch Heritage Museum, the Hispanic
Cultural Division, the New Mexico State Library,
the Arts Division, and the Historic Preservation
Division. Manages the historical, cultural, and
library facilities, sites, and programs of the
state. Also provides for the research, preservation, public presentation, and promotion of the
state's and region's cultural resources.

New Mexico Sculptors Guild
2089 Plaza Thomas, 87505
505-471-6794
A nonprofit corporation composed of active
sculptors.

PEN New Mexico
2860 Plaza Verde, 87505
505-473-4813
The regional chapter of PEN International—a
group of professional novelists, playwrights,
poets, essayists, journalists, editors, translators,
and writers of nonfiction. The New Mexico
chapter, consisting of about 200 members,
sponsors readings, dinner programs, and workshops. PEN's Right to Write Committee supports
imprisoned, threatened, and exiled writers
worldwide; protests censorship; and fosters the
unhampered transmission of written expression
across linguistic and cultural boundaries by
encouraging bilingual and multicultural writing
and publishing. Issues a directory and bimonth-
ly newsletter.

Recursos de Santa Fe
826 Camino del Monte Rey, Suite A-3, 87501
505-982-9301
An educational nonprofit organization specializing in professional destination management
services for museum, academic, professional,
and special interest groups. Recursos offers
unique tours, seminars, and writers conferences focusing on traditional and contemporary
aspects of art, culture, history, literature, cuisine, and natural history of the multicultural
Southwest and the Americas.

Santa Fe Artists League
PO Box 6961, 87502
505-471-0705
A group of local artists presenting ongoing
juried shows in the parking lot of the First
National Bank building on Santa Fe Plaza.

Children and animals take to the streets for the Pet Parade during La Fiesta de Santa Fe. Photograph by Mark Nohl

Santa Fe Arts Commission
200 Lincoln Avenue
PO Box 909, 87504-0909
505-984-6707
Provides leadership by and for city government
in supporting arts and cultural affairs.
Recommends programs and policies to develop, sustain, and promote artistic excellence in
the community.

Santa Fe Council for the Arts
PO Box 6863, 87502
505-988-1878
Sponsors visual arts and crafts events including
the Contemporary Spanish Market, two New
Mexico arts markets in Cathedral Park, Santa Fe
Plaza arts booths, studio tours, and gallery
exhibits. Presents seminars, workshops, and
panel discussions; publishes the *Arts Advocate*
newsletter; and organizes project sponsorships
for artists and emerging arts groups.

Santa Fe Fiesta Council
PO Box 4516, 87501
505-988-7575
Organizes each year's La Fiesta de Santa Fe and
oversees selection of the Fiesta Queen and her
Court, selection of Diego de Vargas and his
staff, and preparations for the Fiesta Ball.

Santa Fe Gallery Association
PO Box 9248, 87504
505-982-1648

Santa Fe Institute of Fine Arts
1807 Second Street
PO Box 9608, 87504
505-983-6157
Offers artist-conducted visual arts education in
a studio setting.

Santa Fe Society of Artists
PO Box 2031, 87504
505-473-5595
A group of local artists offering educational
programs in city schools and exhibitions in
Cathedral Park.

School of American Research
PO Box 2188, 87504
505-982-3584
Supports and conducts worldwide anthropological research. The school operates a
research center; maintains a 7,000-piece collection of Indian pottery, jewelry, basketry,
paintings, textiles, and costumes; releases 10
yearly anthropological publications; conducts
archaeological research; administers a Native
American scholarship program and
Wetherhead Fellowship program; and offers
advanced seminars.

**Southwest Traditional and Bluegrass
Music Association**
PO Box 6523, 87502
505-471-3462
Offers public education in traditional forms of
acoustic American and Spanish music. The
association sponsors an annual winter concert,
a summer concert series featuring local musicians, and the Santa Fe Banjo and Fiddle
Contest.

Southwestern Association on Indian Affairs
509 Camino de los Márquez, 87501
505-983-5220
Organizes each summer's Santa Fe Indian
Market, the world's oldest, largest, and most
prestigious display of Indian art. SWAIA also
sponsors the Santa Fe Powwow.

Spanish Colonial Arts Society
PO Box 1611, 87504
505-983-4038
Sponsors the Traditional Spanish Market and
Winter Market. Also maintains the world's
largest collection of Spanish Colonial arts,
housed at the Museum of New Mexico.

Western States Arts Federation
236 Montezuma Avenue, 87501
505-988-1166
A partnership of 12 Western state arts agencies
providing support, programs, services, and
educational outreach to Western initiatives in
the folk arts, literature, performing arts, and
visual arts. WESTAF also sponsors a Western
States Book Awards competition in fiction,
poetry, and creative nonfiction.

Witter Bynner Foundation for Poetry
PO Box 10169, 87504
505-988-3251
Established in 1972 to provide grant support to
nonprofit organizations offering programs in
poetry.

LIBRARIES
Fogelson Library Center
College of Santa Fe
1600 St. Michael's Drive, 87501
505-473-6576

Museum of New Mexico History Library
110 Washington Avenue
PO Box 2087, 87504
505-827-6470
Associated with the Museum of New Mexico's
Palace of the Governors history museum and
noted for its extraordinary collections of Southwest
and Spanish Colonial material, New Mexican historical material, and Adolph Bandelier Papers.

New Mexico Records and Archives Center
404 Montezuma Avenue, 87505
505-827-7332
Responsible for the custody, care, preservation,
and disposition of all public records created by
state agencies. Open to the public.

New Mexico State Library
300 Don Gaspar Avenue, 87503
505-827-3800
Services include circulation and reference,
materials for the blind and physically disabled,
and several bookmobiles. The state library
assists other libraries through consultation,
grants-in-aid, training, technical assistance, and
coordination of an interlibrary loan service. A
part of the New Mexico Office of Cultural Affairs.

Santa Fe Public Library
145 Washington Avenue, 87501
505-984-6780

St. John's College Meem Library
1160 Camino Cruz Blanca, 87501
505-984-6041

PUBLIC ART
Bataan Memorial Building
Galisteo Street and Cerrillos Road
Gilbert Guzman
Oil painting
Federal Courthouse Building
Lincoln Avenue and Federal Place
William Penhallow Henderson
Landscape mural panels
New Deal Art

Fountainhead Rock
Water Street and Don Gaspar Avenue
Thomas Lipps and *George Gonzales*
Stone fountain and benches

La Familia Medical Center
1121 Alto Street
Tim Klabunde
"Mother and Child"—steel sculpture

Joseph Montoya Building
1100 St. Francis Drive
Celia C. Kimball
Mural

Museum of Fine Arts Front Walkway
Lincoln and Palace Avenues
Vladan Stiha
"Artist Walk of Fame"—bronze plaques

Museum of Fine Arts Patio
107 East Palace Avenue
Will Shuster
Pueblo Indian murals
New Deal Art

Museum of New Mexico History Library
110 Washington Avenue
Olive Rush
"The Library Reaches People"—mural in fresco
New Deal Art

New Mexico State Library Southwest Room
300 Don Gaspar Avenue
Gilberto Guzman
Historical mural

New Mexico State Printing Facility
2641 Siringo Road
Two-dimensional pieces by numerous artists, including *David Lauren Bass, Nancy Day, Madonna Dunbar, Anne Farrell, Russell Hamilton, Jo Moore, Pamela Parsons, Barbara Tomasko Quimby,* and *Morgan Thomas.*

Peralta Park
Paseo de Peralta
Dave McGary
"The Founding of Santa Fe"—bronze monument

Public Parking Garage
Sandoval and Water Streets
Rudolf Hunziker
"Mesa"—stucco frieze

Monica Roybal Center
737 Agua Fria Street
Sam Leyba
"Sueños de Juventud"—mural

Harold L. Runnels Building
New Mexico Health and Environment Department
1190 St. Francis Drive
Carlos Carulo
"Inherent Vaults"— oil painting
Carlos and Sam Leyba
"Herbalism and Medicine in New Mexico"—mural

Sanbusco Center
Montezuma Street
Bob Haozous
"Bear with Planes with Clouds with Fish"—steel sculpture

Santa Fe Airport
Airport Road
Reynaldo "Sonny" Rivera
"Don Pedro de Peralta"—bronze sculpture

Santa Fe City Hall
Lincoln and Marcy Streets
Andrea Bacigalupa
"San Francisco de Asís"—bronze sculpture
Jerry R. West
"Recuerdos y Sueños de Santa Fe"—mural

Santa Fe Community College
Richards Avenue
Sculptures and two-dimensional pieces by
numerous artists, including *Russell Adams,*
Susan Contreras, Eddie Dominguez,
Frank Ettenberg, Richard Hogan, Juane
Quick to See Smith, and *Bernadette Vigil.*

Santa Fe Plaza
Obelisk monument to honor New Mexico's citizens who died in the Civil War. The memorial
was called the Soldiers Monument when it was
constructed between 1866 and 1868 by the
New Mexico Territorial Legislature.

Santa Fe Public Library
145 Washington Avenue
Hannah Ludins Small
Children and books—stone sculpture
New Deal Art

St. Francis Cathedral
131 Cathedral Place
J. Jusko
"Archbishop Jean Baptiste Lamy"—bronze statue
Donna Quasthoff
History of the Catholic Church in New
Mexico—bronze doors relief panels

State Capitol Grounds
Old Santa Fe Trail
Glenna Goodacre
"Basket Carriers"—bronze sculpture

Torreón Park
West Alameda
E. Pedro Romero
"El Torreón de El Torreón"—sculpture/tile
mural

TALPA

NM 518, 2 miles south of Ranchos de Taos
This small community dappled with prehistoric
pit houses once lodged the settlement of Llano
Quemado, excavated by the Smithsonian
Institution. Spanish villagers arrived in Talpa in
the late 18th century.

TAOS

US 64 at NM 68
About 6,000 years ago, nomadic hunter-gatherers passed through the Taos area searching
for game. The first permanent residents,
descendants of the Anasazi, arrived around AD
900. By 1540, when conquistador Hernando
de Alvarado entered the Río Grande Valley,
Taos Indians were already living in their present-day dwellings. European influence took
root when Padre de Zamora founded the first
Catholic mission in the region around 1600.
With the 1617 founding of the Spanish village
of Taos two miles south of the pueblo, the
town became the northernmost outpost of
Spanish Colonial America and the third permanent European settlement in what was to
become the United States. The town served as
a supply base for French and Anglo mountain
men, the home and burial place of frontiers-
man Kit Carson, and the site of 1847 uprisings
against the United States. In the early 1900s,
Taos emerged as a colony for artists and writers. Taos today is said to have more art galleries and studios per capita than any other
town in the United States.

Indians gather on the grass and a horse waits by the café in this 1953 view of Taos Plaza. Courtesy Museum of New Mexico, neg. 59072

MUSEUMS AND EXHIBIT SPACES

Ernest Blumenschein Home and Museum
222 Ledoux Street
PO Drawer CCC, 87571
505-758-0505
The home and studio of Ernest L. Blumenschein, one of the six founders of the Taos
Society of Artists in 1912. The 1797 adobe
home is maintained much as it was when the
artist lived here. Unusual European antiques,
hand-carved furniture of Spanish Colonial
design, and original art fill the 11 rooms open
to the public. Exhibits display the work of
Blumenschein and other great Taos artists.
Fee. ☺△

Governor Bent Museum
117 Bent Street
PO Box 153, 87571
505-758-2376
A history museum in the house built around
1830 for Governor Charles Bent, New Mexico's
first American governor. Also the site of Bent's
murder during the anti-United States resistance
of 1847. A gallery in the home features both
early and contemporary Taos art. Fee. ☺▢

Harwood Foundation Museum and Library
238 Ledoux Street
PO Box 766, 87571
505-758-3063
A Pueblo Revival-style research library and art
museum showcasing Taos art from 1898 to the

present; Patrocinio Barela sculptures; 19th-century *santos* (carved images of the saints) and *retablos* (religious paintings on wood); historic photographs; Persian miniatures; Río Grande tinwork; and Spanish Colonial furniture. New Mexico's second-oldest museum. ◉▢

Kit Carson Home and Historical Museum
Old Kit Carson Road
PO Drawer CCC, 87571
505-758-0505
Mountain man and scout Kit Carson purchased this 12-room adobe home in 1843 as a wedding gift for his bride, Josefa Jaramillo. Three of the rooms are furnished as they might have been over the 25 years Carson lived here with his family. Exhibits include gun and mountain man displays, Spanish and early American furniture, arms and munitions, fur-trapping equipment, costumes and textiles, Indian and archaeological artifacts, religious articles, tools and farm equipment, and photographs. ◉▢△

Martínez Hacienda
Ranchitos Road, 2 miles west of Taos Plaza
PO Drawer CCC, 87571
505-758-0505
Situated on the banks of the Río Pueblo, this 21-room fortresslike building with massive adobe walls and no exterior windows is one of the few remaining Spanish Colonial haciendas open to the public. Originally built in 1780 as a refuge against Comanche invaders, the hacienda was enlarged by Don Antonio Severino Martínez in the early 19th century. Period rooms illustrate the rugged lifestyle typical of northern New Mexico in the early 1800s. Artisans present weaving, quilting, woodcarving, and other folk art demonstrations. Fee. ◉▢

Millicent Rogers Museum
1504 Museum Road
PO Box A, 87571
505-758-2462
An art and anthropology museum that exhibits Southwestern Indian pottery, jewelry, textiles, and paintings; the María Martínez family collection of pottery; and religious and secular arts and crafts of Hispanic New Mexico. Fee.

Nicolai Fechin Institute and Home
227 Paseo del Pueblo Norte
PO Box 832, 87571
505-758-1710
The adobe home of Russian émigré artist Nicolai Fechin was built in 1928 with hand-carved doors, windows, gates, posts, fireplaces, and other features reminiscent of a Russian country home. Fechin's furnishings and art objects remain on site. The institute uses the house and studio for Fechin exhibits as well as the sale of posters, cards, and books. ◉▢

Van Vechten-Lineberry Taos Art Museum
501 North Pueblo Road
PO Box 1848, 87571-1848
505-758-2690
Exhibits the works of Taos Society of Artists founders Ernest Blumenschein, E. Martin Hennings, Oscar E. Berninghaus, and others. The museum was established in 1994 by Edwin C. and Novella Lineberry in memory of Edwin's first wife, the late Diane Van Vechten, who studied with many of the artists. Van Vechten's oil paintings and other works are also on display. Fee.

HISTORIC BUILDINGS AND SITES
D. H. Lawrence Ranch and Shrine
San Cristóbal
NM 522, 13 miles north of Taos
The Kiowa Ranch, given to D. H. Lawrence and his

COMMUNITY EVENTS

Meet the Artist Series
Taos Inn
125 Paseo del Norte
505-758-2233
Tuesday and Thursday evening discussions, studio tours, on-the-spot demonstrations, slide shows, and performances involving nationally known Taos artists. The program runs May 15th to June 21st, and October 15th to December 15th.

Old Taos Trade Fair
Martínez Hacienda
Ranchitos Road
505-758-7505
A reenactment of Spanish Colonial life in the 1820s, featuring authentic music, weaving, baking and carving demonstrations, and native foods and crafts. Held the last weekend of September.

Taos Fall Arts Festival
Various locations
PO Drawer I, 87571
505-758-3873
Two weeks of exhibitions, lectures, an arts and crafts fair, a wool festival, and more than 80 gallery shows. Major art shows include Taos Invites Taos and Taos Open. Held mid-September to early October.

Taos Mountain Balloon Rally
Weimer Field
PO Drawer I, 87571
800-732-8267
Tethered hot-air balloon rides, a Balloominaries de Taos glow, parade, picnic, and ball in late October.

wife Frieda between 1924 and 1925 by art champion Mabel Dodge Luhan, was home to the writer and occasional painter in the last years of his life. After he died, Frieda continued to live at their home and in 1934 built a small white shrine on the grounds for Lawrence's ashes. Upon her death, she was buried in front of the shrine, and the ranch was willed to the University of New Mexico on the condition that 10 acres of the property, including the shrine, remain open to the public. The ranch is currently used for university seminars.

Kit Carson Park and Cemetery
Paseo del Pueblo Sur
In 1868, Christopher "Kit" Carson—legendary guide, scout, soldier, and trapper—died in Fort Lyons, Colorado. The following year, his body and his wife Josefa's were brought home to Taos. Others buried in this 22-acre park include art benefactor Mabel Dodge Luhan and soldiers killed in the 1847 rebellion protesting the United States annexation of New Mexico.

La Loma Plaza Historic District
Western edge of Taos
This small residential area, settled around 1795, is considered one of the two most well-preserved defensive plazas in New Mexico; the other is in Chimayó. Among the buildings preserved on La Loma's Plaza is beautiful San Antonio Chapel, built in the late 1850s. ◑□

Mabel Dodge Luhan House
240 Morada Lane
PO Box 3400, 87571
505-758-9456
The estate of wealthy New Yorker Mabel Dodge who, active in art and literary circles, moved to Taos in the 1920s and married Tony Lujan of Taos Pueblo. The estate is now owned by Las Palomas de Taos, a nonprofit learning center that

conducts workshops, institutes, and special programs on the Southwest. Off-season, the estate operates as a bed and breakfast. Fee. ⊚□△

Pueblo Revolt Site
NM 68, south of Taos
The 1680 Pueblo Revolt began at Taos Pueblo when Popé, a religious leader driven out of San Juan Pueblo by Spanish authorities, sent runners to the region's pueblos. The runners carried a knotted cord designating the number of days until the uprising was to occur. Tiwa warriors from Taos and Picurís moved south on August 10th to lay siege to Santa Fe.

Taos Canyon
NM 150, north of Taos
Site at which the Indians of Taos Pueblo were defeated by Governor Don Diego de Vargas in September 1696, during one of the last battles of the Spanish reconquest of New Mexico.

Taos Downtown Historic District
Areas adjacent to Taos Plaza
Established in the late 1700s, this district—known as Don Fernando de Taos—is one of the oldest settlements in the Taos Valley. The architecture surrounding the central Plaza reflects its history as a meeting place of many cultures; Spanish Colonial and Territorial-style buildings stand beside Mission and Spanish-Pueblo Revival-style buildings. The layout of the district signifies its origin as a fortified settlement and its later role as a center of trade for northern New Mexico. ⊚□

Taos Plaza
Taos Plaza became an arena for commercial and political activity in the late 1800s, when it began hosting an annual trade fair for Spanish settlers, Taos Indians, and roving Comanches. During

Taos Poetry Circus
5275 NDCBU, 87571
505-758-1800
A literary event featuring the World Heavyweight Championship Poetry Bout. Held in June.

Taos Spring Arts Celebration
Various locations
PO Drawer I, 87571
505-758-0516
Three weeks of visual, performing, and literary arts exhibits and demonstrations in May.

Taste of Taos
Río Grande Hall
PO Drawer I, 87571
800-732-8267
A gala food and wine event held in conjunction with the Taos Mountain Balloon Rally in late October.

Wool Festival
Kit Carson State Park
505-776-2925
An arts and crafts fair featuring shearing, spinning, and weaving demonstrations; lamb delicacies; and beautiful handmade items for sale. Held the first weekend in October.

Yuletide in Taos
Various locations
PO Drawer I, 87571
800-732-8267
An early December excursion into the tradition, culture, and arts of northern New Mexico. Preholiday events include romantic *farolito* tours, candlelight dinners, dance performances, and ski valley festivities.

that time, the Plaza was also a focal point for French and Anglo trappers. Over the course of the 20th century, it has swelled with an influx of artists and writers. ☉▢

Vásquez de Coronado's Route
NM 68, south of Taos
The trail taken by Captain Hernando de Alvarado who, under orders from Francisco Vásquez de Coronado in 1540, left Tiguex, near present-day Bernalillo, for Taos Pueblo in his exploration of the Southwestern pueblos. Captain Francisco de Barrionuevo passed this way the following year, also en route to Taos Pueblo.

PERFORMING ARTS
Taos School of Music Summer Chamber Music Festival
PO Box 1879, 87571
505-776-2388
Presents classical and contemporary chamber music concerts by the American String Quartet, the Muir String Quartet, pianist Robert McDonald, and gifted students from around the world. Performances take place at the Taos Community Auditorium and Hotel St. Bernard at Taos Ski Valley from mid-June through early August.

CULTURAL ORGANIZATIONS
Society of the Muse of the Southwest
PO Box 3225, 87571
505-758-0081
A writers' organization that sponsors literary arts throughout northern New Mexico, offering readings, workshops, and other programs. Publishes a yearly anthology.

Taos Art Association
133 Paseo del Norte, 87571
505-758-2052
Showcases visual and performing arts in the Stables Art Center, located in the historic 1898 Manby-Thorne House. The association presents the work of local artists in thematic exhibits as well as films, lectures, gallery talks, concerts, dance recitals, arts festivals, drama, workshops, and traveling exhibitions.

LIBRARIES
Harwood Public Library
238 Ledoux Street
PO Box 766, 87571
505-758-3063

PUBLIC ART
Armstrong Burke Fine Arts Gallery
Old Taos County Courthouse
Taos Plaza
Emil Bisttram, Victor Higgins, Ward Lockwood, and *Bert Phillips*
Murals in fresco
New Deal Art

El Prado
US 64, 2 miles north of Taos
Enriqueta and Juanita Jaramillo
"Un Puno de Tierra"—mural

Mary Medina Building
Cruz Alta Road
Maye Torres
"Reaching for the Light"—mixed media

Paseo del Pueblo Sur
George Chacon
"El Santero"—mural
Gray Mercer
"Red Horse"—sculpture

The appearance of Taos Pueblo has changed little since this photograph was taken in 1950. Photograph by Tyler Dingee, courtesy Museum of New Mexico, neg. 120216

Taos Community Auditorium
Paseo del Pueblo Sur
Ted Egri
"Worlds Within"—sculpture

TAOS PUEBLO

NM 64, 2 miles north of Taos
PO Box 1846, 87571
505-758-9593
Taos Pueblo has survived nearly 1,000 years of volatile history, punctuated by invasions of the Spaniards in the 1540s, the Pueblo Revolt of 1680, and the Taos rebellion against the United States government in 1847. The pueblo's two large multistoried dwellings—typical of local 12th-century building styles—face each other across a clear stream running through the central plaza, much as they did when the first Spanish explorers arrived in 1540. *Hornos* (outdoor ovens) are still in use, as is stream-drawn water. Today's Tiwa-speaking descendants of the original Chaco or Anasazi inhabitants are widely admired for their red-brown micaceous pottery, silver jewelry, sculpture, painting, beadwork, carved flutes, and handcrafted moccasins, boots, and drums. ☉□△☺

COMMUNITY EVENTS

Dances to Commemorate the Christmas Season
Procession of the Virgin ceremony with dances and bonfires on December 24th, followed by Deer or Matachines Dances on Christmas Day.

New Year's Day Celebration
A Mass, procession, and dances.

San Antonio Feast Day
A Corn Dance on June 13th.

San Juan Feast Day
A Corn Dance on June 24th.

Santa Ana Feast Day
A Corn Dance on July 26th.

Santa Cruz Feast Day
Blessing of the fields followed by a Corn Dance and footraces on May 3rd.

Santiago Feast Day
A Corn Dance on July 25th.

Taos Pueblo Feast Day
A celebration of San Gerónimo Eve, with Vespers at San Jerome Chapel and a sundown dance, followed by the Feast of San Gerónimo, with a midmorning Mass, procession, arts and crafts trade fair, relay races, and pole climbing by Koshares (clowns). Held September 29th and 30th.

Taos Pueblo Powwow
El Prado—US 64 at NM 150
2 miles north of Taos
505-758-8626
Competition in traditional and fancy Indian dances. Also an arts and crafts fair. Held in July.

Three Kings Day
Transfer of the Canes of Authority, ceremonializing the installation of new tribal officers on January 6th.

TESUQUE PUEBLO

US 84-285, 10 miles north of Santa Fe
505-983-2667
Noted for its very early contact with Europeans, Tesuque is considered one of the most traditional Tewa-speaking pueblos. The Tesuque people played an important role in the Pueblo Revolt of 1680. In today's largely agricultural community, farmers produce natural food and artists create brightly painted unfired pottery as well as classic red or gray-brown pots decorated with animal figures and symbolic designs. ◐▢

COMMUNITY EVENTS

Blessing of the Fields
A Corn Dance held in late May or early June.

Dances to Commemorate the Christmas Season
Traditional dances during Christmas week.

Tesuque Pueblo Feast Day
A midmorning Mass and procession, followed by Buffalo, Comanche, Corn, Deer, and Flag Dances. Held on November 12th.

Three Kings Day
Transfer of the Canes of Authority to new tribal officers on January 6th.

TIERRA AMARILLA

US 84 at US 64
This region was part of a large community land grant made to Manuel Martínez and other settlers in 1832. Settlement was delayed, however, by Ute, Jicarilla Apache, and Navajo raids. Eventually established as Nutritas, Tierra Amarilla became the Río Arriba County seat in 1880. In 1967, the town was a focus of conflict between National Guardsmen and land rights activists led by Reies López Tijerina.

COMMUNITY EVENTS
Fiesta de Santo Niño
A religious procession, parade, and village celebration on Labor Day weekend.

HISTORIC BUILDINGS AND SITES
El Vado Dam
NM 112, 14 miles west of Tierra Amarilla
Completed in 1935, this dam is a rare example of the extensive use of steel in reservoir construction. ◉

Tierra Amarilla Historic District
The village and isolated farmhouses of Tierra Amarilla are among the best preserved examples of late-19th-century Hispanic New Mexico's settlement patterns, folk architecture, and building techniques. The structures date from about 1860. ◉▢

TRUCHAS

NM 76, 17 miles northeast of Española
This land along the Río Truchas was granted in 1754 by Governor Tomás Vélez Cachupín to families from Santa Cruz and Chimayó. Because Nuestra Señora del Rosario de Truchas was on the northern frontier, and subject to attack by Plains Indians, the governor stipulated that the houses form a square with only one entrance. The small village on the High Road to Taos was the set for Robert Redford's 1988 film *The Milagro Beanfield War,* based on John Nichols's popular novel by the same name.

VELARDE

NM 68, 14 miles north of Española
Founded in 1875, this small Spanish farming community was first named La Jolla. Famous for its finely woven blankets, the village marked the point at which the Camino Real (Royal Road) left the Río Grande and followed a canyon northeast to Embudo Creek, where it began a climb over the mountains to Taos. Present-day Velarde is known for its bounteous apple orchards.

HISTORIC BUILDINGS AND SITES
Los Luceros Hacienda (formerly Los Luceros County Couthouse)
NM 68, 3 miles south of Velarde
The old Los Luceros County Courthouse, dating back to 1601, later became a fort and then a *hacienda* for a prominent local family. ◉

From the top of Capulín Volcano in New Mexico's northeast corner, visitors can view the vast *llano*, the high plains that stretch on to a dusty horizon 100 miles away. Few signs of human habitation mar the solitude. Anyone asked to list vacation destinations would be unlikely to think of northeastern New Mexico—a reality that gives the region special allure. Almost nothing here is touristy.

Abandoned wheat mills, forts, and wagon ruts recall pioneer life in a landscape that is still frontier today. Sheltered from the biting winter winds of the *llano* by the eastern slope of the Sangre de Cristo Mountains, the unpretentious historic districts in Ratón, Cimarrón, and Las Vegas suggest what Santa Fe and Taos might be like if they had never been discovered by pleasure travelers. The northeastern region offers up its history raw and unromanticized: Folsom Man who camped here 12,000 years ago for however long it took to eat a mastodon; the small detachment of Texan soldiers who tried to seize northern New Mexico for the Confederacy; the holy man who lived for years on Hermit's Peak. Their memories linger in the silence of the *llano*.

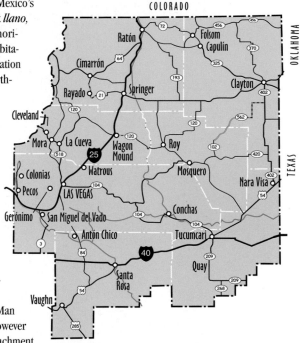

ANTÓN CHICO

US 84, 25 miles south of Las Vegas
Established through an 1822 land grant, Antón Chico was built according to the predominant blueprint of the times: connecting structures enclosed the Plaza, providing protection against Comanche attacks. The village is situated along the northern portion of the Pecos River and exemplifies traditional 19th-century Hispanic central-plaza community design. ◉❑

A rodeo rider dismounts a bucking horse the easy way.
Photograph by Mark Kane

CAPULÍN

US 64-87, 28 miles east of Ratón
When the area roamed by train robber Thomas "Black Jack" Ketchum in the late 1800s opened for homesteading in the early 20th century, it became a bustling trade center. In 1909, the town was named Dedman, for a Santa Fe Railway superintendent; in 1914, it was renamed after nearby Capulín Volcano. The word *capulín* is Spanish for chokecherries, which proliferate in the area. The land once plowed by homesteaders is now a cattle range. Only a few houses and stores have endured the passage of time.

Ringed by a roadway to the top, Capulín Volcano rises 1,500 feet above the surrounding rangeland. Photograph by Mark Nohl

MUSEUMS AND EXHIBIT SPACES
Capulín Volcano National Monument
NM 325, 3.5 miles north of Capulín
PO Box 40, 88414
505-278-2201
A natural history park, featuring a 1,500-foot, unusually symmetrical volcanic cinder cone— the remains of a volcano thought to have been active at least 7,000 years ago. A visitor center offers a library and natural history collection as well as interpretive programs for self-guided tours into the crater. Fee.

HISTORIC BUILDINGS AND SITES
Goodnight-Loving Trail
Southeast of Capulín

The route cut through Trinchera Pass in 1868 by Texas longhorn rancher Charles Goodnight. His goal: to circumvent Ratón Pass by forging an easier, shorter, toll-free cattle trail.

CIMARRÓN

US 64, at NM 58 and NM 21
Located on the Mountain Branch of the Santa Fe Trail, this truly Wild West town was settled around a stage station in the mid-1840s. In 1857, it became the home of Lucien B. Maxwell—buffalo hunter, entrepreneur, and eventual purchaser of the 1.74 million-acre Maxwell Land Grant, which extended over gold deposits, timber country, and grasslands.

Between 1862 and 1876, the town served as agency headquarters for the Ute Indians, after which disputes over boundaries and ownership of the grant culminated in the Colfax County War. Over this period of time, Cimarrón (Wild Place), named for the area's untamed horses and sheep, came to be the "cowboy capital of northern New Mexico."

MUSEUMS AND EXHIBIT SPACES

Kit Carson Museum
NM 21
Philmont Scout Ranch, 87714
505-376-2281
A history museum focusing on early settlement of the area, fur trading, and the Santa Fe Trail. Also featured is a replica of the adobe home built here by Kit Carson (see Rayado, page 95), Maxwell's friend. Open June through August.

Old Mill Museum
NM 21, Old Town Cimarrón
505-376-2662
Housed in Aztec Mill, built in 1864 to furnish grain to the Indians, the museum exhibits regional artifacts, memorabilia, and early photographs. Open May through September. Fee.

Philmont Museum
NM 21, 4 miles south of Cimarrón
Philmont Scout Ranch, 87714
505-376-2281
An art and history museum chronicling the development of Philmont and the surrounding area, and repository for the 6,000-volume Ernest Thompson Seton library. The museum, housed in Villa Philmonte—the restored home of Philmont benefactor Waite Phillips—is open June through August.

HISTORIC BUILDINGS AND SITES

Black Jack's Hideout
Turkey Creek Canyon
US 64, 5 miles west of Cimarrón
Turkey Creek Canyon became history when the outlaw gang of Thomas "Black Jack" Ketchum used it as a hideout. After a train robbery in July 1899, a posse surprised the gunmen in their canyon hideaway, a bloody battle ensued, and the outlaws scattered—resulting in the breakup of the Ketchum gang.

Cimarrón Historic District
The majority of Cimarrón's adobe and stone buildings were constructed in the mid-19th century. Still standing, with only minor modifications, are the county courthouse, the Old Stone Jail, the St. James Hotel, and Maxwell's 1864 stone flour mill. ⊚☐

Philmont Scout Ranch
NM 21, 4 miles south of Cimarrón
505-376-2281
Oklahoma oilman Waite Phillips gave this 127,000-acre property to the Boy Scouts of America in the late 1930s. Philmont, the first National Boy Scout Camp ever established, now hosts thousands of young men each year from all over the world.

Santa Fe Trail
US 64, between Cimarrón and Ratón
One of the few off-the-federal-highway-system roads that trace the route traveled by William Becknell, the first Santa Fe Trail trader. Becknell entered Santa Fe in 1821 after Mexico's independence from Spain, opening the border of Spanish New Mexico to Anglo travelers. At this point on the trail, the Mountain Branch over Ratón Pass divided: one fork turned west to Cimarrón, then south,

joining the other, more direct, route at
Rayado.

St. James Hotel
NM 21, Old Town Cimarrón
Route 1, Box 2, 87714
505-376-2664
Built in 1875 by Henri Lambert, chef for
President Abraham Lincoln and General Ulysses
S. Grant, the hotel boasts a long list of famous
guests, including Zane Grey, Annie Oakley,
Buffalo Bill Cody, and Billy the Kid. Ten rooms
have been refurbished to evoke their original
Victorian splendor. ☺

LIBRARIES
Ernest Thompson Seton Memorial Library
Philmont Scout Ranch, 87714
505-376-2281
Houses the works and personal collections of
Ernest Thompson Seton—author, artist, natural-
ist, and cofounder of the Boy Scouts of America.
A 6,000-volume library encompassing the natur-
al and political history of the Southwest.

Rural Bookmobile Northeast
PO Box 97, 87714
505-376-2474

PUBLIC ART
Village Hall Complex
Pat Loree
"Cimarrón"—acrylic mural

CLAYTON

US 64-87 at US 56
Trade caravans and homesteaders traveling the
Cimarrón Cutoff of the Santa Fe Trail to avoid
the rocky, mountainous terrain of Ratón passed
just north of the area that was to become
Clayton, their ruts still visible. Years later, in
1887, Clayton was founded by the Colorado and
Southern Railroad. Named for the son of cattleman and ex-senator Stephen W. Dorsey, one of
the town's developers, Clayton, with its rich
grasslands, became a major turn-of-the-century
livestock shipping center for herds from the
Pecos Valley and Texas Panhandle.

MUSEUMS AND EXHIBIT SPACES
Clayton School Museum
Clayton High School
323 South Fifth Street, 88415
505-374-9611
Chronicles local WPA projects and area development during the Great Depression. Open by
appointment.

Herzstein Memorial Museum
South Second and Walnut Streets
PO Box 75, 88415
505-374-2977
Dedicated to the preservation and interpretation of Union County history from prehistoric
times through the homesteading era, including
development of the Santa Fe Trail. Hosts an
open house the last weekend in April.

HISTORIC BUILDINGS AND SITES

Clayton Lake State Park
NM 370, 12 miles north of Clayton
Rural Route Box 20, Seneca, 88437
505-374-8808
One of the most extensive dinosaur trackways
in North America, with more than 500 imprints
from eight species of dinosaurs, including the
handprints of a flying pterodactyl. Fee.

Eklund Hotel
15 Main Street
Constructed of native sandstone in 1892 by John
C. Hill, range manager for cattleman Stephen
Dorsey, the building is an excellent example of
turn-of-the-century architecture. Later won in a
poker game by Carl Eklund, the establishment
was advertised as "the only first-class hotel
between Trinidad and Fort Worth." ◉

Rabbit Ear Mountain
NM 370, north of Clayton
These two striking mounds were the first features
visible to Santa Fe Trail travelers crossing into New
Mexico from Oklahoma. An important landmark
for caravans, the mountain signified that about 200
miles remained before reaching Santa Fe. ◉□△

Santa Fe Trail
NM 406, 20 miles northeast of Clayton
Trail ruts can still be seen in the dry soil where
the Cimarrón Cutoff of the Santa Fe Trail crosses Union County. McNee's Crossing marks the
site of the first Fourth of July celebration in
what is now New Mexico; the year was 1831.

Sheriff's Office
Downtown Clayton, next to the courthouse
The north wall of the sheriff's office is where
Black Jack Ketchum, leader of a notorious band
of train robbers, was hanged in 1901. Two

COMMUNITY EVENTS

Clayton Arts Festival
American Legion Hall
PO Box 562, 88415
505-374-2700
Fine arts, crafts, and purchase awards
on the first weekend in October.

**Clayton Independence Day
Celebration**
Union County Fairgrounds
505-374-9250
The community's largest celebration,
including an arts and crafts show,
dances, a rodeo, barbecue, street
parade, and fireworks.

Dinosaur Days
Downtown area
PO Box 476, 88415
505-374-9253
An open-air bazaar featuring an Old
Western Dance complete with costumes
and old-fashioned dance prizes. Also a
free tour of dinosaur tracks at Clayton
Lake State Park. Held in mid-April.

years earlier, he had surrendered to local
authorities after being wounded in Folsom.

Wagon Ruts
US 56-64, 1 mile east of Clayton
Although the main route of the Santa Fe Trail
passed north of Rabbit Ear Mountain, early caravans traveled south of the mounds. The ruts seen
here are probably those of the Kenton, Oklahoma-
to-Clayton freight route of the early 1800s—a
route that may well have followed the path carved
by the Santa Fe Trail pack-mule trains.

CULTURAL ORGANIZATIONS
Clayton Arts Council
302 Monroe Street
PO Box 517, 88415
505-374-2416
An umbrella group for other cultural organizations and host of the Clayton Arts Festival.

Shrine of the Testaments
PO Box 486, 88415
505-374-9693
A nonprofit organization dedicated to art and education, and owner of 45 oil paintings by the late Jan Maters, a Dutch-born artist.

Union County Historical Society
PO Box 75, 88415
505-374-9508
Maintains the Herzstein Memorial Museum and sponsors programs on regional history.

LIBRARIES
Albert W. Thompson Memorial Library
17 Chestnut Street, 88415
505-374-9423

PUBLIC ART
Chamber of Commerce
1103 South First Street
Larry Smith
"Life-Size Dinosaurs"—foam and mixed media

CLEVELAND

NM 518, 3 miles northwest of Mora
Originally called San Antonio, this village north of Mora was renamed in the late 1800s in honor of President Grover Cleveland. Soon afterward, a group of Irishmen led by Dan

COMMUNITY EVENTS
Cleveland Roller Millfest
Cleveland Roller Mill Museum
NM 518
505-387-2645
Arts and crafts, history talks, and craft demonstrations in early August.

Cassidy settled in the village. Cassidy operated a general store, and his compatriots became merchants and farmers.

MUSEUMS AND EXHIBIT SPACES
Cleveland Roller Mill Museum
NM 518
PO Box 287, 87715
505-387-2645
This three-story adobe roller mill played a major role in the agricultural economy of northern New Mexico for 80 years. Built and equipped in 1877, the facility became one of the two largest mills in the western United States. When it closed in 1957, it was the last functioning flour mill in the Mora Valley. The Cleveland Roller Mill remains fully operable. Exhibits trace the history of regional flour production. Fee. ◉☐

CULTURAL ORGANIZATIONS
Historic Mora Valley Foundation
PO Box 287, 87715
505-387-2645
Works to preserve, interpret, and promote Mora Valley history, specifically the installations, exhibits, and public programming at the Cleveland Roller Mill Museum. Sponsor of the Cleveland Roller Millfest.

COLONIAS

NM 379, 12 miles north of I-40 juncture
Part of the Antón Chico Land Grant established
in 1822, the village situated along the northern
portion of the Pecos River, 30 miles downstream from Antón Chico, was not established
until the mid-1860s. At that point, Colonias de
San José, unlike most other Spanish settlements
of the time, was laid out in a grid rather than
around a plaza. Today's village contains 23 of
the historic buildings, all on the verge of ruina-
tion. Colonias is one of three Antón Chico Land
Grant settlements in which 19th-century
Hispanic frontier traditions endure. ◎□

HISTORIC BUILDINGS AND SITES
La Placita de Abajo Historic District
NM 379, 11 miles north of I-40 juncture
Established in the last quarter of the 19th century, this district was built according to traditional central-plaza community design: most
structures were connected and faced the Plaza,
providing protection against attacks by disloca-
ed Indians. All that remains of this historic settlement a mile downstream from Colonias is 1
standing building and 17 ruins. ◎□

CONCHAS DAM

NM 104, 31 miles north of Tucumcari
The oldest and one of the largest US Army Corps
of Engineers water projects in New Mexico.
Begun under the Emergency Relief Act of 1935,
the dam became operational in the summer of
1939, protecting the Canadian River Valley. Today,
the $16-million project provides flood control as
well as water storage for irrigation and conservation, and serves as a recreational facility to more
than a quarter of a million people each year. ◎

FOLSOM

NM 72 at NM 456, 32 miles east of Ratón
Situated on the southern slopes of the Ratón
Mountains, this turn-of-the-century ranching
and railroad town was named after Grover
Cleveland's wife, Frances Folsom. The name
became history in 1925, when a cowboy riding
in an arroyo west of town came upon prehistoric spear points and bones of animals, indi-
cating occupation of the area 12,000 years earlier by a hunting-and-gathering culture.
Evidence of Folsom Man pushed back the
timetable of human habitation in North America
about 8,000 years. Folsom today is the center
of a large cattle industry.

MUSEUMS AND EXHIBIT SPACES
Folsom Museum
Main Street, 88419
505-278-2122
Preserves the pioneering spirit of the region,
including the discovery of Folsom Man. The
museum is housed in the Doherty Mercantile
Building, completed around 1896. ◎

HISTORIC BUILDINGS AND SITES
Folsom Hotel
Grand Avenue and Wall Street
A rock building, constructed in the early 1890s
to serve as the first mercantile store in Folsom.
◎□

Folsom Site
Dead Horse Gulch, 8 miles west of Folsom
Archaeological discoveries at this site in 1925
proved the early arrival of humans in the
Americas. Folsom Man, based on the spear-
heads and mastadon skeletons he left behind,
dates back about 12,000 years. □△

COMMUNITY EVENTS
Folsom July Jam
Downtown Folsom
505-278-2102
Sponsored by the Emergency Medical
Technicians from Folsom, Capulín, and
Des Moines, the event features entertain-
ment by area bands, special activities for
children, and a variety of booths.

GLORIETA PASS

I-25, 14 miles east of Santa Fe
The decisive battle of the Civil War in New
Mexico was fought at the summit of Glorieta

Pass on March 28, 1862. Union troops dashed
Southern hopes for a takeover of New Mexico—
and ultimately the West—when a party of Union
volunteers from Colorado burned Confederate
supply wagons in Glorieta's Apache Canyon. The
pass also served as a gateway through the
mountains for Francisco Vásquez de Coronado's
1541 exploration of the plains in preparation
for the Spanish friars' conversion expeditions of
the 1600s, for Apache and Comanche entry into
Pueblo country, and for the Santa Fe Trail excur-
sions of the 1820s to 1880s. ⊚◻

HISTORIC BUILDINGS AND SITES
Pigeon Ranch
I-25, 14 miles east of Santa Fe
This stagecoach stop along the Santa Fe Trail

A waterwheel powers this 19th-century grist mill in the historic district of La Cueva. Photograph by Mark Nohl

became part of the Glorieta Pass Civil War Battlefield in 1862. It is the only roofed structure to have withstood the battle. ◎

LA CUEVA

NM 518 at NM 442, 6 miles east of Mora
La Cueva (The Cave), first settled in the 1850s, became the commercial center for the Mora Land Grant. The 33,000-acre historic district contains a water-powered grist mill; a mercantile store and storage buildings; the town's original San Rafael Church, built in the late 1800s; and a ranch house with outbuildings. The ranch house, constructed in 1851 by La Cueva founder Vicente Romero, was visited by General William Tecumseh Sherman and other prominent figures. ◎□

LAS VEGAS

I-25, at NM 104 and NM 518
Home to the Paleo Indians in 8,000 BC, Las Vegas (The Meadows) was established as a Mexican settlement in 1835, after which it became a prime—and prosperous—stop on the Santa Fe Trail and, later, the Atchison, Topeka & Santa Fe Railway. In booming Las Vegas, General Stephen Watts Kearny announced the annexation of New Mexico by the United States on August 15, 1846. During the Confederate occupation of Santa Fe in 1862, the town served as territorial capital. Nicknamed the "Land of Sun, Silence, and Adobe" in the late 1800s, Las Vegas was hardly silent: its community supported an opera house, social and literary clubs, an orchestra, a theater, and by 1893, a university.

MUSEUMS AND EXHIBIT SPACES
António Sanchez Cultural Center
166 Bridge Street, 87701
505-425-8829
Organizes traveling exhibits and showcases photographs, paintings, historical artifacts, and the work of local artists.

Arrott Art Gallery
Donnelly Library
New Mexico Highlands University
National Avenue, 87701
505-454-3332
A fine arts gallery offering continuous shows and exhibits.

Rough Riders Memorial and City Museum
727 Grand Avenue
PO Box 179, 87701
505-425-8726
Displays Teddy Roosevelt memorabilia, artifacts from the Spanish American War of 1898, Indian relics, and other aspects of Las Vegas history.

HISTORIC BUILDINGS AND SITES
Adele Ilfeld Auditorium
New Mexico Highlands University
National Avenue
This architecturally significant structure was begun in 1919 and completed in 1931. The brown brick building has arches, Doric columns, and a Romanesque Revival-style front facade of brownstone. The project was funded by the New Mexico State Legislature and the Ilfeld family, in memory of Adele Ilfeld, wife of business tycoon Charles Ilfeld. ◎□

Atchison, Topeka & Santa Fe Railway Roundhouse
South end of Railroad Avenue
The 34-stall roundhouse was built in 1917 to

replace the 9-stall structure of 1880—an expansion needed to sustain the railroad enterprise that eventually made Las Vegas the transportation capital of northeastern New Mexico. In the 1920s, more than 400 employees were serving 20 or more locomotives daily as they ended their runs at this division headquarters. ⊚□

Bridge Street Historic District
Bridge Street and vicinity
Most of the buildings along this 800-foot-long section of Bridge Street were constructed between 1880 and 1910. They stand as powerful reminders of a 19th-century business district that underwent successful transition from a wagon road settlement to a commercially developed area. ⊚□

Carnegie Park Historic District
North of Douglas Avenue, surrounding Library Park
One of the finest examples of 19th-century landscape architecture in New Mexico, this district exemplifies the French Beaux Arts principles of symmetry and long vistas of green space terminating in a monument or a building. Here, the centerpiece is the Carnegie Library.

Castañeda Hotel
524 Railroad Avenue, 87701
505-425-9985
Built in 1898 to 1899 as a luxurious Fred Harvey hotel, the Castañeda boasted amenities unique to the Harvey chain and served as an active community center. Noted guests included Theodore Roosevelt and William Jennings

Electric trolleys cross the Gallinas River Bridge in this 1904 view of Las Vegas. Photograph courtesy Museum of New Mexico, neg. 9463

Bryan. The Castañeda, La Fonda in Santa Fe, the Montezuma Hotel near Las Vegas, and the Hotel Clovis in Clovis are the only Fred Harvey establishments still standing in New Mexico. ☉

Douglas-Sixth Street and Railroad Avenue Historic Districts
Visible in the Douglas-Sixth Street area are some of the finest 19th-century Victorian commercial buildings in New Mexico, including the city's banks, the Masonic Temple, the Duncan Opera House, the YMCA, and City Hall. The Victorian structures along Railroad Avenue once served as mercantile houses, hotels, saloons, and dance halls. ☉□

Hermit's Peak
I-25, west of Las Vegas
This 10,263-foot granite outcropping was an important landmark on the Santa Fe Trail. From 1863 to 1867, it was also home to Giovanni Marie Augustini, an Italian recluse and holy man who had walked the Trail from Kansas. When he wasn't healing the sick or creating well-publicized miracles, the hermit was carving crucifixes and religious articles, which he traded for food. After spending four years here, Augustini moved to the Organ Mountains in southwestern New Mexico, where he was found murdered in 1869.

Las Vegas Plaza Historic District
Las Vegas Plaza and vicinity
The Plaza was the central business square for the town's founders—34 families who had moved here from San Miguel del Vado in 1835. Most of the buildings that remain were erected between 1880 and 1900. Only the Dice Apartments, modified on the exterior, predate the Mexican War of 1846. ☉□

Las Vegas Railroad and Power Company Building
North 12th Street, between San Francisco and Baca Streets
Completed in 1907, the building served as a center of both service and production at a time when the town's electricity was generated locally and mass transportation was provided by electric trolley cars. ☉□

Library Park Historic District
Library Park and vicinity
Library Park's central square is dominated by a Neoclassical Revival structure and surrounding buildings of frame and brick—a Midwestern design imported from Chicago in 1879 via the Santa Fe Railway. Another Midwestern adaptation is the library, one of the few Carnegie public libraries in the state. ☉□

Lincoln Park Historic District
South side of New Town
A turn-of-the-century park and neighborhood featuring Victorian-era architecture and tree-lined streets. ☉□

Montezuma Hotel
NM 65, 5 miles north of Las Vegas
PO Box 248, 87731
505-454-1461
Originally a 77-room stone hotel constructed in 1880 near natural hot springs, the building was purchased by the Atchison, Topeka & Santa Fe Railway in 1882 and converted into a 300-room luxury facility to lure wealthy tourists. The renovated Montezuma—standing more than four stories high and designed in Queen Anne style at a cost of more than $200,000—was considered the most elegant hotel in the Far West. Less than two years after its opening, however, it burned to the ground. Rebuilt, it met with

COMMUNITY EVENTS

July Fiesta
Plaza Park
505-425-8631
A traditional fiesta, with a parade, music, dance, mariachis, an art show, fishing derby, fireworks, and food on the Fourth of July weekend.

Las Vegas Rails 'n' Trails Days
Historic Roundhouse
Grand Avenue
505-425-8631
Commemorating the historic Santa Fe Trail and the arrival of the Atchison, Topeka & Santa Fe Railway, this return-to-the-Old West event features historic tours, a parade, a crafts show, antiques, a Western Art Show, fiddler's contest, barbecue, rodeo, and country-and-western dance. Held in early June.

People's Fair and Places with a Past
Carnegie Park
505-425-8631
A look inside select historic homes and buildings, in conjunction with arts and crafts, food, and live entertainment. Held in late August.

Southwest Culture Festival
New Mexico Highlands University
National Avenue
505-425-3745
Art shows, lectures, workshops, dancing, and music in mid-July.

more fires as well as financial troubles. In 1903, the Montezuma closed its doors to hotel guests and spent the next 77 years under the ownership of the YMCA, the Baptist Church, then a Catholic seminary. In 1982, the Armand Hammer United World College of the American West opened on the property. ◉▢

Old Town Residential District
Neighborhoods north and east of Old Town Plaza
This district—composed of 340 houses, 2 churches, and a few commercial buildings— represents the historic residential architecture typical of West Las Vegas. The structures form an intact record of the area's transition from the Spanish-Mexican adobe tradition to the Anglo-American, industrial-age, eclectic style characteristic of the period spanning 1850 to 1915. ◉▢

Plaza Hotel
230 North Plaza
Built in 1880, this hotel was the premier reception point for visiting businessmen and ranchers, and the principal gathering place for community meetings, banquets, and dances. The Plaza was superseded by the more luxurious Castañeda Hotel in 1899. ◉

WCTU Fountain in Fountain Park
Intersection of Lincoln Street and Grand and Manzanares Avenues
In this small, triangular park stands a large stone fountain erected in 1896 by the local Women's Christian Temperance Union. The now inoperative fountain embodies two facets of local culture from the pre-1900 boom era: the frontiersmen's excessive imbibing of alcoholic beverages in the town's saloons and the campaign of dedicated women to create a wholesome environment in Las Vegas. ◉▢

Originally built as a resort hotel, Montezuma Castle now houses the Armand Hammer United World College of the American West.
Photograph by Mark Nohl

CULTURAL ORGANIZATIONS
Las Vegas Arts Council
PO Box 2603, 87701
505-425-1085
Provides arts services to the communities of Las Vegas, Mora, Montezuma, and Wagon Mound. Sponsors a six-week children's summer project culminating in a production involving 250 to 300 local children. The group also sponsors the Las Vegas People's Fair.

LIBRARIES
Carnegie Public Library
500 National Avenue, 87701
505-454-1401
One of many libraries built throughout the United States by philanthropist Andrew Carnegie. Completed in 1903 and modeled after Thomas Jefferson's Monticello, the building exemplifies Neoclassical Revival architecture.

PUBLIC ART
Las Vegas Medical Center
Hot Springs Boulevard
David Ellis
"We are the smell of the rain / Sun on the skin / We are heaven and earth and / Peace in the heart"—ceramic tile mural

Luna Vocational Technical Institute
Camp Luna site, NM 65
Francisco Le Febre
"La Education"—mural
Kim Martin
Steel obelisk
Caroline Rackley
"Mesa Helices"—textile/woven sculpture

New Mexico Highlands University Administration Building
National Avenue
Lloyd Moylan
"The Dissemination of Education in New Mexico"—mural in fresco
New Deal Art

LOGAN

US 54 at NM 39
Located on the Canadian River, this trading center for ranchers was named after Captain H. Logan, a Texas ranger who filed a claim on the site around the turn of the 20th century.

MUSEUMS AND EXHIBIT SPACES
McFarland Brothers Bank
Main Street
A one-story bank building constructed in 1904 of native sandstone at a cost of $1,000. The structure is considered a good example of stone masonry using red stone indigenous to the area. ◑

Shollenberger Mercantile Company Building
Main Street
A structure built in 1911 of native sandstone from a Canadian River quarry about two miles south of town. ◑

MORA

NM 518 at NM 434
Settled by farmers in 1818, the village of Mora was originally called L'eau des Morts (Water of the Dead), because a French beaver-trapping party found human bones in what is now called the Mora River. Early residents were an eclectic mix of Spanish, Mexican, Irish, German, Syrian, and French ancestry. Life in Mora quickly became tumultuous, filled with murders, lynchings, and terrorism spilling over from brash Las Vegas to the south.

HISTORIC BUILDINGS AND SITES
Mora Historic District
With the founding of nearby Fort Union in 1851, Mora evolved from a predominantly Hispanic agricultural settlement into the region's business and governmental center. Mills, granaries, stores, churches, and residences sprang up throughout town. Mora today exhibits a range of 19th- to early-20th-century Hispanic folk architecture as diverse as any in New Mexico. ◑□

St. Vrain's Mill
NM 434, 1 block north of NM 518
Constructed in 1864, this grinding mill was owned and operated by Ceran St. Vrain. Grinding the wheat grown in nearby valleys helped meet the demand for flour at nearby Fort Union. The mill was also used to generate electricity until early in the 20th century. ◑□

LIBRARIES
David Cargo Public Library
NM 518
PO Box 638, 87732
505-387-5029

MOSQUERO

NM 39, 74 miles north of Tucumcari
The small village of Mosquero (Swarm of Flies), situated atop a carbon dioxide gas field, prospered throughout the 1920s and 1930s by producing dry ice.

HISTORIC BUILDINGS AND SITES
Goodnight-Loving Trail
NM 39, northwest of Mosquero
After leaving Fort Sumner, the Goodnight-Loving Trail forked in two directions. This branch, developed by Oliver Loving in 1866, followed the Pecos River to Las Vegas, then the Santa Fe Trail to Ratón Pass. Until the arrival of the railroad in 1880, numerous Texas cattle drives followed this route to northern markets in Colorado and Wyoming.

NARA VISA

US 54 at NM 402
Named for a sheepherder who lived here in the 1880s, the town grew up with the Rock Island Railroad's arrival in 1902.

MUSEUMS AND EXHIBIT SPACES
Brams & Bradley Memorial Museum
NM 402, 2 miles south of Amistad
HCR 62, Box 17, 88430
505-633-2251
Originally part of a homestead established in 1906, the building housed a catalog mail-order business. The structure remains unaltered and contains its original furnishings. Open by appointment.

HISTORIC BUILDINGS AND SITES
Nara Visa School
US 54, .5 miles east of NM 402 intersection
A 1936 WPA project featuring an adobe gymnasium, shower house, storage building, generator building, pump house, windmill, and playground equipment, including a merry-go-round, slide, swings, and seesaw. ⊚☐

PECOS

I-25 at NM 63, 21 miles east of Santa Fe
The small Hispanic village in the upper Pecos River Valley was founded around 1700 and called Levy until 1883. Pecos has long served as gateway to the Pecos Wilderness and a large portion of the Sangre de Cristo Mountains.

MUSEUMS AND EXHIBIT SPACES
Pecos National Historical Park
NM 63, 2 miles south of Pecos
PO Drawer 418, 87552
505-757-6414
The area of Pecos was inhabited 12,000 years ago by mammoth, bison, and camel hunters. From 1,100 to 500 years ago, it was populated by pottery makers, hunters, and jewelers who traded extensively with the Plains Indians. When Spanish explorers arrived in the mid-1500s, Pecos was among the most resplendent and highly populated pueblos they encountered. Drought, famine, and disease led to evacuation of the pueblo in 1838, at which point the survivors relocated to Jémez Pueblo, north of Albuquerque. Next to the ruins of Pecos Pueblo—which rose four or five stories in height and contained 600 rooms—are the remains of 17th- and 18th-century Spanish Colonial missions. The park, which recently acquired 5,500 acres of the Glorieta Civil War Battlefield and the adjacent Forked Lightning Ranch, now encompasses hundreds of archaeological sites as well as two structures: Kozlowski's Ranch on the Santa Fe Trail and the Tex Austin House. Included are a visitor center, a 1.25-mile ruins trail, and 2.5 miles of the Pecos River. ⊚☐△

RATÓN

I-25 at US 64

The town of Ratón emerged in 1879 from the
Willow Springs freight stop on the Santa Fe Trail,
which became strewn with railroad repair shops
as soon as tracks were laid for railways to cross
Ratón Pass. As Trail travel gave way to train travel, valuable coal deposits attracted early settlers
to this town at the base of the pass. With its railroad yards and nearby coalfields, Ratón came to
be known as the "Pittsburgh of the West."

MUSEUMS AND EXHIBIT SPACES

Old Pass Gallery
140 South First Street
PO Box 774, 87740
505-445-2052
Located in the historic Cook Building constructed in 1892, Old Pass displays the works of local
and regional artists.

Ratón Museum
216 South First Street, 87740
505-445-8979
A history and art museum housed in the 1906
Coors Building. The museum's permanent and
temporary exhibits feature regional artifacts
associated with ranching, coal mining, railroading, and pioneer life; original works by New
Mexican artists; and a large photo collection.
Additional offerings include lectures and a visiting scholar program.

Sugarite Canyon State Park
NM 526, 10 miles northeast of Ratón
505-445-5607
The park contains historic exhibits, lakes, and
campsites. A visitor center offers information
on early mining activities in the area. Fee.

HISTORIC BUILDINGS AND SITES

Dawson Cemetery
US 64, 14 miles northeast of Cimarrón
A graveyard for European immigrants who dominated the company town of Dawson, the largest
coal-mining community in the former Ratón coal-
field. In the early 1900s, Dawson experienced two
large mine explosions, killing nearly 400 workers,
the majority of whom are buried here. ◉☐

Ratón Downtown Historic District
First Street vicinity
These 20 acres include a five-city-block area
containing the town's original business section.
Most of the buildings still standing were constructed during the late 19th and early 20th
centuries to serve as hotels, saloons, stores,
warehouses, and railroad facilities. ◉☐

Ratón Pass
I-25, at the Colorado-New Mexico border
This important pass on the Mountain Branch of
the Santa Fe Trail was used by Brigadier General
Stephen Watts Kearny in his 1846 invasion of
New Mexico, and by the Colorado Union volun-
teers who helped defeat the Confederates in New
Mexico in 1862. Four years later, mountain man
Richens L. "Uncle Dick" Wootton cleared the
pass of trees and established a tollgate at the
border, which he operated until 1879, when the
Santa Fe Railway bought the road. ☐△

Shuler Theater
131 North Second Street
505-445-5520
Constructed in 1915, during the mayoral term
of Dr. J. J. Shuler, the auditorium was considered one of the finest theaters in the Southwest.
It was used for plays and other performing arts,
as well as community meetings and events. The
theater was restored in the early 1980s. ◉

COMMUNITY EVENTS
Ratón International Arts Show and Crafts Fair
International State Bank in Ripley Park
505-445-3689
A juried event featuring the work of in-state and out-of-state artists. Held in mid-August.

Santa Fe Trail Rendezvous
National Rifle Association Whittington Center
505-445-3689
A mountain man rendezvous, complete with blackpowder shoots, tomahawk and knife throwing, and a tepee village. Held in mid-June.

CULTURAL ORGANIZATIONS
Ratón Arts and Humanities Council
140 South First Street
PO Box 774, 87440
505-445-2052
Sponsors a performing arts series, Hispanic cultural programming, cooperative humanities presentations, and development of a permanent visual arts center. The council also manages the historic Cook Building and serves as a resource for arts information and publicity.

LIBRARIES
Arthur Johnson Memorial Library
244 Cook Avenue, 87740
505-445-9711

PUBLIC ART
El Portal Hotel
101 North Third Street
Manville Chapman and *William Warder*
Murals
New Deal Art

Ratón Convention Center
941 North Third Street
Two-dimensional pieces by numerous artists, including *Lois D. Dolch, Glenda Lenz, Jim Mullings,* and *Marvin W. Newton.*

Ratón Post Office
245 Park Avenue
Joseph A. Fleck
"Butterfield Mail"—mural
"Unloading Mail at Ratón"—mural
New Deal Art

Shuler Theater Foyer
131 North Second Street
Manville Chapman
Murals
New Deal Art

RAYADO

NM 21, 12 miles south of Cimarrón
Rayado, the first permanent colony on the Beaubin-Miranda Land Grant, was settled in 1848. Between 1861 and 1880, the village functioned as a rest stop and trading area along the Mountain Branch of the Santa Fe Trail. During this time, Kit Carson built a house in the village (see page 81). In 1929, the village was purchased by Oklahoma oilman Waite Phillips, who donated it to the Boy Scouts of America in 1941. Rayado now forms the southeastern corner of Philmont Scout Ranch and, aside from the Kit Carson Museum, is available for exterior viewing. The village consists of the Maxwell-Abreu home and outlying buildings constructed from 1848 to 1857. ◉☐

SAN GERÓNIMO

Forest Road 18 at Tecolote Creek, 2 miles southwest of NM 283

The 26 weathered adobe, rock, and log buildings that now comprise the village of San Gerónimo were once part of a thriving community of several hundred buildings situated on the Mountain Branch of the Santa Fe Trail. In the 19th century, the village was one of the largest and most prosperous trade centers in the eastern Sangre de Cristo Mountains. When communal land use began to provoke fierce Spanish-American conflict, San Gerónimo served as headquarters of Las Gorras Blancas (The White Caps), one of the most significant late-19th-century protest movements in the Southwest. Today's villagers retain their early agricultural customs, irrigating crops in the creek bottom by means of an *acequia madre* (mother ditch) and grazing animals in the hills of the valley. ☉▢

SAN MIGUEL DEL VADO

NM 3, 3 miles south of I-25

Founded around 1806 by the Ribera family of Santa Fe, this village took root where Santa Fe Trail wagon trains crossed the Pecos River. By the 1820s, when wagon traffic had increased along the Trail, San Miguel boasted a population of 1,000. In 1835, a small band of San Miguel residents moved north and founded Las Vegas. The prize of the historic district today is its massive village church, constructed between 1805 and 1806—a twin-towered building with rock walls 3 feet thick and 20 feet high. ☉▢

SANTA ROSA

I-40 at US 54

Spanish explorer António de Espejo passed through this area in 1583, as did Gaspar Castaño de Sosa in 1590. Settled as a land grant around 1865, the village was known as Agua Negra Chiquita (Little Black Water) and was situated on the ranch of politician Don Celso Baca y Baca. In 1897, when Baca built a chapel in the community and dedicated it to Santa Rosa de Lima—the first canonized saint in the New World—the town took her name as well. With the arrival of the Southern Pacific Railroad in 1901, the quiet village of Santa Rosa mushroomed into a trade center for nearby farms and ranches. The present-day town is known for its natural springs and lakes, including Park Lake, the "world's largest free swimming pool."

HISTORIC BUILDINGS AND SITES
Grzelachowski House and Store
Puerto de Luna
NM 91, 10 miles south of Santa Rosa
The Territorial-style building was constructed in the 1870s by Alexander Grzelachowski, a Polish-born Roman Catholic priest who in 1851 came to Las Vegas, New Mexico, to serve the parish of Bishop Lamy. After the Civil War, Grzelachowski left the priesthood to become a merchant, rancher, and father of nine children. In time, he moved his family and successful mercantile business to Puerto de Luna, where he built this popular store and meeting place. ☉▢

Trail of the Forty-Niners
I-40, west of US 84 exit
Paralleling I-40 to Albuquerque is a section of the Arkansas-to-New Mexico wagon road

opened in 1849 by Captain Randolph B. Marcy
and Lieutenant James H. Simpson in an attempt
to give gold-seekers an alternative to the Santa
Fe Trail route to California. Marcy's Road, as it
came to be called, was popular among the
Forty-Niners, though never as well traveled as
the Santa Fe Trail.

LIBRARIES
Moise Memorial Library
208 Fifth Street, 88435
505-472-3101

SPRINGER

I-25 at US 56
What began as a railroad worker camp in the
rich grasslands of the Maxwell Land Grant near
the Cimarrón Cutoff of the Santa Fe Trail developed into an important shipping point for cattle
en route to slaughterhouses and packing companies in Kansas City and Chicago. Founded
with the coming of the railroad in 1879,
Springer got off to a violent start in the con-
cluding period of the Colfax County War, a dis-
pute between land grant owners and settlers.
Even so, in 1882, the town was designated the
county seat of Colfax County—a distinction that
lasted until 1897 when, after a heated political
battle, the county seat was moved to Ratón.

HISTORIC BUILDINGS AND SITES
Dorsey Mansion
US 56, 30 miles northeast of Springer
A two-story log-and-stone mansion built between
1878 and 1886 by cattle baron and former US
senator from Arkansas, Stephen W. Dorsey. Here,
party guests and a wide array of visitors were
treated to indoor plumbing, gas-powered lighting, and a lavishly decorated swimming pool—
uncommon amenities on the northeastern plains
of New Mexico in the 1880s. Between Dorsey's
1892 departure from Colfax County and the early
1970s, the Gothic Revival "castle" functioned as
a tuberculosis sanitorium, post office, private
home, and general store. ☉☐

Point of Rocks
US 56, .25 miles east of Springer
This geological formation in Jicarilla Apache
country was a major landmark on the Santa Fe
Trail. Nearby, in 1849, the family of Santa Fe
merchant J. W. White was attacked; the military

party organized to rescue his wife and daughter included Kit Carson.

CULTURAL ORGANIZATIONS
Santa Fe Trail Museum and Historical Society
614 Maxwell Avenue
PO Box 323, 87747
505-483-2701
Situated in the county courthouse built in 1881, this history museum features art exhibits and artifacts pertaining to the Santa Fe Trail and early pioneer life. Fee.

LIBRARIES
Fred Macaron Library
PO Box 726, 87747
505-483-2848

TUCUMCARI

I-40, at NM 209 and NM 104
On the western edge of a watering place frequented by mastodons and giant bison, this region lured migrating humans as well: Stone Age game hunters, conquistadores, bands of plains and mountain Indians, pioneers, and outlaws. Between the mid-1700s and the military campaigns of 1874, the area attracted raiding Comanches and Comancheros (New Mexicans who traded with the Comanches) too. With the coming of the railroad in 1898, the small community of Liberty, eight miles to the north, moved southward to form the nucleus of Tucumcari at the juncture of two railroad lines. Incorporated in 1908, Tucumcari has prospered from its proximity not only to rail transport but to Route 66 and the irrigation district created in the 1930s by the building of Conchas Dam on the Canadian River.

MUSEUMS AND EXHIBIT SPACES
Tucumcari Historical Institute Museum
416 South Adams Street, 88401
505-461-4201
This history and folk art museum, housed in a 1904 courthouse, showcases items ranging from 12,000 BC Indian artifacts to a 1926 fire truck. Fee.

HISTORIC BUILDINGS AND SITES
Blue Swallow Motel
815 East Tucumcari Boulevard
The pre-World War II tourist motor court became an icon of Route 66 folklore. ☺☐

Comanche Country
I-40, west of Tucumcari
By 1700, Comanche refugees from Texas had acquired horses and begun moving westward into the Tucumcari area. After driving out the Jicarilla Apache people, they launched continuous raids on New Mexico's eastern frontier, posing a threat to Indian, Spanish, and Anglo settlements for more than a century. The Comanches were defeated by US Army troops in 1874.

Fort Bascom
NM 104, 8 miles north of Tucumcari
Fort Bascom was built in 1863 to protect the area from Comanche attacks. The installation was used in Kit Carson's campaign against Comanche warriors in 1864 and in General Philip Sheridan's in 1868. The stronghold was also used to control the Comancheros. Fort Bascom was abandoned in 1870.

Route 66
The nation's first paved road linking the East and West Coasts entered New Mexico east of Tucumcari in 1926 and sliced 375 miles across

the north-central portion of the state. Scores of roadside structures promoting automobile tourism across the transcontinental artery have endured the passage of time here, remaining unobscured by modern interstate highways.

Tucumcari Mountain
Rising 1,000 feet above the surrounding plain, Tucumcari Mountain has long been a landmark for travelers along the Canadian River. Captain Randolph B. Marcy led an expedition past the mountain in 1849, while blazing a trail from Arkansas to California.

CULTURAL ORGANIZATIONS
Quay County Arts and Humanities Council
1410 South Fifth Street, 88401
505-461-2551

LIBRARIES
Kenneth Schlientz Memorial Library
602 South Second Street, 88401
505-461-0295

Rural Bookmobile East
PO Box 1163, 88401
505-461-1206

PUBLIC ART
Quay County Courthouse
Ben Carlton
"Coronado"—mural
New Deal Art

Tucumcari Area Vocational School
Sculptures by numerous artists, including *James Beville, Bill Curry, K.O. Dewey, Janette Fister, William Hise, Ben Mead, Mabel Mirabal, Scott Lane*, and *Yoni Sinor.*

COMMUNITY EVENTS
Billy the Kid Pageant
Caprock Amphitheatre
505-576-2455
A historical drama set in a natural stone amphitheater on the edge of the Llano Estacado. Runs from mid-June to mid-August.

C.R.A.F.T. Fair
Quay County Exhibit Center
505-461-0725
An early December event featuring local craftmakers.

Mesa Redondo Cowboy Camp Meeting
NM 18, 12 miles south of Tucumcari
505-769-0425
An old-time gospel-singing and camp-preaching fellowship held in late July.

Piñata Festival
Quay County Exhibit Center
505-461-1694
Events include the crowning of Prince Tocom and Princess Kari—the town's legendary Apache namesakes—as well as one of the largest parades in New Mexico. Held in mid-June.

Tucumcari Arts and Crafts Fair
Quay County Exhibit Center
505-461-3133
Features local New Mexico artists during the first week in June.

Skeletons of century-old artillery lie scattered around old Fort Union. Photograph by Mark Nohl

VAUGHN

US 54, at US 285 and US 60
Dubbed "the intersection of the nation's central plains," Vaughn connects routes to Kansas City, the Gulf of Mexico, and Mexico City. A source of bountiful grazing land and a shipping point for nearby cattle and sheep ranches, the town emerged following the arrival of two transcontinental railroads: the El Paso and Rock Island Line from the South in 1902, and the Belén Cutoff of the Santa Fe Railway from the West in 1907. A civil engineer named Vaughn helped build the Santa Fe line through the area.

LIBRARIES
Huntsinger Public Library
PO Box 278, 88353
505-584-2580

WAGON MOUND

I-25 at NM 120
This volcanic mesa shaped like the top of a covered wagon was the westernmost great landmark on the Santa Fe Trail. Here, travelers could cross from the Cimarrón Cutoff to Fort Union which, on the Mountain Branch of the Trail, afforded protection from Indian attack. The two branches joined at Watrous, 23 miles south of Wagon Mound. ◉□△

WATROUS

I-25 at NM 161
Juncture of the Santa Fe Trail's Mountain Branch and Cimarrón Cutoff, this spot was originally called La Junta (The Junction). In 1879,

with the coming of the railroad, it was named for Samuel B. Watrous, a prominent local rancher. The village of Watrous, which grew up around the 20-room house and stage station built 30 years earlier by the rancher, served as a place for wagon trains to organize before entering hostile Indian territory. ๑△

MUSEUMS AND EXHIBIT SPACES
Fort Union National Monument
NM 161, 8 miles north of I-25 junction
Watrous, 87753
505-425-8025
Active from 1851 to 1890, Fort Union was staffed with Army personnel plus more than 400 civilians to guard the Santa Fe Trail from attack by Indians. Following the Civil War, the fort became the primary supply depot for other military posts in the Southwest. In 1890, when the railroad replaced wagon trains, the US Army abandoned the fort. A military museum on the grounds features Santa Fe Trail exhibits and artifacts. Fee. ๑▢

HISTORIC BUILDINGS AND SITES
Loma Parda
NM 161, 6 miles northwest of Watrous
A ghost town once known as "Sodom on the Mora" for the recreational diversions it offered the soldiers stationed at nearby Fort Union in the late 19th century. Loma Parda was renowned for its prostitutes, gambling, and powerful rotgut. ๑

Santa Fe Trail
I-25, east of Watrous
Part of the original trade route opened by William Becknell in 1821 to link Missouri river towns with Santa Fe, New Mexico. This portion of the trail marks the joining of its two main arteries: the Cimarrón Cutoff and the Mountain Branch. Travel over the trail ceased with the coming of the railroad in 1879. ๑

COMMUNITY EVENTS
Living History Portrayal of Frontier Garrison Life
Fort Union National Monument
505-425-8025
Lectures and demonstrations on the subjects of muskets, women on the frontier, the infantry, cavalry, Fort Union and the Civil War, and the Santa Fe Trail. Presentations run from Memorial Day to Labor Day.

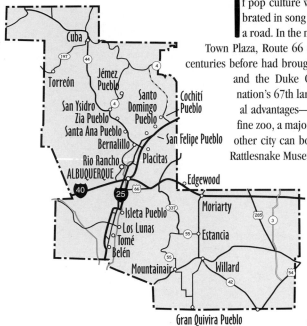

I f pop culture were a highway, it would be Route 66, celebrated in song and television show, an American Dream of a road. In the mid-1920s, at a spot near Albuquerque's Old Town Plaza, Route 66 crossed the Camino Real, the highway that centuries before had brought Spanish settlers north from Mexico City, and the Duke City was born. Modern Albuquerque, the nation's 67th largest city, has more than its share of cultural advantages—various performing arts, ethnic festivals, a fine zoo, a major university—plus a few special touches. No other city can boast the likes of the American International Rattlesnake Museum, let alone the bilingual repertory theater group La Compania de Teatro, the colorful Gathering of Nations Powwow, or the city's hallmark event, the International Balloon Fiesta.

Visitors who venture beyond the city limits of contemporary Albuquerque soon discover a far older heritage. No fewer than eight Indian pueblos surround the Albuquerque metropolitan area. Strange symbols pecked in stone at Petroglyph National Monument carry messages from a lost ancient time. Ruins at Salinas Pueblo Missions National Monument bear mute witness to early Spanish missionary efforts to convert the native people of New Mexico. A few miles away, the whimsical side of central New Mexico is reflected in Mountainair's Rancho Bonito and Shaffer Hotel—amazing folk art creations that present a different kind of "Pop" culture.

ALBUQUERQUE

I-40 at I-25
The Albuquerque area was inhabited more than 12,000 (some say as many as 20,000 or 25,000) years ago by bands of hunter-gatherers, and from AD 1100 to 1300 by Anasazi Indians. In 1540, Francisco Vásquez de Coronado's expedition arrived en route from Mexico, in search of the mythical Seven Cities of Cíbola. Within the century, members of subsequent expeditions settled in the fertile farmland along

Bernalillo residents honor the town's patron saint in the annual Fiesta de San Lorenzo. Photograph by Mark Nohl

the Río Grande. Resettled and founded in 1706 as the Villa of San Felipe de Alburquerque (the first *r* was later dropped)—in homage to Spain's Duke of Alburquerque, who, at the time, was the viceroy in Mexico City—the town consisted of a small chapel and a cluster of adobe homes built around a plaza. Through the Plaza passed oxcart caravans on their way from Mexico to Santa Fe along the Camino Real (Royal Road), seeking refuge from attacks by nomadic Indian tribes in the Río Abajo, the lower Río Grande Valley. With the 1880 arrival of the railroad two miles east of Old Town Plaza, a new town, composed largely of Anglos, took root along the tracks, and a horse-drawn streetcar transported residents between the two communities. Albuquerque was incorporated as a town in 1885, and as a city six years later.

MUSEUMS AND EXHIBIT SPACES

Albuquerque Center for Peace and Justice
144 Harvard Drive SE, 87106
505-268-9557
Mounts small, rotating exhibits, and maintains a collection of peace and justice posters.

Albuquerque Children's Museum
800 Río Grande Boulevard NW, Suite 10, 87104
505-842-5525
Presents hands-on exhibits and demonstrations for children of all ages. Permanent exhibits feature The Arts and Imagination, How Things Work, and Communication and Heritage. Fee.

Albuquerque Museum of Art and History
2000 Mountain Road NW
PO Box 1293, 87103
505-243-7255
A city-operated museum adjacent to Old Town, featuring decorative arts, fine arts and crafts, costumes, photographs, and cultural artifacts from 20,000 BC to the present, including centuries of Spanish Colonial items. The facility houses children's exhibits, a sculpture garden, and an extensive library.

American International Rattlesnake Museum
202 San Felipe Street NW, 87104
505-242-6569
Displays the world's greatest diversity of rare and unusual rattlesnakes and related artifacts and memorabilia. The museum also presents a video and runs a gift shop.

Enabled Arts Center Gallery
2017 Yale Boulevard SE, 87106
505-766-9620

Offers a studio arts program to youth and adults with disabilities. Services include career development, one-on-one instruction with professional artists and teachers, apprenticeships, supported employment, residencies, and multicultural projects in both visual and performing arts. The gallery and a gift shop of arts and crafts produced at the center are open to the public. Serves ages 14 and up.

Explora Science Center
40 First Plaza, Suite 68, 87102
505-842-6188
Presents hands-on science exhibits for children and adults. Fee.

Geology and Meteoritic Museum
University of New Mexico
200 Yale Boulevard NE, Room 107, 87131
505-277-4204
Showcases the geology of our solar system. Rare meteorites from Mars and the asteroids sit side by side with minerals, rocks, and fossils from Earth. Special exhibits are devoted to the geology of New Mexico and to meteorites recovered within the state.

Indian Pueblo Cultural Center
2401 12th Street NW, 87104
505-843-7270
This high-profile institution, directed by New Mexico's 19 pueblo governors, houses a performing space, museum, gift shop, and restaurant. The center hosts events ranging from Indian ceremonies and dances to arts and crafts fairs.

Jonson Gallery of the University of New Mexico Art Museum
University of New Mexico
1909 Las Lomas Road NE, 87131
505-277-4967

Offers changing exhibitions of work by contemporary experimental artists and Raymond Jonson (1891–1982), a prolific New Mexican artist and teacher. The collection includes 2,000 works of art.

Maxwell Museum of Anthropology
University of New Mexico
University Boulevard, 87131
505-277-4404
Features international work, with special emphasis on crafted items by native cultures of the American Southwest, such as Mimbres and Pueblo pottery, American Indian baskets and jewelry, and Navajo weaving.

Museum of Southwestern Biology
University of New Mexico
Yale Boulevard, 87131
505-277-3411
Features plants, mammals, birds, reptiles, amphibians, and fish of the Southwest. The museum, affiliated with the university's Biology Department, offers educational programs and temporary exhibits. Open to the public by appointment.

Jurassic beasts are among the biggest attractions at the New Mexico Museum of Natural History and Science. Photograph by Mark Nohl

National Atomic Museum
Kirtland Air Force Base
Building 20358
Wyoming Boulevard, 87185-5400
505-845-6670
Traces the history of the top-secret Manhattan Project, beginning with a copy of the letter from Albert Einstein to President Franklin Roosevelt encouraging development of the atomic bomb. Offerings include a 53-minute film entitled *The Ten Seconds That Shook the World;* full-scale models of missiles as well as a B-52 bomber and F-105D fighter bomber; and a library. Visitors must obtain a pass at the Wyoming Gate entrance to the base.

New Mexico Museum of Natural History and Science
1801 Mountain Road NW, 87104
505-841-8837
New Mexico's most visited museum—a high-tech masterpiece containing permanent and changing exhibits on zoology, botany, geology, and paleontology. Displays include a walk-through volcano, an ice-age cave, live sharks and other sea animals, and an "Evolator," a time machine that transports passengers 38

million years into New Mexico's past. The facility also offers a large-format theater experience, lectures, summer camps, field trips, workshops, and seminars. A part of the New Mexico Office of Cultural Affairs. Fee.

New Mexico State Fair Fine Arts Gallery
State Fairgrounds, Gate 3
PO Box 8546, 87198
505-265-1791
Showcases the State Fair's permanent collection of fine arts, and organizes a juried art exhibition, temporary exhibits, and a sales gallery.

Petroglyph National Monument
6900 Unser Boulevard NW, 87120
505-897-8814
Chipped into the black volcanic boulders along the 17-mile West Mesa escarpment that defines the western edge of Albuquerque are more than 15,000 ancient Indian rock drawings. Strewn among the rock art, much of which dates back at least 1,000 years, are crosses inscribed by early Spanish settlers who may have viewed some of the Indian figures as demonic. Fee.

Pueblo Indian Museum
Indian Pueblo Cultural Center
2401 12th Street NW, 87104
505-843-7270
Portrays the history of New Mexico's 19 Indian pueblos. A permanent exhibit on the lower level depicts the development of Pueblo culture from prehistoric times to the present. Changing exhibits on the upper level feature murals and other works by contemporary Pueblo artists. Attractions include a large gift shop, an Indian restaurant, and native dancing and craft demonstrations. Fee.

Río Grande Nature Center State Park
2901 Candelaria NW, 87102
505-344-7240
A migratory bird sanctuary with a visitor center containing fauna and flora exhibits. Fee.

Río Grande Zoological Park
903 10th Street SW, 87102
505-843-7413
A collection of more than 1,200 mammals, birds, reptiles, and amphibians from around the world. Features include a children's zoo, snack bars, a gift shop, and guided tours on request. The zoo also provides educational programs in the schools and for parents. Fee.

Simms Fine Arts Center
Albuquerque Academy
6400 Wyoming Boulevard NE, 87109
505-828-3338
Changing exhibits highlight the work of professional artists, students, and faculty members. The center also presents about a dozen theatrical performances each year, ranging from full-length musicals and historical plays to contemporary dramas and comedies.

South Broadway Cultural Center
1025 Broadway SE, 87102
505-848-1320
A multicultural meeting place offering art exhibits, films, classes, workshops, performing arts, and a film and video rental program. The center consists of a gallery and a small performing space with technical lighting and sound systems. Administered by the City of Albuquerque and supported in part by the nonprofit Friends of the South Broadway Cultural Center.

Spanish History Museum
2221 Lead Avenue SE, 87106
505-268-9981
Chronicles New Mexico's Spanish history and
Colonial period. The education-oriented museum contains a library with more than 300
monographs and research papers. Fee.

Tinkertown Museum
121 Sandía Crest Road
PO Box 303, Sandía Park, 87047
505-281-5233
Offers a unique exhibit of an animated, minia-
ture hand-carved Western town. Included are a
turn-of-the-century potter's studio and more
than 6,000 objects on display. Fee.

Turquoise Museum
2107 Central Avenue NW, 87104
800-821-7443
Features one-of-a-kind showpieces from
around the world, a simulated turquoise mine,
and a gift shop.

University Art Museum
University of New Mexico Fine Arts Center, 87131
505-277-4001
Displays 19th- and 20th-century American and
European sculpture, paintings, and other works
on paper, and maintains a major collection of
photographs and prints. The museum also
hosts a changing exhibition program, lectures,
and gallery talks.

HISTORIC BUILDINGS AND SITES
Albuquerque Municipal Airport Building (old)
Yale Boulevard SE
One of the few surviving airports constructed by
the WPA in the 1930s. The $875,000 building
stands as testimony of the boom-era war years
in Albuquerque, symbol of a critical time in

United States aviation history, and a rare example of Pueblo Revival architecture in an institu-
tional setting. The airport began operation in
1928 and was used for passenger and freight
transport until 1942. ◎□

Albuquerque Public Library (old)
423 Central Avenue NE
Constructed in 1925 in the Spanish-Pueblo Revival
style of the times. The building's interior—including its impressive fireplaces—was decorated by
prominent Santa Fe artist Gustave Baumann. ◎

Armijo School
1021 Isleta Boulevard SE
Built in 1914 in one of Albuquerque's oldest
communities, the Armijo School has for 80
years served as a South Valley landmark. ◎□

Fourth Ward Historic District
West of downtown area
Home to many of the city's most influential citizens in the 1905-to-1923 period. The fine residences, built between 1880 and about 1930
reflect architectural styles ranging from bungalow and Queen Anne to hipped box and
Spanish-Pueblo Revival. ◎□

Hilton Hotel (old)
125 Second Street NW
Built in 1939, this was the last of Albuquerque's
great "Southwestern" hotels—establishments
that fused modern building techniques with traditional New Mexico decor. ◎□

**Historic Residences of Downtown
Albuquerque**
North of Central Avenue
Adjacent to historic Old Albuquerque—the
Spanish community founded in 1706—this pri-
marily residential area reflects nearly every

Fewer than 3,000 people lived in Albuquerque in 1880 when the first railroad arrived. Photograph by George C. Bennett, courtesy Museum of New Mexico, neg. 14568

architectural style used in the city between 1860 and 1930. ◉▢

Huning Highlands Historic District
Grand Avenue area
A sector of town named for Franz Huning, a German immigrant who moved to New Mexico in the mid-1800s and by the 1880s had become a prominent Albuquerque citizen. Here, turn-of-the-century building styles run the gamut from Queen Anne to Italianate. ◉▢

Kearny's Route
I-25, between Albuquerque and Santa Fe
Brigadier General Stephen Watts Kearny and his United States forces invaded New Mexico on August 1, 1846. On August 18th, he raised the American flag in Santa Fe, after which he marched unopposed along this route into Bernalillo and Albuquerque. As a result of the occupation, New Mexico was declared a territory of the United States.

KiMo Theater
423 Central Avenue NW
505-848-1370
This gem of historic Route 66 epitomizes the 1920s Art Deco interpretation of American Indian motifs. The lobby is decorated with Carl von Hassler murals depicting Indian pueblos of the area, flamboyant wrought-iron wild turkeys, and buffalo skulls with illuminated eye sockets. Renovated in 1980, the 750-seat KiMo hosts a full schedule of theatrical events. ◉▢

Los Griegos Historic District
3 miles north of downtown area
The only 19th-century community in Albuquerque's agricultural North Valley to have retained its architectural continuity and cultural traditions, most of which were rooted in 18th-century Spanish customs. ◉▢

Los Poblanos Historic District
Río Grande Valley, north of Albuquerque
One of the few remaining stretches of uninterrupted farmland and riverside cottonwood

bosque in the Río Grande Valley north of Albuquerque. Whereas most of the district's structures date back to 1850, three of the houses were designed by Santa Fe architect John Gaw Meem in the 1930s. ◉□

Manzano Day School (formerly La Glorieta)
1801 Central Avenue
La Glorieta, a focal point of regional activity for more than a century, is among the most important historical residences in the city. Two wings of the building date back to the Civil War period. With subsequent additions, the four-sided adobe encircled a *placita* (little plaza), and served as home to such influential families as the Hunings and Fergussons. Today, it houses a school. ◉□

Monte Vista Fire Station
3201 Central Avenue NW
This Spanish-Pueblo Revival-style building was erected with WPA funds in 1936. ◉□

Nob Hill Business Center
3500 Central Avenue SE
Albuquerque's first drive-in shopping center—a U-shaped facility constructed just after World War II in the old East Heights area. Its original streamlined Moderne detailing and many of its initial neon signs are intact. ◉□

Occidental Insurance Company Building
119 Third Street SW
Dominating the corner of Third Street and Gold Avenue, the Occidental Building was considered Albuquerque's most artistic facility when it was built around 1917. The structure was designed by architect Henry Trost of El Paso, Texas, and opened to the public on August 1, 1917. Its prominent arches, columns, and bas-relief terra cotta were modeled after the Doge's Palace in Venice, Italy. ◉□

Old Town Plaza
Central Avenue west to Río Grande Boulevard
This historic area formed the Villa of San Felipe de Alburquerque on the banks of the Río Grande in 1706. Today, Indians and other artisans sell their wares on the streets that line the square. The Plaza's San Felipe de Neri Church is as central to the neighborhood's religious life now as it was in 1793, when it was built.

Pueblo Revolt Site
I-25, between Santa Fe and Albuquerque, near Santa Domingo Pueblo
In August 1680, the Pueblo Indians staged a dramatic revolt against Spanish rule. Forced to evacuate Santa Fe by bands of Tanos, Tewas, and Tiwas, Governor Otermín led the retreating Spanish colonists south through Keres pueblo country.

San Felipe de Neri Church
Old Town Plaza
PO Box 7007, 87194
505-243-4628
A repository for more than two and a half centuries of history—and nearly all of the city's post-Spanish past—this church was built in 1792. (The parish itself was established in 1706, but the original church was destroyed by a flood in 1791.) The Spanish Colonial-style structure, named for Albuquerque's patron saint, has enormous adobe walls and an elaborate, handcrafted interior. ◉□

Sandía Cave
NM 44, 11 miles east of Bernalillo
More than 50 years ago, University of New Mexico archaeologists found stone tools, weapons, and bones of extinct animals in this limestone cave. The artifacts are said to date back to 23,000 BC, providing some of the earli-

est evidence of human habitation in the United States. ⊚□△

Silver Hill Historic District
Bordered by Central and Lead Avenues
Albuquerque's first suburban subdivision straddles a large hill above the flood plain of the Río Grande. Built just after World War I, Silver Hill quickly became a middle-class neighborhood populated mostly by newcomers to the city during the 1920s. The long rows of regularly spaced houses, each with a manicured lawn, reveal a variety of architectural styles. ⊚□

Spruce Park Historic District
University Boulevard area, west of the University of New Mexico
This district contains the city's greatest concentration and widest variety of 1920s and 1930s residential architectural designs. Mediterranean-style homes with red-tile roofs sit beside Gothic cottages, Spanish-Pueblo Revival adobes, and streamlined Moderne houses. The neighborhood, well preserved, is still thriving. ⊚□

Watson Historic District
Lomas Boulevard and Mountain Road
These 1940s Pueblo Revival-style adobes north of Old Town, distinguished for their wise planning and judicious use of native materials and crafts, are the achievement of Albuquerque designer and builder Leon Watson. ⊚

Whittlesey House
201 Highland Circle SE
A rustic log-and-stone building designed by Charles Whittlesey, architect for Santa Fe Railway hotels and stations, including the Alvarado Hotel in Albuquerque and the famous El Tovar Hotel at the Grand Canyon. Built in 1903 and modeled after a Norwegian villa, the

house is currently headquarters for the Albuquerque Press Club. ⊚

PERFORMING ARTS

Albuquerque Children's Theatre
4139 Prospect Avenue NE, 87110
505-888-3644
Live theater for, by, and with children.

Albuquerque Civic Light Opera Association
4201 Ellison Street NE, 87109
505-345-6577
Offers the best of Broadway in five musical productions each year at Popejoy Hall on the University of New Mexico campus. Currently in its third decade, the ACLOA is the largest community producer of musical theater in the nation.

Albuquerque Little Theater
224 San Pasquale Avenue SW, 87104
505-242-4750
Combining local talent with a staff of professionals, this nonprofit community theater company produces comedies, dramas, musicals, and mysteries in one of Albuquerque's most charming historic facilities. Sized for intimacy and designed by Southwestern architect John Gaw Meem, the theater offers a lobby, lounge, and art gallery.

Albuquerque Philharmonic Orchestra
2631 Vista Larga Drive NE, 87106
505-265-0283
This group of local amateur musicians performs four free concerts each year in different Albuquerque locations.

Artists of Indian America
6636 Mossman Place NE, 87110
505-881-4093
Committed to social and cultural improvement among American Indian people, the performing

arts organization brings top Indian talent to schools and communities in New Mexico. Events include concerts, workshops, performances, and opportunities for personal contact.

Ballet en Fuego: Latin Dance Revue
156 Calle Arroyo Seco NW, 87105
505-836-7579
A professional, Albuquerque-based dance company offering an extensive Mexican, Spanish, and contemporary Latin dance repertoire performed in colorful costume.

Chamber Orchestra of Albuquerque
PO Box 35081, 87176
505-881-0844
Conducted by David Oberg, the 31-musician professional orchestra performs six classical subscription concerts, an all-baroque concert, a concert with the University of New Mexico Chorus, several ensemble programs, and concerts for children and seniors. Major soloists of national and international acclaim appear regularly with the group. Most concerts are performed at St. John's United Methodist Church.

D.A.N.C.E., Inc.
9017 Natalie Avenue NE, 87111
Offers educational ballet programs for New Mexico elementary school children as well as performances by Ballet West, Paul Taylor, and San Francisco Ballet principals.

Danzantes
PO Box 4613, 87196
505-247-9640
This contemporary dance-and-theater ensemble performs the work of choreographer and artistic director Alicia Perea.

Bill Evans Dance Company
PO Box 2815, Corrales, 87048
505-898-1531
A professional contemporary dance company in residence at the University of New Mexico. The group, under the direction of Bill Evans, performs an original modern and jazz/tap choreography three or four times a year at the KiMo Theater and the university's Rodey Theater and Popejoy Hall in addition to touring other New Mexico communities. The company also presents the Bill Evans Summer Institute of Dance, an intensive workshop for students and professionals throughout the nation. Several institute performances are open to the public.

Experimental Theatre
University of New Mexico Fine Arts Center
505-277-4402
A 120-seat facility, this black-box venue houses experimental plays, dance, and performance art.

Guerreros de Chicomostoc
157 Willow Road NW, 87107
505-242-6545
This group of Aztec dancers presents pre-Columbian warrior ritual dances from central Mexico, complete with authentic vestments and musical instruments.

June Music Festival of Albuquerque
9910 Indian School Road NE, Suite 201, 87112
505-294-2468
A program of six chamber music concerts featuring international ensembles. Held in Woodward Hall on the University of New Mexico campus.

Keller Hall Series
University of New Mexico Fine Arts Center
505-277-4402
Music concerts featuring faculty and guest-artist

performances as well as student recitals.

La Compania de Teatro de Alburquerque
PO Box 884, 87103
505-242-7929
One of 10 major Hispanic theater companies in the nation, community-based La Compania offers a season of four plays from both modern and classical English and Spanish repertoires.

La Zarzuela de Alburquerque
3301 San Rafael SE, 87106
505-265-0821
This volunteer community organization performs *zarzuela*—musical comedy in the traditional Spanish folk operetta genre.

Mother's Day Concert at the Río Grande Zoo
Río Grande Zoological Park
903 10th Street SW, 87102
505-842-8565
Performed by the New Mexico Symphony Orchestra.

Música Antigua de Albuquerque
1017 Roma NE, 87106
505-842-9613
An ensemble composed of six professionals specializing in medieval, Renaissance, and baroque music. Performances highlight voice and such authentic period instruments as the

The New Mexico Symphony Orchestra is the state's largest professional arts organization. Photograph by Mark Nohl

viola da gamba, recorder, crumhorn, vielle, medieval harp, shawm, and harpsicord. Subscription series concerts are offered in both Albuquerque and Santa Fe.

New Mexi-Chords
PO Box 22076, 87154
505-242-4451
Albuquerque's only barbershop chorus, presenting an annual show in mid-May at the University of New Mexico's Popejoy Hall.

New Mexico Ballet Company
3620 Wyoming Boulevard NE, Suite 105D, 87111
505-292-4245
A resident ballet company presenting classical repertory and original works choreographed by artistic director David Chavez. Performances take place October through May at the University of New Mexico's Popejoy Hall.

New Mexico Jazz Workshop
PO Box 1925, 87103
505-255-9798
Sponsors such musical events as Jazz under the Stars, a summer Saturday evening series at the Albuquerque Museum; Women's Voices, an early June tribute to the state's best female jazz vocalists and musicians, held at the Río Grande Zoo; a guest artist series showcasing major jazz artists in concert at various locations in Albuquerque, from November to March; and

Jazz Education for Children, a school-year program held at the Albuquerque Museum.

New Mexico Symphony Orchestra
3301 Menaul Boulevard NE
PO Box 30208, 87190-0208
505-881-9590
The state's largest professional arts organization presents classical, pops, special events, outdoor, statewide tour, and school concerts. A special Mother's Day concert is performed at the Río Grande Zoo.

New Mexico Women Composers Guild
9704 Aztec Road NE, 87111
505-292-0253
An organization founded in 1980 to pursue creative expression in music and to extend professional status to women composers. Public performances include concerts at the University of New Mexico's Keller Hall and in communities, retirement centers, schools, and hospitals throughout the state.

New Mexico Woodwind Quintet
7450 Prairie Road NE, 87109
505-898-7600
The group's chamber music concerts in the Albuquerque area highlight local composers and musicians.

Opera Southwest
515 15th Street NW, 87104
505-242-5837
Produces two or three operas featuring local and imported talent each fall and winter season. Performances are usually held at the KiMo Theater or Popejoy Hall.

Quintessence-Choral Artists of the Southwest
7521 Bear Canyon Road NE, 87109
505-821-0309
This Albuquerque-based ensemble of 30 professional singers directed by Michael G. Cooke performs a diverse repertoire of works.

Sun Dance Inc.
PO Box 82273, 87198
505-268-8756
Specializes in concerts and conventions featuring modern flamenco, tap/rhythm, ballet by the Bill Evans Dance Company, Ritmo Flamenco, and Dance España.

Sweet Adelines
3408 Gladden Court NE, 87110
505-889-3269
An international organization of 24,000 vocalists in women's barbershop choruses. The local branch, Enchanted Mesa Chorus, presents an annual fall show and performs for conventions, organizations, churches, and other groups.

Tapestry Players
PO Box 12897, 87195
505-877-6615
This multiethnic theater company performs original and innovative scripts about relationships between culturally diverse people.

Teatro Consejo
1710 Centro Familiar SW, 87105
505-873-1604
A community-based teenage theater company dedicated to substance abuse education. Plays are performed at the KiMo Theater, and puppet shows tour city schools.

University of New Mexico Theater Arts Department
Rodey Theater, on campus
505-277-4402
Offers four main-stage theater productions, three dance concerts, and student presentations.

Vortex Theatre
2004 ½ Central Avenue SE, 87106
505-247-8600
The Vortex presents 10 shows, including world premieres, in genres ranging from classical to modern. Some of the most innovative theater in Albuquerque.

CULTURAL ORGANIZATIONS
Albuquerque Arts Alliance
PO Box 27657, 87125-07657
505-243-4971
A nonprofit organization offering advocacy and referral services to individuals and groups engaged in the arts.

Albuquerque Community Foundation
PO Box 36960, 87176
505-883-6240
Provides grants to nonprofit arts and cultural organizations.

Albuquerque United Artists
PO Box 1808, 87103
505-243-0531
A nonprofit contemporary arts organization composed of local artists committed to the promotion of visual arts throughout the region, from the Río Grande Zoo to the state penitentiary. Sponsors Visions of Excellence, a statewide juried exhibition at the State Fairgrounds.

Hispanic Culture Foundation
4060 St. Joseph's Place
PO Box 7279, 87194
505-831-8360
Dedicated to identifying, preserving, enhancing, and promoting New Mexico's 400-year-long Hispanic heritage. The foundation sponsors major programs in Technical Assistance/Special Projects and Arts and Humanities Education, including a summer institute on language and culture for elementary and secondary school students.

New Mexico Endowment for the Humanities
209 Oñate Hall
University of New Mexico, 87131
505-277-3705
Grants up to $200,000 per year throughout the state and manages a statewide speakers bureau.

Senior Arts
PO Box 4679, 87196
505-877-4430
This nonprofit organization hires prominent local artists to give workshops and performances in public senior centers. Activities include music, dance, theater, literature, and visual arts—with emphasis on the traditional arts of New Mexico.

Very Special Arts New Mexico
2017 Yale Boulevard SE
PO Box 7784, 87194
505-768-5188
Affiliated with the John F. Kennedy Center for the Performing Arts, this group demonstrates the value of the arts in the lives of children and adults with disabilities. Programs include Very Special Arts Festivals; the Buen Viaje Dancers, a touring group of adult performers with disabilities; Arts Accessibility Initiatives; and the Enabled Arts Center gallery, gift shop, and studio arts program for people with disabilities.

(continued on page 116)

COMMUNITY EVENTS

**Albuquerque
International
Balloon Fiesta**
Balloon Fiesta Park
505-821-1000
More than 650 hot-air
balloons participate in
an opening-day parade,
daily mass ascensions,
competitions, precision
parachuting, and
evening balloon glows.
Held the first Saturday
through second Sunday
in October.

**American Indian
Week**
Indian Pueblo Cultural
Center
2401 12th Street NW,
87104
505-843-7270
A week-long tribute to the American Indian,
focusing on cultures and traditions as well as
major social and political concerns. Held the
third week in April.

ARTSCRAWL
121 Tijeras Avenue NE, 87102
505-842-9918
Albuquerque's monthly self-guided gallery tour.
Maps are available by phone.

Arts in the Park
Albuquerque Parks
505-768-3483
Outdoor entertainment provided by musicians,
dancers, clowns, and jugglers on Sunday afternoons, Memorial Day to Labor Day.

Albuquerque International Balloon Fiesta. Photograph by Mark Nohl

**East Mountain
Rendezvous**
Sandía Peak Ski Area
505-281-5099
A community fair cel-
ebrating the return of
mountain men from
winter trapping.
Booths, music, food,
and more in early
August.

**Fiesta Artistica:
Gathering of Native
American Arts**
Albuquerque
Convention Center
505-768-3483
A juried visual arts
exhibit and sale, fea-
turing regional artists
in early May.

Footsteps across New Mexico
303 Romero Street NW, 87107
505-243-4656
A high-tech, 30-minute multimedia presentation
on New Mexico and its prolific past. Fee.

Founder's Day Weekend
Old Town
505-768-3483
A parade, historical presentations, and entertainment on the weekend nearest April 23rd.

Gathering of Nations Powwow
University Arena
University Boulevard and Stadium Boulevard SE
PO Box 75102, 87194
505-836-2810
A gathering of more than 5,000 American Indian

dancers, singers, and traders in mid-April. North America's largest powwow, with more than 300 participating tribes.

Grecian Festival
St. George Greek Orthodox Church
308 High Street SE, 87102
505-242-2212
Greek food, dancing, and arts and crafts on the first weekend in October.

Indian National Finals Rodeo
Tingley Coliseum, State Fairgrounds
505-255-1791
A competition among American Indian rodeo riders from the United States and Canada for prize money and the title of World Champion Indian Cowboy. Event includes Indian arts and crafts, a powwow, ceremonial dance competition, and Miss Indian Rodeo Pageant. Held in mid-November.

Las Posadas de Barelas
Barelas Community Center and vicinity
505-848-1343
This annual Christmas Eve pageant re-creates the night of Jesus' birth. Events include singing in the streets and a church celebration, followed by refreshments at the Barelas Community Center.

Magnífico! Albuquerque Festival of the Arts
PO Box 26866, 87125
505-842-9918
A 17-day citywide celebration of the visual, performing, literary, and culinary arts. Highlights of the more than 200 events include the Art of Albuquerque Show, Dance Magnífico!, Magnífico Mariachi Symphony

LIBRARIES
Albuquerque Public Library
501 Copper Avenue NW, 87102
505-768-5140

Ernie Pyle Home and Library
900 Girard Boulevard SE, 87106
505-265-2065
The memorabilia-filled home of the Pulitzer Prize-winning war correspondent is now a public library.

Menaul Historical Library of the Southwest
301 Menaul Boulevard NE, 87107
505-345-7727

University of New Mexico General Library
University of New Mexico Campus, 87131
505-277-4241

PUBLIC ART
Third Street and Tijeras Avenue NW
Glenna Goodacre
"Sidewalk Society"—bronze sculpture

60th Street at Central Avenue NW
Joe Stephenson, Richard Brandt, and *Michael "Giant" LeSage*
"Paz y Unidad"—painted wall

1500 Broadway NW
Pedro Romero
"New Mexico Lowrider Bench"—ceramic tile sculpture

Albuquerque Fire Academy
11500 Sunset Gardens SW
Evelyn Rosenberg
"Fire Work"—metal reliefs

Albuquerque International Airport Art Collection
Yale Boulevard
Assembled by the City of Albuquerque Public
Art Program, the collection appearing through-
out the terminal building is composed of the
work of 90 New Mexican artists, including *Pop
Chalee, Laura Gachupin, Miguel
Gandert, Glenna Goodacre, R. C.
Gorman, Betty Hahn, Wilson Hurley,
Beaumont Newhall, Gary Niblett, Ben
Ortega, Tim Prythero, Senaida and
Emilio Romero, Fritz Scholder, Luis
Tapia, Horacio Valdez*, and *Pablita
Velarde.* Represented are sculptures, ceram-
ics, stonework, paintings, photography, textiles,
and jewelry.

Albuquerque Museum of Art and History
2000 Mountain Road NW
More than 30 outdoor sculptures representing
the work of such artists as *Ed Haddaway,
Doug Hyde, Luis Jimenez, Jesus Moroles,
Nora Naranjo-Morse, Fritz Scholder,* and
Sebastian.

Arenal Boulevard
Federico Armijo
"The River"—travertine marble

Carrie Tingley Hospital
1127 University Boulevard NE
Oliver LaGrone
"Tender Mercies"—sculpture

**Central Avenue and Girard Boulevard/
Central Avenue and Washington Street**
Terry Conrad and *Joan Weissman*
"Nob Hill Gateways"—steel, neon, concrete,
and ceramic tiles

Spectacular, and Intimate Evening with an
Artist series, as well as a chile cook-off and
a literary fair. Held in May.

Native American Arts and Crafts Fair
Indian Pueblo Cultural Center
2401 12th Street NW, 87104
505-843-7270
A large assembly of American Indian artisans, special activities, and Indian dances.
Held in early July.

**New Mexico Arts and Crafts Fair:
Summer Festival of the Arts**
State Fairgrounds
550 San Mateo Boulevard NE, Suite 111,
87109
505-884-9043
An open-air festival in which more than
200 New Mexican artists display and sell
juried original calligraphy, ceramics, jewelry, leatherwork, macramé, drawings, paintings, prints, sculpture, stitchery, weavings,
and woodwork. Special events include
entertainment, demonstrations, children's
activities, and concessions. Held the last
full weekend in June.

New Mexico State Fair
State Fairgrounds
PO Box 8546, 87198
505-265-1791
The eighth largest state fair in the nation,
complete with thoroughbred and quarter-
horse racing, Professional Rodeo Cowboys
Association events, entertainment by
recording stars, a midway, reconstructed
Indian and Spanish villages, livestock
shows, and arts and crafts. A 17-day event
beginning the Friday after Labor Day.

Río Grande Arts and Crafts Festival
State Fairgrounds
11200 Montgomery NE, Suite 8, 87111
505-292-7457
Spring and fall juried shows with more
than 170 exhibitors, entertainment, artist
demonstrations, food, and children's activities. Held in mid-March, and late
September or early October.

San Felipe de Neri Fiesta
Old Town Plaza
PO Box 7007, 87194
505-243-4628
Three days of food and entertainment in
honor of Albuquerque's patron saint. Held
the first weekend in June.

Southwest Arts and Crafts Festival
State Fairgrounds Exhibit Hall
525 San Pedro NE, Suite 107, 87108
505-262-2448
More than 150 entrants from across the
nation compete in this invitational juried
show held in mid-November. Fee.

**City/County Building in the Council/
Commission Chambers**
Fifth Street and Marquette Avenue NW
Roy Grinnell
"New Life in Old Albuquerque"—oil painting
Harvey Johnson
"Apprehension of the State Robbers"—oil
painting

Indian Pueblo Cultural Center
2401 12th Street NW
*Norman Pacheco, Arnold Puentes,
Francis Rivera,* and *Margarete Bagshaw-
Tindel*
"Shared Traditions: Mind, Body and Spirit:
Pueblo Perspective"—mural

KiMo Theater
423 Central Avenue NW
Carl von Hassler and *A. Rosenthal*
Murals

Loma Linda Community Center
1700 Yale Boulevard SE
David Griggs
"Albuquerque Apparition"—steel and neon

Lomas/Tramway Library Center for Public Art
908 Eastridge Drive NE
Collette Perazio-Itkin
"La Blessure"—sculpture
Sarah Perry
"Gorilla Route #66"—sculpture
Tom Waldron
Steel

Longfellow Elementary School
400 Edith Boulevard NE
Francis Rivera
Acrylic mural

Martíneztown Park
Edith Boulevard and Roma Avenue NE
Luis Jimenez
"Southwest Pietà"—sculpture

North Valley Library
Second Street NW
Evelyn Rosenberg
"Reading Ribbons"—detonography of twisted bronze

Northeast Heights Police Substation
Osuna Road and Wyoming NE
Bill Worthen
Police Officers Memorial—granite sculpture

Pajarito Elementary School
Don Felipe Road SW
Stuart Ashman
"Paja-Saur-Us"—wood

Río Grande Zoo
903 10th Street SW
Catherine A. Gore
"What's for Lunch?"—stained and carved glass
Leonard J. Lee
"To All the Great Animals around the World"—wood railing
Reynaldo "Sonny" Rivera
"Los Cíbolos del Río Grande"—bronze fountain
Michael Semsch
"Wild Things"—sculptured wood corbels

San Mateo Boulevard at Gibson Boulevard SE, Eastern Avenue SE, and Inspiration Drive SE
Barbara Grygutis
"Cruising San Mateo I, II, & III"—ceramic tile sculpture

Summerfest
Civic Plaza
Third Street and Marquette Avenue NW, 87102
505-768-3483
Showcase for the culture and cuisine of Albuquerque's numerous ethnic groups. Held on Saturday evenings throughout the summer.

Visions of Excellence
State Fairgrounds Fine Arts Gallery
PO Box 1808, 87103
505-243-0531
A juried exhibition of New Mexico's artists. Held in May.

Weekend Indian Dances and Craft Demonstrations
Indian Pueblo Cultural Center
2401 12th Street NW, 87104
505-843-7270
Pueblo dances every Saturday and Sunday, 11 am and 2 pm, from mid-April through mid-October.

Weems Artfest
State Fairgrounds
2801 Eubank Boulevard NE, 87112
505-293-6133
A November event featuring the originality of more than 200 artisans throughout the Southwest. Fee.

Senior Multi-Service Center
714 Seventh Street SW
Helen Thompson and *senior artists*
"Historia de Barelas"—tapestry

University of New Mexico
Lomas Boulevard and Stanford Drive NE
Dennis Oppenheim
"Dreams and Nightmares: Journey of a Broken Weave"—sculpture

US Federal Building
421 Gold Avenue SW
Emil Bisttram
"Justice Tempered with Mercy"—mural
New Deal Art
Loran Mozley
"The Rebellion of 1680"—mural
New Deal Art

Zia School Park
440 Jefferson Street NE
Beverly Magennis
"Full Circle"—sandbox/bench

BELÉN

I-25 at NM 47
As Spanish colonization began along the Río Grande south of Albuquerque, a land grant was created to encourage expansion. As a result, colonists from Albuquerque settled in Nuestra Señora de Belén (Our Lady of Bethlehem) in 1740. Situated near the Camino Real (Royal Road), Belén became a farming and ranching town and, with the arrival of the railroad, a crossing point for east-west and north-south rail lines.

MUSEUMS AND EXHIBIT SPACES
P & M Farm Museum
Jarales Road
505-864-8354
Displays an antique collection of farm memorabilia, including buggies, cars, equipment, dolls, and appliances. Fee.

Valencia County Historical Society Museum (formerly Belén Harvey House)
104 North First Street
505-861-0581
Constructed in 1901 in the Mission style popularized by the Santa Fe Railway, this Fred Harvey hotel and restaurant was for decades the most visible and successful public establishment in Belén. The museum features three period rooms. ◉□

HISTORIC BUILDINGS AND SITES
Belén Hotel
200 Becker Street
Built in 1907 by German immigrant Bertha Rutz to serve employees of the Atchison, Topeka & Santa Fe Railway, the hotel is one of Belén's best examples of the decorative brick style of architecture. ◉□

Our Lady of Refuge Chapel
1002 Don Felipe
505-864-1825
A restored Spanish mission chapel built in the mid-1700s by the town's early settlers.

Valencia County Flour Mill
Jarales Road
505-864-0305
A wood-frame and tin mill erected in 1914, when flour milling came to area. Wheat, a staple village crop in the 1880s, remained a primary regional grain until 1930.

COMMUNITY EVENTS
Our Lady of Belén Fiesta
Our Lady of Belén Church
505-864-8043
Burning of the devil, a parade, games,
food booths, and carnival in mid-August.
Río Valley Festival
Anna Becker Park
PO Box 6, 87002
505-864-8091
Arts and crafts, food, and trade booths
in mid-June.

LIBRARIES
Belén Public Library
333 Becker Street, 87002
505-864-7797

Rural Bookmobile West
409 Horner Street, 87002
505-864-1430

PUBLIC ART
Belén Middle School
425 Baca Avenue
Francis Rivera
"Hip Hop History"—acrylic mural

Belén State Office Building
Fifth and Becker Streets
Peter Ruta
"Piñones"—oil painting
Kathleen Tijerina
"Hachita"—oil painting
"Manhattan Cafe"—oil painting
"Whitehouse Cafe"—oil painting
Alex Traube
"Painted Chairs"—oil painting

BERNALILLO

I-25 at NM 44
The Pueblo Indian province of Tiguex, in the
area of Bernalillo, served as winter headquarters for Spanish explorer Francisco Vásquez de
Coronado during his explorations of the
Southwest from 1540 to 1542. The village of
Bernalillo was founded 150 years later, shortly
after the Spanish reconquest of New Mexico by
Diego de Vargas. Vargas died in the adobe-
walled village in 1704. In time, the Hispanic
town became a significant trading and business
center, catering to miners and ranchers, and
later, an important stop on the railroad.

MUSEUMS AND EXHIBIT SPACES
Coronado State Monument
NM 44, 1 mile west of Bernalillo
505-867-5351
Fire pits reveal that this region was occupied by
migrating bands of Indians around 3000 to 4000
BC. In 1540, it became a stopping point for
Francisco Vásquez de Coronado when, in search
of the fabled cities of gold, he came upon 200-
year-old adobe villages inhabited by indigenous
peoples. The Tiwa pueblo of Kuaua, possible site
of Coronado's encampment, dates from 1300 and,
like many Río Grande Valley pueblos, was deserted by the early 1600s. Pueblo ruins, including a
kiva with painted murals on its interior walls, have
been partially reconstructed, and an interpretive
trail winds through the site. A visitor center chronicles the prehistory and history of the valley. A
part of the Museum of New Mexico. Fee. ☺

HISTORIC BUILDINGS AND SITES
Abenicio Salazar Historic District
Buildings dating from 1873 reflect the rural
lifestyle found here over a century ago. Nearby

COMMUNITY EVENTS
Fiesta de San Lorenzo
505-867-4689
Matachines dances, processions, and a
Mass in honor of Bernalillo's patron
saint on August 9th through 11th.

New Mexico Wine & Vine Festival
505-867-3311
Music, food, and wine tasting in early
September.

is Our Lady of Sorrows Church, built in 1719.
The largest and most dominant structure in the
district is Our Lady of Sorrows High School,
constructed in 1922. ◉□

LIBRARIES
Martha Liebert Library
901 Camino del Pueblo
PO Box 638, 87004
505-867-3311

PUBLIC ART
Bernalillo High School
Camino del Pueblo
John Connell
Mural

COCHITÍ PUEBLO

NM 16, 10 miles north of I-25
PO Box 70, 87041
505-465-2244
Established in the 1200s by Keres-speaking
Indians who had migrated east from the cliffs
and caves of the Pajarito Plateau, Cochití
Pueblo experienced little European contact

until Juan de Oñate's colonization campaign of
1598. San Buenaventura de Cochití, a mission
church built here in 1628, was destroyed during the Pueblo rebellion of 1680 and later
restored. The Cochití people are widely known
for crafting double-headed drums, fine jewelry,
and pottery, including the prized storyteller figures that originated here in the 1960s. ◉□

LIBRARIES
Pueblo de Cochití Community Library
PO Box 153, 87072
505-465-2885

COMMUNITY EVENTS
Cochití Pueblo Feast Day
A morning Mass, procession, and after-
noon Corn and Rain Dances on July 14th.

**Dances to Commemorate the
Christmas Season**
Traditional dances during Christmas
week.

Easter Celebration
A Mass, procession, and traditional
dances during Easter week.

New Year's Day Celebration
A Mass, procession, and traditional
dances on January 1st.

Santa Cruz Feast Day
A Corn Dance on May 3rd.

Three Kings Day
Transfer of the Canes of Authority honoring new tribal officers on January 6th.

CORRALES

NM 448, in Albuquerque's North Valley
Formerly the site of several Tiwa Indian pueblos, this region on the banks of the Río Grande was colonized by Spanish farmers in the 17th century. An extensive network of corrals built by founder Juan González gave the village of Corrales its name. Throughout the 18th century, the rich farming village was targeted by Comanche attacks and, until 1851, Navajo raids. During that time, Spanish—and later United States—garrisons used the surrounding valley as a base to protect nearby river settlements, towns, and pueblos from invasions. Today, the North Valley community of Corrales is a peaceful village set within groves of cottonwood, willow, and olive trees.

MUSEUMS AND EXHIBIT SPACES
Los Colores Museum
4499 Corrales Road, 87048
505-898-5077
Housed in the historic Alejandro Gonzáles House, the museum is dedicated to the weaving traditions of Mexico and New Mexico.

HISTORIC BUILDINGS AND SITES
Old San Ysidro Church
Old Church Road
PO Box 1051, 87048
505-897-1150
This church—third to bear the name of San Ysidro, patron saint of farmers and guardian of Albuquerque's North Valley—stands as one of the few surviving examples of 18th- and 19th-century New Mexican Hispanic religious village architecture. The structure was built in the shape of a cross, with three-foot-thick masonry walls hand-plastered with adobe both inside

COMMUNITY EVENTS
Harvest Festival
505-898-5610
Arts and crafts, a parade, a harvest market, and entertainment in mid-October.

San Ysidro Fiesta
PO Box 460, 87048
505-898-1779
Music, dance, food, and entertainment in mid-May.

and out. Hand-hewn corbels support the *viga* ceiling, and hand-adzed lintels top the doors and windows. The building was purchased from the Archdiocese of Santa Fe in 1974. ☉☐

CULTURAL ORGANIZATIONS
Corrales Cultural Arts Council
PO Box 2723, 87048
505-898-7600

Corrales Historical Society
PO Box 1051, 87048
505-898-7221
Promotes a greater understanding of the history and tradition of Corrales. The society maintains the Old San Ysidro Church and other community landmarks, researches the heritage of Corrales, and supports local educational and cultural projects.

LIBRARIES
Corrales Community Library
La Entrada Road
PO Drawer L, 87048
505-897-0733

CUBA

NM 44 at NM 126
Originally called Nacimiento (Nativity), this
farming and ranching community was founded
in the late 18th century by a group of Hispanic
families. Today, Cuba is a lumbering town, trade
center for the Navajo and Jicarilla Apache people, and retreat for campers and hikers.

LIBRARIES
Cuba Community Library
Route 126, Box 426, 87013
505-289-3100

ESTANCIA

NM 41, 17 miles south of Moriarty
Once the bed of an inland sea, Estancia in prehistoric times drew nomadic Indians from
nearby mountains and plains to its copious salt
deposits. Early Spanish inhabitants mined the
salt for transport by oxcart to Mexico, launch-
ing New Mexico's first mining export. Spanish
cattlemen of the 1800s grazed livestock on the
area's rich grasses. The coming of the railroad
in the early 20th century opened the ranchlands
to homesteaders and farmers—and with them,
water wells, windmills, frame houses, and dryland crops. Estancia became the county seat of
Torrance County in 1905 and was incorporated
four years later. Large quantities of beans,
grains, and potatoes were shipped out of the
valley town via New Mexico Central Railway
until the plowing and drought took a heavy toll
on the arid farmland. Estancia, which continued to cultivate pinto beans until the 1950s,
remains an agricultural center.

LIBRARIES
Estancia Public Library
1000 Highland Avenue
PO Box 167, 87016
505-384-2708

PUBLIC ART
Main Street
Frederic Remington reproduction
"Bucking Bronco"—bronze sculpture

ISLETA PUEBLO

I-25 at NM 47
PO Box 1270, 87022
505-869-3111
The Tiwa-speaking pueblo of Isleta (Little Island)
has had a troubled history. When the Pueblo
Revolt began in 1680, many members of the community fled west to Hopi settlements in Arizona;
numerous others retreated south with the Spanish
to El Paso del Norte. After the rebellion, the people returned to their ancestral home, bringing
Hopi mates and children of mixed ancestry. The
returning refugees created a satellite community
called Oraibi. Today's pueblo consists of two small
communities—Oraibi and Chicale—as well as
the main village of Isleta. The mission church built
on Isleta's plaza between 1613 and 1630 is
among 2 out of 80 built on Indian lands to have
survived the Pueblo Revolt; the other is at Acoma.
Although the church at Isleta was burned and
used to pen sheep during the rebellion, its exteri-
or walls remained intact. It was remodeled and
rededicated when the people returned to their
pueblo. Agriculture, pottery making, weaving, and
embroidery are the primary occupations of
today's Isleta tribe. The pueblo operates camping,
picnicking, and fishing facilities. ◉▢

COMMUNITY EVENTS
Dances to Commemorate the Christmas Season
Traditional dances during Christmas week.

Isleta Pueblo Feast Day
San Agustine Feast Day is celebrated with a morning Mass, procession, and afternoon Harvest Dance on September 4th.

San Agustine Celebration
Indian dances, food, and arts and crafts on August 28th.

LIBRARIES
Isleta Pueblo Library Resource Center
PO Box 1270, 87022
505-869-2597

JÉMEZ PUEBLO

NM 4, 9 miles north of NM 44 junction
PO Box 100, 87024
505-834-7359
The present site of Jémez Pueblo has been occupied since the 16th century, although most of its buildings date back to the period following the Pueblo Revolt of 1680. The only remaining Towa-speaking pueblo, Jémez is known for its long-distance runners, excellent dancers, and well-attended fairs and festivals. Today's ceremonials honor Jémez traditions as well as those of the now-extinct pueblo of Pecos, whose survivors migrated here in the 1830s. The Jémez people, like their ancestors, make fine pottery and baskets of plaited yucca leaves, as well as embroidered items, stone sculptures, weavings, jewelry, moccasins, dolls, and drums. The Walatowa (This Is the Place) Visitor Center offers a variety of programs and artist demonstrations. ◉▯

COMMUNITY EVENTS
Dances to Commemorate the Christmas Season
Buffalo Dances during Christmas week.

Jémez Pueblo Feast Day
San Diego Feast Day is celebrated with a midmorning Mass, procession, and Corn Dance on November 12th.

New Year's Day Celebration
Matachines Dances, accompanied by the Pumpkin moiety on native drums and the Turquoise moiety on violin and guitar.

Old Pecos Bull Dance
Our Lady of the Angels Feast Day is celebrated with Bull and Corn Dances on August 2nd.

Our Lady of Guadalupe Feast Day
A midmorning Mass and procession, followed by a Matachines Dance, on December 12th.

Three Kings Day
New tribal officers are honored with a transfer of the Canes of Authority, followed by a huge Buffalo Dance (also called Herd Dance), complete with deer, mountain sheep, antelope, elk, eagle, and hawk dancers. Held on January 6th.

LIBRARIES
Jémez Pueblo Community Library
PO Box 9, 87024
505-834-7678

JÉMEZ SPRINGS

NM 4, 17 miles northeast of NM 44 junction
Once called Hot Springs, this mountain village
grew up around bubbling sulfur-laden springs.
Today, one of the geothermal springs provides
heat to town buildings—some of which serve
as retreat houses for Catholic priests seeking
spiritual and physical replenishment.

MUSEUMS AND EXHIBIT SPACES
Jémez State Monument
NM 4, 1 mile north of Jémez Springs
PO Box 143, 87025
505-829-3530
The now extinct village of Giusewa, 10 miles
upstream from present-day Jémez Pueblo, was
occupied by Jémez Indians before the arrival of
the Spanish in 1541. Adjacent to its ruins lie those
of the red sandstone mission church of San José
de Giusewa, built by Franciscans around 1622.
The monument museum features permanent and
temporary history exhibits as well as a library. A
part of the Museum of New Mexico. Fee.

LIBRARIES
Jémez Springs Community Library
PO Box 597, 87025
505-829-3540

LOS LUNAS

I-25 at NM 6
Named for the Don Diego Luna family, recipi-
ents of the San Clemente Land Grant early in the
1700s and originators of regional sheep ranching in 1808. Over the centuries, the town has
produced many high-profile leaders, including
Solomon Luna, one of New Mexico's principal
political figures when the area was declared a
United States territory in 1846. Los Lunas is the
county seat of Valencia County.

HISTORIC BUILDINGS AND SITES
Atchison, Topeka & Santa Fe Railway Depot
Constructed in 1879, when the railway reached
Los Lunas from Albuquerque, this is one of the
oldest remaining depots in the state. The building is reminiscent of the social and economic
impact the railroad had on Los Lunas. ◎□

Huning Mercantile and House
Main Street and Los Lentes
The square adobe building and interior courtyard were constructed in the 1840s. Although
the structure has been remodeled several times,
it retains its original character. ◎

Luna Mansion
NM 314 and NM 6
Constructed in the 1880s, the 14-room Luna
family home is considered the best example of
adobe Victorian architecture in New Mexico.
The mansion is now a restaurant that preserves
the family history in a display of photographs
and memorabilia. ◎□

LIBRARIES
Los Lunas Community Library
460 Main Street
PO Box 1209, 87031
505-865-6779

PUBLIC ART
Los Lunas Senior Center
Don Pasquale Road
Juan and Patricia Navarette
Banco—cement masonry

MORIARTY

I-25 at NM 41
Named in the 1880s after an Irish homesteader
who settled in this Estancia Valley town to cure
his rheumatism, Moriarty must have been the
needed remedy, for the Irishman spent the next
50 years as a vigorous sheep rancher. Located
on Old Route 66, present-day Moriarty is a
farming, ranching, and tourism center.

MUSEUMS AND EXHIBIT SPACES
Moriarty Historical Society Museum
777 Old US Route 66 SW
PO Box 1366, 87035
505-832-4764
The museum, housed in Moriarty's first fire station, exhibits local history artifacts.

HISTORIC BUILDINGS AND SITES
Gregg's Trail
I-40, 10 miles east of Moriarty
Josiah Gregg, merchant and pioneer historian
of the Santa Fe Trail, made four expeditions to
Santa Fe from Van Buren, Arkansas. On his last,
from 1839 to 1840, he blazed a new route
south along the Canadian River, then southwest
through the region that was to become
Moriarty. His trail became a favorite among
California-bound gold-seekers in 1849.

LIBRARIES
Moriarty Community Library
201 South Broadway Street
PO Box 1917, 87035
505-832-6919

MOUNTAINAIR

US 60 at NM 55
The Mountainair region was occupied by Tompiro
and eastern Tiwa Pueblo Indians from prehistoric
times through the mid-17th century. When
Spanish priests and soldiers arrived in 1598, they
found flourishing communities inhabited by people they called Las Humanas. Churches were built,
and for about 80 years, the settlement served as a
locus for Franciscan missionaries in the area.
Drought, disease, and marauding Plains Indians
forced evacuation of the churches and pueblos
alike. In 1902, when homesteading settlements
began appearing along newly placed railroad
tracks, Mountainair was founded as a center for
area ranchers and dryland farmers. Until the
drought of the 1940s, the town was known as the
Pinto Bean Capital of the World.

MUSEUMS AND EXHIBIT SPACES
Salinas Pueblo Missions National Monument
US 60 at NM 55
PO Box 496, 87036
505-847-2585
A unique complex of prehistoric Indian pueblo
and associated 17th-century Franciscan mission
ruins, this monument preserves the first century
of American Indian and European contact in
what is now the United States. The complex
includes Abó, Quarai, and Gran Quivira
Pueblos, all situated within a few miles of the
Mountainair-based visitor center. Fee. ☉☐△

HISTORIC BUILDINGS AND SITES
Atchison, Topeka & Santa Fe Railway Depot
A 1907 depot built in California Mission style, with stucco and a red-tiled roof. ⊚

Mountainair Community Building
Roosevelt Avenue at Beal Street
A public works project designed by local architect Everett Crist, and erected from 1934 to 1936 using sandstone from nearby Goat Canyon at the former Abó Mission. The building's auditorium became one of New Mexico Governor Clyde Tingley's political symbols for New Deal programs. ⊚☐

Rancho Bonito
NM 55, 1.5 miles south of Mountainair
This colorful creation by Clem "Pop" Shaffer, New Mexico's most prolific folk art environmentalist, served as his studio, playground, and hideaway. ⊚☐

Shaffer Hotel
Broadway
The Southwestern Art Deco hotel and its unique animal and geometric carvings were designed and built by Pop Shaffer, folk artist and environmentalist. ⊚☐

LIBRARIES
Mountainair Civic Library
110 North Roosevelt Street
PO Box 100, 87036
505-847-2321

PERALTA

NM 304, 6 miles east of Belén
Named for the first family to settle along this portion of the Camino Real, Peralta became the site of one of the last skirmishes of the Civil War in New Mexico. On April 15, 1862, the Sibley Brigade, retreating to Texas, camped at the *hacienda* of Governor Henry Connelly, outside of Peralta. Here, the Confederates were routed by Union forces under the command of Colonel Edward R. S. Canby.

HISTORIC BUILDINGS AND SITES
Our Lady of Guadalupe Catholic Church
A well-maintained adobe church built between 1879 and 1888. ⊚

CULTURAL ORGANIZATIONS
Society for the Preservation of American Indian Culture
PO Box 854, 87042

PLACITAS

NM 44, 6 miles off I-25
Placitas (Little Plazas, or Little Towns) consists of a grouping of small 18th-century villages built by Hispanic farmers and expanded upon by 19th-century farmers, ranchers, and miners. The original villages of Las Huertas, Ojo de la Casa, Tecolote, and Tejón were fortified to protect residents from Apache Indian attacks. Today's community of small farms and ranches sustains many of the agricultural traditions observed in the old villages.

PERFORMING ARTS
The Placitas Artists Series
PO Box 944, 87043
505-867-2471
Presents nine concerts and art exhibitions in the community's Presbyterian Church, and sponsors a fall Hispanic music festival at Our Lady of Sorrows Catholic Church Social Center in Bernalillo. Featured musicians include the resident Helios Quartet on strings as well as

guest artists. The Series promotes the work of local artists and musicians, conducts outreach programs in the schools, commissions work from New Mexican composers, and exposes local audiences to the music of Latin American composers.

RIO RANCHO

NM 528, northwest edge of Albuquerque
The settlement originated as open grazing land on the Thompson Ranch carved from the 18th-century Alameda Land Grant. Site of an early 1960s land development project, Rio Rancho has become New Mexico's fastest growing city.

CULTURAL ORGANIZATIONS
Storytellers International
PO Box 15517, 87174
505-897-0713
Dedicated to preserving cultures and increasing communication through the art of storytelling. The organization sponsors a Storyfiesta in April, featuring expert storytellers from around the world, as well as educational programs serving more than 15,000 pueblo-, public-, and private-school children each year.

COMMUNITY EVENTS
Springfest
1463 Rio Rancho Drive, Suite D, 87124
505-892-1533
A weekend festival featuring a Friday evening concert followed by arts and crafts, a business expo, food court, and ongoing entertainment. Held the third weekend in May. Fee.

LIBRARIES
Rio Rancho Public Library
950 Pine Tree Road SE
PO Box 15670, 87174
505-891-7244

SAN FELIPE PUEBLO

I-25, 11 miles north of Bernalillo
PO Box A, 87001
505-867-3381
Migrating from their ancestral home on the Pajarito Plateau, the San Felipe people established a village on a bluff overlooking the Río Grande before moving to their present location along the river in the early 1700s. Here, they raised corn, hay, grains, fruit, and other crops, and conducted elaborate ceremonies—as a result of which their earthen plaza, worn down three feet below ground level, resembles a sunken bowl. One of the most culturally conservative Keres-speaking pueblos, San Felipe has retained its religion and customs despite relentless pressure to assimilate. Today's villagers, still known for their colorful ceremonies, are skilled potters and beaders, specializing in heishi necklaces. ☉

COMMUNITY EVENTS
Candlemas Day
A Buffalo Dance on February 2nd.
Easter Celebration
A Mass, procession, and dances.
San Felipe Pueblo Feast Day
An all-day Corn Dance with male choral accompaniment and hundreds of participants. Held on May 1st.
Three Kings Day
Transfer of the Canes of Authority honoring new tribal leaders on January 6th.

LIBRARIES
San Felipe Pueblo Library
PO Box A, 87001
505-867-5234

SAN YSIDRO

NM 44 at NM 4
Named for St. Isadore, patron saint of farmers, this parcel of land was established on the San Ysidro Land Grant. In May 1786, the property was given to Salvador Sandoval and Antonio de Armenta, the chief justice stationed at Jémez Pueblo. In commemoration of the event, villagers celebrate San Ysidro Feast Day each year on May 15th by carrying the statue of the saint through the village and into the fields.

HISTORIC BUILDINGS AND SITES
Vásquez de Coronado's Route
San Ysidro
Site of the trail taken in the fall of 1540 by Francisco Vásquez de Coronado and his army as they headed east from Zuni. At San Ysidro, the advance guard followed the Río Grande from the Isleta area to Alcanfor, a pueblo near present-day Bernalillo, where the men camped for two winters.

SANDÍA PUEBLO

I-25 at Bernalillo
PO Box 6008, Bernalillo, 87004
505-867-3317
Sandía Pueblo, called Na-Fiat (Sandy Place, or Dusty) in the Tiwa language, was established in 1300 along the Río Grande, where its early inhabitants irrigated large plots of land to grow food. Today, the Sandía people are still among the most successful Pueblo farmers, although the

COMMUNITY EVENTS
Sandía Pueblo Feast Day
San Antonio Feast Day is celebrated on June 13th with a midmorning Mass followed by a procession and afternoon Corn Dance—the pueblo's only festival open to the public.

acreage devoted to farming has been reduced. During the Pueblo Revolt of 1680, the retreating Spaniards burned the mission church and convent; rather than submit to Spanish rule following the reconquest, the Sandía people fled the pueblo and joined Hopi tribes in Arizona. After nearly 60 years of exile and cultural interbreeding, they were granted permission to return to their ancestral home and start life anew. The remains of the early village of Sandía are still visible, and the narrow plaza—in ongoing use—has been worn concave by moccasined feet. Bien-Mur Indian Market Center offers visitors a wide variety of pottery, jewelry, and other crafts.

LIBRARIES
Sandía Pueblo Resource Center
PO Box 6008, Bernalillo, 87004
505-867-2876

SANTA ANA PUEBLO

NM 44, 12 miles northwest of Bernalillo
2 Dove Road, Bernalillo, 87004
505-867-3301
The early history of Keres-speaking Santa Ana (Ta'ma'ya) Pueblo, lies buried beneath the Pueblo Revolt of 1680. After the Spanish reconquest of the New Mexican territory between 1692 and 1694, the present-day pueblo site was

COMMUNITY EVENTS

Dances to Commemorate the Christmas Season
A variety of traditional dances during Christmas week.

Easter Celebration
A Mass, procession, and traditional dances.

New Year's Day Celebration
A Mass, procession, and traditional dances in the afternoon.

San Juan Feast Day
A Corn Dance on June 24th.

San Pedro and San Pablo Feast Days
A Corn Dance on June 29th.

Santa Ana Pueblo Feast Day
A morning Mass, procession, and afternoon Corn Dance on July 26th.

Three Kings Day
Transfer of the Canes of Authority to honor new tribal officers on January 6th.

founded on the north side of the Jémez River. Most Santa Ana people now farm along the Rió Grande, returning to their ancestral home for special ceremonials. Their blue corn products and other organic produce are marketed through Santa Ana Agricultural Enterprises, a tribal initiative. The Ta'ma'ya Cooperative Association sells food as well as crafts. Traditional crafts, most of which are on the wane, include woven belts and headbands, polychrome pottery, paintings, and wood crosses inlaid with straw. ◑☐

LIBRARIES
Santa Ana Pueblo Community Library
2 Dove Road, Bernalillo, 87004
505-867-3301

SANTO DOMINGO PUEBLO

I-25 at NM 22
PO Box 99, 87052
505-465-2214
Here, in 1598, Oñate met with 38 Pueblo leaders, who gave him permission to settle in the region. In the early years of the Spanish occupation of New Mexico, Keres-speaking Santo Domingo Pueblo functioned as ecclesiastical headquarters of the province. The Franciscan priests-in-residence, who served in missions scattered throughout the area, did not survive the Pueblo rebellion of 1680. Santo Domingo today is the largest of the Río Grande pueblos and among the most conservative; ceremonial observances form the core of the social structure. This essentially farming community supplements its income through the sale of ancient forms of pottery, jewelry, beadwork, and woven rugs. The Santa Domingo people have become known nationwide for their expertise as traders. ◑☐

LIBRARIES
Santo Domingo Library
PO Box 99, 87052
505-465-2214

TIJERAS

I-40, at NM 14 and NM 337
True to its name, Tijeras (Scissors) sits at the intersection of two long canyons whose outlines resemble open scissors. Since prehistoric times, this pass between the Sandía and

SANTO DOMINGO PUEBLO COMMUNITY EVENTS

Dances to Commemorate the Christmas Season
Traditional dances during Christmas week.

Easter Celebration
A Mass, procession, and traditional dances.

New Year's Day Celebration
A morning Mass followed by a procession and such traditional ceremonials as the Turtle and Matachines Dances.

San Juan Feast Day
A rooster pull on June 24th.

San Pedro and San Pablo Feast Days
A rooster pull on June 29th.

Santiago Feast Day
A rooster pull on July 25th.

Santo Domingo Pueblo Feast Day
An all-day Corn Dance with more than 500 participants—enacted in honor of St. Dominic, patron saint of the pueblo. Held on August 4th.

Santo Domingo Pueblo Indian Arts and Crafts Market
An open-air Labor Day weekend fair featuring the work of about 350 artists.

Three Kings Day
Transfer of the Canes of Authority honoring new tribal leaders on January 6th.

Manzano Mountains has served as a travel route between eastern New Mexico and the Río Grande Valley. During the Spanish Colonial period, Tijeras was known as Cañon de Carnue.

MUSEUMS AND EXHIBIT SPACES

Old Church of Santo Niño Museum
Displays local history exhibits in a church built in 1929.

CULTURAL ORGANIZATIONS

Turquoise Trail Arts Council
15 Futurity Place, 87509
505-281-2098

TOMÉ

NM 314, 9 miles north of Belén
This small farming village on the banks of the Río Grande was home to Tomé Domínguez de Mendoza, who fled during the 1680 Pueblo Revolt and never returned. Resettled by *genízaros* (Hispanicized Indians) as part of the Tomé Land Grant in 1739, the village came under constant attack by dispossesed Apache and Comanche Indians. Even so, it grew to be an important community on New Mexico's north-south trade route. The old Plaza of Tomé is now shaded with giant cottonwoods, creating a pastoral setting for the faithful who visit the crosses atop Mount Calvario, site of Mendoza's long-ago abode.

MUSEUMS AND EXHIBIT SPACES

Immaculate Conception Parish Museum
NM 47, 9 miles north of Belén
PO Box 100, 87060
505-865-7497
A religious history and folk art museum featuring relics, paintings, statues, and *santos* (painted or carved wooden images of the saints).

COMMUNITY EVENTS
Easter Procession
Mount Calvario
Each year's Good Friday pilgrimage cul-
minates in an Easter sunrise procession
to the top of Mount Calvario.

HISTORIC BUILDINGS AND SITES
Tomé Jail
Tomé Plaza
A courthouse and jail built in 1875, with four-
foot-thick walls of black igneous rock quarried
from a nearby volcanic formation. ◉☐

ZIA PUEBLO

NM 44, 19 miles north of Bernalillo
135 Capitol Square Drive, 87053-6013
505-867-3304
The pueblo of Zia has been inhabited since
1250, when Keres-speaking Indians arrived from
a settlement farther up the Jémez River. In
Spanish Colonial times, Zia was one of the
largest and most important Keres pueblos of the
Río Grande region. The revolt of 1680 and the
burning of the pueblo by Otermín in 1681, however, reduced the tribe's population by about
600—a loss that increased dramatically during
the Spanish reconquest. Today's agricultural and
ranching community, although small, has a
strong sense of identity. Its ancient sun symbol is
highly visible: the Zia emblem of perfect friend-
ship among united cultures is the official state
insignia, appearing on the state flag and license
plates and in the floor plan of the State Capitol
Building in Santa Fe. In addition, Zia has produced watercolor and oil painters of national
acclaim, as well as outstanding earthtone pottery,

COMMUNITY EVENTS
**Dances to Commemorate the
Christmas Season**
Traditional dances during Christmas week.
Easter Celebration
A Mass, procession, and traditional
dances.
Three Kings Day
A ceremony honoring new tribal leaders
on January 6th.
Zia Pueblo Feast Day
Our Lady of Assumption Feast Day, cele-
brated with a colorful Corn Dance on
August 15th.

distinguished by its geometric designs and floral,
deer, and bird motifs. Valued for its vessels used
largely as water containers and dough bowls, Zia
served as the main source of pottery for the
pueblos until World War II. ◉☐

LIBRARIES
Zia Enrichment Library
162B Zia Boulevard, 87053-6002
505-867-3304

PUBLIC ART
Zia Pueblo Community Building
Antonio Gachupin
Bow and arrow
Bernard Gachupin
Leather shields and rock painting
Bob Gachupin
Stone sculpture
Antonio T. Medina
Stone sculpture
Edwin Shije
Buckskin hide

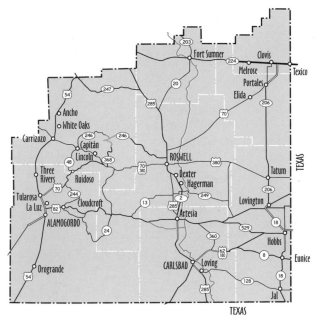

Southeastern New Mexico's cultural heritage has been preserved in countless Westerns. Just over a century ago, cattle barons and hired gunslingers took lawlessness to legendary extremes. The Lincoln County War and its aftermath spawned numerous efforts to propagate the enigmatic career and untimely demise of the state's favorite antihero, Billy the Kid.

The region's rugged wildness has been preserved in other ways as well. The expanse of gypsum dunes at White Sands is remembered in history as the place where the nuclear age dawned in a mushroom cloud. Carlsbad Caverns imprints summer visitors with haunting memories of the nightly flight of Mexican freetail bats, a species that outnumbers the human population of southeastern New Mexico 2-to-1.

In this land best known for rowdiness and turbulence, many travelers are surprised to find, pulling in to Roswell, the Roswell Museum and Art Center, one of the state's finest repositories of art; numerous works by the area's renowned artist Peter Hurd; and, courtesy of a handful of philanthropic oil and ranching tycoons, a repertory theater and a symphony orchestra. Elsewhere, the region offers incomparable collections at the Smokey Bear Museum, the Confederate Air Force Museum, the Space Center, and the Cowboy Hall of Fame.

ALAMOGORDO

US 54 at US 70
Brothers Charles B. and John A. Eddy, promoters of the El Paso & Northeastern Railroad, founded Alamogordo (Large Cottonwood) in 1898. The following year, it was designated the county seat of Otero County. For decades, Alamogordo served as a junction with a railroad line to a lumbering operation in the nearby Sacramento Mountains and as a center for ranchers and farmers. However, with the establishment of military installations in the area—Holloman Air Force Base during World War II

The St.Francis de Paula Fiesta has been a tradition in Tularosa since 1868.
Photograph by Pamela Porter

and White Sands Missile Range in the 1950s—the town took on a new role. The first atomic bomb was exploded 60 miles northwest of Alamogordo on July 16, 1945, and ever since, the community's focus has been science related.

MUSEUMS AND EXHIBIT SPACES
Space Center
Top of NM 2001
PO Box 533, 88311-0533
505-437-2840
Celebrating the history, technology, and daring of space exploration, the center encompasses a five-story International Space Hall of Fame Museum; the Clyde W. Tombaugh Space Theater, featuring a planetarium equipped with an

An antique Saturn rocket aims skyward in front of the Space Center in Alamogordo. Photograph by Mark Nohl

Omnimax projector system; and the John P. Stapp Air and Space Park, Astronaut Memorial Garden, and Shuttle Camp for children. A part of the New Mexico Office of Cultural Affairs. Fee.

Toy Train Depot
1991 North White Sands Boulevard, 88310
505-437-2855
A turn-of-the-century train depot with hundreds of model and toy trains plus a large layout of historic Alamogordo.

Tularosa Basin Historical Museum
1301 White Sands Boulevard
PO Box 518, 88310
505-437-4760
Exhibits include Mogollón Indian artifacts, cloud-climbing railroad photos, fossils, antique clothing, mining and farming equipment, Casas Grandes pottery, and a Trinity Site display.

White Sands National Monument
US 70-82, 14 miles southwest of Alamogordo
505-479-6124
Nearly 300 square miles of white gypsum dunes 30 to 40 feet high, constituting the world's largest gypsum dunefield. The constantly moving waves of "sand" were chosen as the testing site for the first atomic bomb. A natural history museum is located on the grounds. Fee.

HISTORIC BUILDINGS AND SITES
Dog Canyon in Oliver Lee Memorial State Park
US 54, 8 miles south of Alamogordo
505-437-8284
The earliest occupation of Dog Canyon dates back more than 5,000 years. Several groups of Apache Indians camped in the canyon about 500 years ago, and continued to inhabit the area through the late 19th century—even

though by that time, the canyon was a primary water source on pioneer Oliver Lee's million-acre Circle Cross cattle range. A museum in the park records the area's history. Fee.

Trinity Site
White Sands Missile Range
Site of the first atomic bomb explosion. The missile range is open to the public on the first Saturdays of April and October. □△

PERFORMING ARTS
Flickinger Center for the Arts
1110 New York Avenue
PO Box 1214, 88310
505-437-2202
This performing and visual arts space presents a September-to-April season of theater, music, and dance, plus a summer outdoor music series. The lobby features monthly shows of local artists' work.

CULTURAL ORGANIZATIONS
Theatre New Mexico
507 Zia Avenue, 88310
505-437-7740
This statewide affiliate of the five-state Southwest Theatre Association sponsors theater workshops. In odd-numbered years, the organization hosts a state-level competition for the American Association of Community Theaters.

LIBRARIES
Alamogordo Public Library
920 Oregon Avenue, 88310
505-439-4140

COMMUNITY EVENTS
Cottonwood Festival
Alameda Park
505-437-6120
An arts and crafts show with juried and nonjuried categories as well as food and entertainment on Labor Day weekend.
Flight Fest
Space Center
505-437-2840
An amateur model rocketry competition and show in June.
International Space Hall of Fame Induction
Space Center
505-437-2840
A yearly inauguration into the center's hall of fame of a handful of major contributors to space research and exploration. Held in late September.
Saturday in the Park
Washington Park
505-434-2867
Arts and crafts booths and demonstrations from the Holloman Air Force Base in mid-May.

PUBLIC ART
Lincoln National Forest Service Building
1101 New York Avenue
Peter Hurd
"Sun and Rain"—fresco
New Deal Art

Murray Morgan Office Building
411 East 10th Street
Two-dimensional pieces by numerous artists, including *Henri Barnhart, Pat Beatty, Dorothy Bell-Knapp, Dorsey Bonnel, Dara Ann Embury-Limes, Alice Orient*

Keil, Ernie Lee Miller, Carroll Robbins, Penny Simpson, Scott Swens, Ann Templeton, and *Sonja Williams*.

New Mexico School for the Visually Handicapped
1900 North White Sands Boulevard
Francis Rivera
"Teachers Pride"—mural

ANCHO

NM 349, 2 miles east of US 54 intersection
This mining and railroad town was developed in 1899. The houses and commercial structures were built of factory-made, light-colored bricks used throughout turn-of-the-century New Mexico. Ancho is now a ghost town.

MUSEUMS AND EXHIBIT SPACES
My House of Old Things
Ancho Railroad Depot
505-437-6120
A history museum within the original depot building constructed in 1902, when the railroad first made its way into Ancho. Fee. ☉

ARTESIA

US 285 at US 82
Beginning in 1866, the area now known as Artesia lay along the Pecos Valley cattle trails used by longhorn barons Charles Goodnight, Oliver Loving, and John S. Chisum. Chisum eventually bought land and established a ranch here. In 1903, the town, named for its many artesian wells, sprang up in Chisum's vast cattle empire. Oil, discovered here in 1923, proved a boon to the town's economy. The farming, ranching, and oil industries continue to play a prominent role in Artesia.

MUSEUMS AND EXHIBIT SPACES
Artesia Historical Museum and Art Center
505 West Richardson Avenue, 88210
505-748-2390
The museum chronicles local and Pecos Valley history via photography, Indian relics, a 1930s kitchen plus children's room with try-on clothes and hats, farm and ranch artifacts, and oil and mineral collections. The art annex features the work of New Mexican artists and traveling exhibits.

PERFORMING ARTS
Center for the Arts
320 West Dallas Avenue, 88210
505-746-4212
An exhibition gallery and performance space presenting local, regional, and national artists.

CULTURAL ORGANIZATIONS
Artesia Arts Council
510 West Main Street
PO Box 782, 88211
505-746-4212
Coordinates activities dedicated to the promotion of visual and performing arts. The council sponsors the Artesia Community Theatre, Writer's Guild, Community Chorale, Story League, and Area Artists Association.

COMMUNITY EVENTS
Art in the Park
Town Park
505-746-4212
An arts and crafts fair on the third weekend in October.

LIBRARIES
Artesia Public Library
306 West Richardson Avenue, 88210
505-746-4252

CAPITÁN

US 380 at NM 48
Between 1876 and 1879, the area witnessed
significant Lincoln County War action. Then, in
1900, Charles B. and John A. Eddy platted the
townsite, originally called Gray, after building a
spur of the El Paso & Northeastern Railroad
from Carrizozo to the Salado coalfields, which
were abandoned the following year. In 1950, a
bear cub with badly burned feet was rescued
from a forest fire within sight of Capitán. The
cub was nursed back to health and flown to a
Washington, DC, zoo to become the living symbol of Smokey Bear in the US Forest Service's
fire prevention program.

MUSEUMS AND EXHIBIT SPACES
Smokey Bear Museum
102 Smokey Bear Boulevard
PO Box 729, 88316
505-354-2298
This log museum houses the stories and memorabilia associated with Smokey Bear.

HISTORIC BUILDINGS AND SITES
Capitán Depot
Built around 1900, when the El Paso &
Northeastern Railroad first entered the newly
named village of Capitán, the depot became a
shipping point for nearby coalfields. Because
there was only one dead-end line into Capitán,
and hence no way to turn around, trains using
the depot had to either back in or back out. ☉

COMMUNITY EVENTS
Smokey Bear Stampede
505-354-3332
This tribute to Smokey Bear features a
parade, fun run, barbecue, Western
dance, and rodeo. Held in early July.

Smokey Bear Historical State Park
118 First Street, 88316
505-354-2748
A visitor center with historical exhibits about
forest fires and the Smokey Bear fire prevention
campaign. Included are a theater as well as
Smokey Bear's grave. Fee.

CARLSBAD

US 285 at US 62-180
Carlsbad was first named Eddy after the 1880s
pioneer cattleman Charles B. Eddy, then
renamed for the famous spa resort of Karlsbad
Springs in Czechoslovakia. In the late 19th century, this part of Pecos River country served as
the center of a major cattle empire.

MUSEUMS AND EXHIBIT SPACES
Carlsbad Caverns National Park
US 62-180, 20 miles south of Carlsbad
3225 National Parks Highway, 88220
505-785-2232
This major national park, first officially
explored in 1922, contains the world's largest
and most spectacular limestone caverns, some
of which are about 25,000 years old. The park
preserves 80 separate caves, 2 historic districts,
pictograph sites, and numerous wildlife and
plant species. Museum exhibits and programs
explain the history, geology, and natural fea-

tures of the area. Guided and self-guided tour options are available. Fee. ⊚☐

Carlsbad Museum and Art Center
418 West Fox Street, 88220
505-887-0276
Features local history; Southwestern relics such as saddles, guns, chuckwagons, and tools; archaeological discoveries; and fine art displays, including the McAdoo collection of paintings, Jack Drake bird carvings, and works by Peter Hurd and Roderick Mead.

Living Desert State Park
1504 Miehls Drive
PO Box 100, 88221
505-887-5516
A zoo and botanical garden highlighting the animals and plants of the Chihuahuan Desert. Exhibits include birds, mountain lions, bobcats, bison, javelinas, and nocturnal animals, as well as cacti and succulents from around the world. Fee.

Million Dollar Museum
US 62-180, 20 miles south of Carlsbad
Main Street, White's City, 88268
505-785-2294
Southeastern New Mexico's largest historical museum—containing 11 rooms filled with doll and dollhouse accessories, 6,000-year-old mummified Indians, Whittling Cowboys Ranch guns, chinaware, antique vehicles, music boxes, and other remnants of the Old West.

Limestone stalagmites in Carlsbad Caverns stand like ancient temple columns. Photograph by Mark Nohl

COMMUNITY EVENTS

Bat Flight Breakfast
Cave entrance to Carlsbad Caverns
National Park
505-785-2232
The return of hundreds of thousands of
Mexican freetail bats from their nighttime escapades. The predawn spectacle
occurs from May until mid-October,
after which the bats migrate to the trop-
ics. The breakfast event takes place
from 5 to 7 am the second Thursday in
August.

Carlsbad Western Week Celebration
505-887-6516
The Old West comes back to life with
nighttime street dances, barbecues,
parades, and rodeos. Held at the
Sheriff's Posse Arena and Carlsbad Civic
Center in early July.

Mescal Roast
Living Desert State Park
505-887-5516
Traditional Mescalero Apache Indian
ceremonies, dances, arts and crafts,
interpretive talks, blessings, and mescal
tasting in mid-May.

September 16th Celebration
San José Plaza
505-887-1381
A parade, food booths, Mexican rodeo,
and dances on the weekend nearest
September 16th.

HISTORIC BUILDINGS AND SITES

Carlsbad Reclamation Project
Canal Street
One of the most extensive privately financed
irrigation projects in the West. The stone dam,
main canals, and great concrete flume built by
the Pecos Irrigation and Investment Company in
1887 still supply water to more than 25,000
acres of fertile land in the Pecos River Valley.
⊚◻

CULTURAL ORGANIZATIONS

Carlsbad Area Arts and Humanities
1213 West Riverside Drive, 88220
505-887-3500

**Southeastern New Mexico Historical
Society**
1510 Grant Street, 88220
505-885-3318

LIBRARIES

Carlsbad Public Library
101 South Halagüeño Street, 88220
505-885-6776

PUBLIC ART

Carlsbad Public Library
101 South Halagüeño Street
Glenna Goodacre
"Indian and Child"—bronze sculpture

Riverwalk Recreation Center
403 Moore Drive
Shelley Horton-Trippe
"Banner Project"—banners

CARRIZOZO

US 54 at US 380
Carrizozo, named after the carrizo reed grass native to the region, was born in 1899 on the El Paso & Northeastern Railroad line. Before that, the area was well known to Billy the Kid, Sheriff Pat Garrett, and Governor Lew Wallace. Carrizozo, county seat of historic Lincoln County, is now a trade center for nearby ranches and a railroad town for the Southern Pacific line. Many of the buildings across from the old depot still bear the ornate woodwork and pressed tin facades of former days.

CLOUDCROFT

US 82, 17 miles east of US 54
Cloudcroft, meaning "cloud in a croft, or meadow," sits 9,000 feet up in the Sacramento Mountains, amid evergreens and aspens. Its seeds were sown in 1898, when the El Paso & Northeastern Railroad ran a narrow-gauge line into the mountains to cut logs for ties. In 1900, the railroad built a luxury hotel at the end of the line. The high-altitude retreat that once provided El Pasoans with a cool respite from the summer heat became a year-round resort for visitors the world over. In wintertime alone, the charming logging town offers a golf course (the highest in the country), ski area (the most southern in the state), snowmobiling, and inner tubing.

MUSEUMS AND EXHIBIT SPACES
Sacramento Mountains Historical Society Museum
US 82
PO Box 435, 88317
505-682-2932
A pioneer village and museum, featuring turn-of-the-century memorabilia. The display is housed in a restored pioneer log cabin. Special offerings include an oral history program and an old-timers reunion. Fee.

Sunspot Solar Observatory
NM 6563, 18 miles south of Cloudcroft
PO Box 62, 88349
505-434-7000
A giant observatory furnished with telescopes and other equipment for monitoring the sun. Maintained by the National Science Foundation, the facility offers exhibits as well as self-guided and guided tours.

HISTORIC BUILDINGS AND SITES
Cloud-Climbing Railroad
US 82, 1 mile west of Cloudcroft
The spur built into the Sacramento Mountains in 1898 by El Paso & Northeastern Railroad owner Charles B. Eddy operated as far as Cloudcroft until 1947. All that remains of it is the Cloudcroft trestle, visible from the highway.

Cloudcroft Lodge
1 Corona Place
PO Box 497, 88317
505-682-2566
Set in a scenic location in the Sacramento Mountains, this is one of the oldest and most prominent of New Mexico's resort hotels. It was constructed in 1900 as a two-story building touted as "The Pavilion: The Breathing Spot of the Southwest." Destroyed by fire in 1909, the lodge was rebuilt, enlarged to three stories, and reopened in 1911, welcoming Mexican revolutionary Pancho Villa as one of its first guests. Rustic, Bavarian-style Cloudcroft Lodge is as popular today as its progenitor was in the early 1900s. ◉

COMMUNITY EVENTS

Christmas in Cloudcroft
Zenith Park
505-682-2733
Crowning of the Snow Queen plus a
skating party, ice sculpture contest,
parade, and lighting tours in mid-
December.

Cloudcroft Oktoberfest
Zenith Park
505-682-2733
Features the town's largest arts and
crafts fair—a juried show with more
than 60 artists from at least 10 states,
competing in pottery, oil, watercolor,
leather, wood, photography, textiles, jewelry, etching, and sculpture. Other events
include a Tenderfoot Express hayride,
music, food booths, a horseshoe tournament, square dances, and guided nature
tours. Held on the first full weekend in
October.

July Jamboree
Zenith Park
505-682-2733
A crafts fair, games, food, hayrides, and
a horseshoe tournament on the weekend
nearest the Fourth of July.

Mayfair
Zenith Park
505-682-2733
Juried arts and crafts, food booths,
hayrides, and horseshoe tournaments on
Memorial Day weekend.

Cloudcroft School
Burro Avenue at Swallow Place
The red brick school, built in 1918, was
designed by Trost and Trost—the El Paso archi-
tectural firm responsible for the design of New
Mexico State University buildings in Las Cruces
and Western New Mexico University buildings in
Silver City. Henry Trost was a student of Frank
Lloyd Wright.

LIBRARIES

Cloudcroft Community Library
Mescalero Avenue at Burro Avenue
PO Box 125, 88317
505-682-2733

CLOVIS

US 60-84 at US 70
The 1932 discovery of huge mammoth bones
and Clovis points in the area revealed that it was
inhabited by a hunting culture about 11,200
years ago (see Blackwater Draw Site, page 158).
Spanish arrivals encountered tall grasslands and
bands of roving Indians. From the 1700s to the
early 1800s, trails cutting through the grasses
were used by Comanche Indian buffalo hunters.
Later in the 19th century, ranchers were drawn
to the area's fertile soil. In 1907, when the Santa
Fe Railway began laying tracks across the plains
of eastern New Mexico, officials decided to turn
the preexisting siding and rough shacks of a
place known as Riley's Switch into a real town
with a real name. Dubbed Clovis—after the king
of the Franks who converted to Christianity in AD
496—by the daughter of a railroad official, the
town became the eastern terminal of the Belén
Cutoff. The railroad opened the region to farmers, who established thriving fields of alfalfa,
sugar beets, and wheat. Clovis today is primarily

Buddy Holly and Waylon Jennings are among the music greats who got their start here in Clovis.
Photograph by Mark Nohl

agricultural and has some of the largest feedlots in the Southwest.

MUSEUMS AND EXHIBIT SPACES

Eula Mae Edwards Museum
Clovis Community College
417 Schepps Boulevard, 88101
505-769-4012
Displays American Indian artifacts.

Hillcrest Park Zoo
10th and Sycamore Streets
505-763-3435
The second largest zoo in New Mexico.

H. A. "Pappy" Thornton Museum
Ned Houk Park
NM 209, 6.5 miles north of Clovis
505-769-3437
Features local farm equipment used before 1926.

HISTORIC BUILDINGS AND SITES

Clovis Central Fire Station
320 Mitchell Street
Constructed in the "motor age" style of architecture, this was the first modern facility erected in Clovis. The fire station was built during the Great Depression and reflects the optimism the Clovisites had in the rapid growth of their community. ☺☐

Clovis City Hall and Fire Station
308 Pile Street
The town's first government building, constructed in 1908. ☺☐

Clovis-Carver Public Library (formerly Clovis Post Office)
701 Main Street
A leading federal project undertaken in 1931, the post office blended Spanish Colonial Revival architecture with Neoclassical styles. ☺☐

Hotel Clovis
210 Main Street
Built in 1931, at the height of the Depression, the hotel was known as the Skyscraper of the Plains. It ranks among the two or three highest quality Art Deco buildings erected in New Mexico. ☺☐

COMMUNITY EVENTS

Cinco de Mayo Fiesta
Our Lady of Guadalupe Church
117 Davis Street, 88101
505-763-4445
Arts and crafts, food booths, and musical entertainment on May 5th.

Clovis Arts and Crafts Show
New Mexico National Guard Armory
601 South Norris Street
505-763-3435
Sponsored by the Clovis Women's Club in late November or early December.

Clovis Music Festival
505-763-3435
Five days of gospel music, fifties rock and roll, and country tunes in celebration of Buddy Holly and Norman Petty. Also a parade, street dance and block party, fifties classic car show, and arts and crafts bazaar. Held in mid-July.

Pioneer Days
Main Street and Fairgrounds
505-763-3435
A parade, arts and crafts fair, rodeo, wild-cow milking, chile cook-off, pageants, and exhibits in honor of the pioneers. Held on the first weekend in June.

Norman Petty Recording Studios
206 North Main Street, 88101
505-767-7565
The studio in which Buddy Holly, Roy Orbison, the Fireballs, Waylon Jennings, and other rock-and-roll greats recorded some of their earliest hits. Artifacts include the drums used during the recording of Holly's "Peggy Sue." Visits by appointment only. Fee.

Old Lyceum Theatre
411 North Main Street
505-763-6085
Constructed between 1919 and 1920, this vaudeville theater hosted such luminaries as Tom Mix, Shirley Temple, and John Philip Sousa. Restored, it is now used for performances and touring groups.

CULTURAL ORGANIZATIONS

High Plains Historical Foundation
313 Prairieview Road, 88101
505-763-6361
Editors of the book *High Plains History,* profiling more than 100 years of east-central New Mexico history.

LIBRARIES

Clovis-Carver Public Library
701 North Main Street, 88101
505-769-7840

PUBLIC ART

Clovis Community College
Schepps Boulevard
Peter Hurd
"White & Gold Twilight"—watercolor painting
Wilson Hurley
"Thunderhead at Last Light"—oil painting

Henriette Wyeth
"Troman's Apple"—pastel
"Blue Well"—oil painting

Curry Field Health Office
1216 Cameo Street
Phyllis Dorough
"GlassWorks"—stained glass panels

Old Post Office Building
Mitchell and Fourth Streets
Paul Lantz
Oil mural
New Deal Art

Play, Inc.
1700 East Seventh Street
Stanley Olivarez
"Sploosh"—life-size geometric figures

DEXTER

NM 2, 10 miles south of Roswell
Situated on the Pecos River, the town is headquarters of the Dexter National Fish Hatchery, a
center for the study and preservation of endan-
gered species of fish in the Southwest. Open to
the public.

LIBRARIES
Dexter Public Library
115 East Second Street
PO Box 249, 88230
505-734-5482

PUBLIC ART
Dexter Schools
100 East Clark Street
Peter Ray James
"Enchanted Migration"—mural

COMMUNITY EVENTS
New Mexico Dairy Day
Lake Van
505-734-5482
Milk-carton boat races, a triathlon, and
an ice cream eating contest in early June.

ELIDA

US 70, 24 miles southwest of Portales
This trading center for ranchers was settled in
1880 by homesteader George Littlefield. By the
turn of the century, Elida boasted a post office,
three general stores, and several shops and
restaurants.

LIBRARIES
Ruth McCowen Public Library
Elida City Hall, 88116
505-274-6376

EUNICE

NM 207 at NM 8
The community of Eunice, started in 1908 by
homesteader John Carson, was named after
his daughter Eunice. In time, the town
became known for its weekly musical productions and drama presentations by the Eunice

COMMUNITY EVENTS
Old-Time Fiddlers' Contest
Community Center
505-394-2132
Concerts and competitions in late July.

Literary Society. Later drought ridden, the community was revived with the discovery of oil in the 1930s.

LIBRARIES
Eunice Public Library
10th and N Streets
PO Box 1629, 88231-1629
505-394-2336

PUBLIC ART
Eunice Public Library
10th and N Streets
Among the numerous pieces on display in the Art Exhibitions Room are a bronze by *Curtis Fort*, oil paintings by *Terry Gill*, and watercolors by *Patrick Light*.

FORT STANTON

NM 214, 2.5 miles south of US 380
Established in 1855 as a frontier outpost on the banks of the Río Bonito, the fort was an active military installation until 1896. At the turn of the century, it became a US Merchant Marine hospital for tuberculosis patients; adjoining the hospital was a cemetery to memorialize the seamen who died from TB. German POWs, held here during World War II, built a performance hall that is still standing. ◉□

PUBLIC ART
Fort Stanton Hospital
NM 214
Gary Yazzie
"Stealing Glances"—oil painting

FORT SUMNER

US 60 at US 84
The town of Fort Sumner grew out of settlements clustered around the adobe fort built in 1862 to guard the Bosque Redondo Indian Reservation. Later a cattle town on the Goodnight-Loving Trail, Fort Sumner again gained notoriety—this time as a hangout for Billy the Kid and his gang and, in 1881, site of the Kid's final confrontation with the law. After construction of the Belén Cutoff of the Santa Fe Railway in 1907, the town became a trading center for Pecos River farmers and cattle ranchers.

MUSEUMS AND EXHIBIT SPACES
Billy the Kid Museum
1601 East Sumner Avenue, 88119
505-355-2380
Displays cowboy memorabilia from the late 1800s, showcasing Billy the Kid, who was shot to death by Sheriff Pat Garrett at the Fort Stanton ranch of Pete Maxwell—nephew of land baron Lucien Maxwell—on July 14, 1881. Fee.

Billy the Kid Outlaw Gang Headquarters Museum
US 60-84
PO Box 1881, Taiban, 88134
505-355-9935
Operated by the Billy the Kid Outlaw Gang, Inc., this historical museum presents exhibits of 1880s paraphernalia. The society is committed to the preservation, protection, and promotion of "America's Most Enduring Legend"; to combating prevarications and discrediting Kid imposters; and to defending New Mexico's history.

Fort Sumner State Monument
Billy the Kid Road
Route 1, Box 356, 88119
505-355-2573
Site of the Bosque Redondo Reservation where, between 1863 and 1868, the US government interred nearly 10,000 Navajos and Apaches—about 3,000 of whom died of exposure, starvation, and disease. The monument also marks the place where in 1881, after the military had abandoned the fort, Pat Garrett killed Billy the Kid. The visitor center features history exhibits, and a living-history program on weekends explains the arms and equipage of frontier soldiers. A part of the Museum of New Mexico. Fee. ⊚□

Old Fort Sumner Museum
172 Billy the Kid Road
PO Box 1881, Taiban, 88134
505-355-2942
Established in 1932, the museum exhibits official historical documents, including handwritten letters by Billy the Kid and Pat Garrett, and the coroner's reports. Also featured are Howard Suttle oil paintings depicting the story of Billy the Kid, cowboy memorabilia from the 1860s, and period antiques and artifacts. Behind the museum lies the Maxwell family cemetery, containing the remains of Billy the Kid, his colleagues Tom O'Folliard and Charlie Bowdre, Lucien Maxwell, and his son Pete. The Kid's grave site is encased in iron. Fee.

HISTORIC BUILDINGS AND SITES
Goodnight-Loving Trail
The often-traveled cattle trail, spanning 2,000 miles from Texas to Wyoming, was blazed in 1866 by Charles Goodnight and Oliver Loving. After crossing into New Mexico, the trail followed the Pecos River north to Fort Sumner, where cattle were slaughtered to feed the Navajos and Apaches imprisoned at the Bosque Redondo Reservation.

Llano Estacado
US 60-84, between Fort Sumner and Clovis
The vast Llano Estacado (Staked Plains), with its fortresslike escarpments, was home turf to nomadic Indians and countless buffalo herds when the Francisco Vásquez de Coronado expedition arrived in 1541. Later, it became a target for Comanchero activity. In the mid-19th century, this portion of the great plateau evolved into a center for cattle ranchers. Early-20th-century homesteaders were the first people to set down roots in the area.

CULTURAL ORGANIZATIONS
Mid-Pecos Historical Society
1321 Avenue F, 88119
Compiles and preserves the history of Fort Sumner and De Baca County.

COMMUNITY EVENTS
Billy the Kid–Pat Garrett Historical Days
Billy the Kid Outlaw Gang Headquarters Museum
US 60-84
PO Box 1881, Taiban, 88134
505-355-9935
Mid-July music performances and other festivities sponsored by the New Mexico Billy the Kid–Pat Garrett Historical Society.

Old Fort Days Celebration
505-355-7393
An arts and crafts show, music festival, Billy the Kid drama, rodeo, parade, and other activities in early June.

LIBRARIES
Fort Sumner Public Library
1400 Mesquite, 88119
505-355-2832

PUBLIC ART
De Baca County Courthouse
514 Avenue C
Russell Vernon Hunter
"The Last Frontier"—murals
New Deal Art

HAGERMAN

NM 2, 17 miles south of Roswell
A farming and ranching community named
for J. J. Hagerman in 1906, when his son was
governor of New Mexico. Hagerman, president of a small railroad and mining enterprise, had developed a system of irrigation in
the area.

LIBRARIES
Hagerman Community Library
209 East Argyle Street
PO Box 247, 88232
505-752-3204

HIGH ROLLS

US 82, 9 miles east of US 54 intersection
This fruit-growing village on Fresnal Creek
was cartoonist Bill Mauldin's hometown.

COMMUNITY EVENTS
Apple Festival
US 82
Welcomes the apple harvest with home-
made apple cider, apple pies, arts and
crafts, and fiddle playing in mid-October.
Also takes place in the nearby communi-
ty of Mountain Park.
Cherry Festival
US 82
505-437-6120
Arts and crafts, cherry picking, and food
booths in mid-June to celebrate the
ripening cherry orchards. Also takes
place in the nearby community of
Mountain Park.

HOBBS

US 62-180 at NM 18
Named in 1907 for the family of James Hobbs,
believed to be the first homesteaders in the
region, the site became a trading village for
nearby ranchers. Following the Midwest Oil
Company's January 1928 discovery of oil in
Hobbs, all of Lea County sprang into visibility
for being at the heart of high-yield oil-produc-
ing country. The state's petroleum now comes
primarily from the Hobbs area.

MUSEUMS AND EXHIBIT SPACES
Confederate Air Force Museum
Hobbs-Lea County Airport
PO Box 1260, 88240
505-397-3202
Features operable World War II aircraft and
memorabilia.

Lea County Cowboy Hall of Fame and Western Heritage Center
New Mexico Junior College
5317 Lovington Highway, 88240
505-392-1275
Portrays the history of Lea County as seen from the perspective of Indians, buffalo hunters, soldiers, open-range homesteaders, and settlers. Exhibits spotlight outstanding county ranchers and rodeo performers.

Linam Ranch Museum
US 62-180 at Carlsbad Highway
505-393-4784
Depicts early ranching history. Visits by appointment only.

PERFORMING ARTS
Southwest Symphony Orchestra
PO Box 101, 88240
505-392-6877
The chamber-size group of about 35 musicians presents two or three concerts each season. The group also sponsors the Southwest Symphony Band, composed of professional and nonprofessional musicians.

LIBRARIES
Hobbs Public Library
509 North Shipp, 88240
505-397-9328

COMMUNITY EVENTS
Cinco de Mayo Celebration
City parks
505-393-8054
Entertainment, food booths, crowning of the queen, and a jalapeño-eating contest on the first full weekend in May.

Hobbs Arts and Crafts Festival
Lea County Cultural Center
New Mexico Junior College
505-393-5933
Local arts and crafts exhibits held in mid-August.

Hobbs Hoedown Days
Lea County Cultural Center
505-397-3202
A dance, parade, and arts and crafts fair in mid-September.

June Teenth Celebration
Washington Park
505-397-3202
Black awareness activities, arts and crafts show, and plays in mid-June.

Llano Estacado Party and Cowboy Hall of Fame Induction
Western Heritage Center
5317 Lovington Highway, 88240
505-392-5518
A Western art show accompanying Cowboy Hall of Fame induction ceremonies in October.

Staked Plains Roundup
Western Heritage Center
5317 Lovington Highway, 88240
505-392-5518
Cowboy poetry, storytellers, Western music, and demonstrations in saddle making, boot making, blacksmithing, wool spinning, quilting, and rawhide braiding. Also exhibits of wagons, tepees, animals, and other Western heritage artifacts. Held in late September.

Scarborough Memorial Library
College of the Southwest
Campus Highway 18, 88240
505-392-6561
The library's Southwest Heritage Room contains the Thelma A. Webber collection of prehistoric Indian, early settler, ranch, and oilfield artifacts.

PUBLIC ART
Hobbs State Office Building
2120 North Alto
Ali Baudoin
"Earth Cooler"—stainless steel sculpture

New Mexico Junior College
5317 Lovington Highway
Wanda Dansereau
"Bahozonie"—oil painting
Terry N. Gill
"New Mexico Hacienda"—watercolor painting
"Pink Mesa"—oil painting
"Santa Fe Adobe"—oil painting
Helen Gwinn
"Spring Pricklies"—watercolor painting
Anne Lane
"American Image"—pastel drawing

JAL

NM 18 at NM 128
This authentic brand-name town originated in the late 1880s, when the Cowden Company of Midland, Texas, decided to expand into the stirrup-high grama grass of the New Mexico Territory and selected a watering place there as its over-the-border headquarters. To stock the virgin ranch land, the company bought a herd of cattle from Texan John A. Lynch—whose brand, JAL, emblazoned from shoulder to hip

on the imported animals, became a familiar sight in the area. Cowboys began calling the rangeland JAL, a moniker that stuck when the region sprouted a town in the early 1900s. In the mid-1920s, oil and gas were discovered beneath the no-longer-stirrup-high grasses. Today, Jal is a hub of oil, gas, farming, and ranching activity.

LIBRARIES
Woolworth Community Library
Third and Utah Streets
PO Box 1249, 88252
505-395-3268

LA LUZ

US 54, 5 miles north of Alamogordo
This lush, verdant, agricultural community, long celebrated for its abundant water supply, was founded by Spanish settlers in the 1860s. Called El Presidio until the 1870s, the village was originally composed of small, flat-roofed adobes; between 1880 and 1900, Anglo ranchers and land speculators began introducing Victorian-style touches such as complex pitch roofs and wood detailing. Today, the La Luz Townsite Historic District features several historic treasures, including the old Nuestra Señora de La Luz Church, built in 1896, and La Luz Pottery Factory, first constructed as a home by Antonio Baca in the 1860s. The Baca house served as a stagecoach stop and post office before it was purchased in 1928 by Rhode Island emigrant Roland Hazard, who converted it to the large pottery plant known for producing vast quantities of urns and roof tiles. ◉□

Billy the Kid made a daring jailbreak from the Lincoln County Courthouse, shown here in a 1905 photograph. Photograph courtesy Museum of New Mexico, neg. 54418

LINCOLN

US 380, 57 miles west of Roswell
Settled in 1849, the place the Spaniards called "The Little Town by the Pretty River" was not destined for serenity—despite the fortified tower the villagers had built at its center. In 1869, the town's name was changed to honor President Abraham Lincoln, and the place was designated the county seat of newly formed Lincoln County, which encompassed far more territory than it does today. Bitter competition soon developed between ranchers and store-keepers vying for lucrative beef contracts at nearby Fort Stanton, erupting, in February 1878, in five months of bloody conflict known as the Lincoln County War. Avenging the assassination of rancher and merchant John H. Tunstall, Billy

the Kid killed the murderers, remaining an out-law until he was captured in December 1880, and even afterward. Jailed four months later in the Lincoln courthouse to await hanging, he escaped within weeks, killed two guards, and eventually hid out at the Maxwell ranch in Fort Sumner, where the law finally caught up with him. In July 1881, he was killed in a bedroom of the ranch by his former friend Sheriff Pat Garrett. The town of Lincoln became a huge memorial to this period in history. ◉□△

MUSEUMS AND EXHIBIT SPACES
La Paloma Museum
US 380
PO Box 43, 88338
505-653-4828
Displays a collection of more than 5,000

antiques and other artifacts dating from 1860 to 1920. Fee.

Lincoln State Monument
US 380
PO Box 98, 88338
505-653-4372
This historic site encompasses a history museum; late-19th-century houses; old Lincoln County Courthouse; the Tunstall Store; San Juan Church; the torreón (rock tower), built in 1850; and much more. A part of the Museum of New Mexico. Fee.

Torreón
US 380
505-653-4372
The sturdy rock tower in which early settlers hid during Indian raids stands in the center of Lincoln.

Wortley Hotel
US 380
505-653-4500
Co-owned by Patrick F. Garrett, sheriff of Lincoln County, this boardinghouse figured prominently in the 1878 conflict and its aftermath. Reconstructed in 1960, the Wortley offers old-fashioned lace comfort and brass beds. Open in the summer months.

CULTURAL ORGANIZATIONS
Lincoln County Heritage Trust
PO Box 98, 88338
505-653-4025
Maintains and operates historic houses, the La Paloma museum store, and a Historical Center featuring exhibits on the Apache Indians, buffalo soldiers (black troops stationed in the West after the Civil War), Lincoln County War, and Billy the Kid. The center also offers a slide show, seasonal guided tours, and special events. Fee.

Lincoln County Historical Society
PO Box 91, 88338
505-653-4047
Sponsors historical programs about the Lincoln area.

PUBLIC ART
Lincoln County Courthouse
Fred Faudie
"Billy the Kid"—acrylic painting

LOVING

US 285, 10 miles south of Carlsbad
This watering place on the Goodnight-Loving Trail was named Vough by Swiss residents in the late 1800s, and later called Florence. The small town took its present name after John Loving, one of the first men to herd cattle up the Pecos River Valley from Texas, was fatally wounded on a cattle drive along the trail.

COMMUNITY EVENTS
Lincoln County Fair
County Fairgrounds
505-354-2234
An arts and crafts fair, livestock judging, and rodeo in mid-August.

Old Lincoln Days
505-653-4372
A Billy the Kid pageant, parade, living-history demonstrations, arts and crafts, food booths, and an old-fashioned fiddlers' contest. Held in early August.

HISTORIC BUILDINGS AND SITES
Espejo's Trail
NM 285, between Malaga and the Texas border
Don Antonio de Espejo, leader of the third
Spanish expedition to explore New Mexico,
passed this way on his return to Mexico City in
1583. After learning of the martyrdom suffered
by two Franciscan friars left behind during an
earlier expedition, he explored the Pueblo
country, then followed the Pecos River Valley
south.

LIBRARIES
Loving Community Library
PO Box 1358, 88256
505-745-3509

LOVINGTON

US 82 at NM 18
Lovington, on the Llano Estacado, was named for
Robert Florence Love, who founded the town on
his homestead in 1908. The cattle- and sheep-
ranching community, known for its irrigated
farming, joined the rich oil empire of southeastern New Mexico after the discovery of the

---

COMMUNITY EVENTS
**Southeastern New Mexico Arts and
Crafts Festival**
Lea County Fairgrounds
505-396-5311
An event featuring more than 100
exhibitors from New Mexico, Texas,
Colorado, Washington, and other
Western states. No commercially manu-
factured items are allowed in this early
November show.

Denton Pool following World War II. Lovington is
the county seat of Lea County, the leading oil-
producing county in the United States.

MUSEUMS AND EXHIBIT SPACES
Lea County Museum
103 South Love Street
PO Box 1195, 88260
505-396-5311
The history museum, located in the
Commercial Hotel built around 1918, displays
artifacts from a local dugout house, the R. F.
Love House, and more. The rooms are furnished and decorated with relics collected
from Lea County residents.

LIBRARIES
Lovington Public Library
115 South Main Street, 88260
505-396-3144

PUBLIC ART
Lovington Public Library
115 South Main Street
Sculpture and two-dimensional pieces by
numerous artists, including *Herbert Bryant,
Bernice Castleberry, Janett Evans, David
Irion, Helen Nave, Suzy Shipp, Betty
McCrory South,* and *Connie Walstad.*

MELROSE

US 60-84, 24 miles west of Clovis
This railroad and ranching center on the Llano
Estacado was called Brownhorn from 1882
until 1906 because it was midway between the
Brown and Horn Ranches. In 1906, Santa Fe
Railway officials named the community after
Melrose, Ohio.

COMMUNITY EVENTS

Easter Pageant
Roger Parks Ranch
Brownhorn Road, 1 mile south of
Melrose
505-253-4530
A Passion play and Easter breakfast. The
play is enacted in caves once used by
Billy the Kid.

Melrose Old-Timers' Days
Melrose Town Park
505-253-4530
A parade, rodeo, and community barbecue in mid-August.

HISTORIC BUILDINGS AND SITES

**Hart Youth Ranch (formerly Pigpin
Ranch)**
NM 267, 3 miles south of Melrose
PO Box 315, 88124
505-253-4278
The original ranch house was built in 1887
with timbers from Pete Maxwell's Fort
Sumner home, where Billy the Kid was killed
by Sheriff Pat Garrett in 1881. Visitors are
welcome.

PUBLIC ART

Melrose Public School Library
Howard Schleeter
Five mural panels
New Deal Art

MESCALERO APACHE RESERVATION

US 70, 16 miles east of Tularosa
PO Box 176, 88340
505-671-4494
The Indians living on the 460,000-acre Mescalero
Apache Reservation are descendants of
Athabascan nomads who migrated south from
Canada along the front range of the Rocky
Mountains and, by the 15th century, into the
parched, arid lands of southern New Mexico. The
Mescalero branch took its name from the mescal
cactus, which supplied food, beverage, fiber, and
stakes for ceremonial tepees. In 1873, when the
Mescaleros were confined to the mountainous
reservation, they began building tepees with ever-
green branches in lieu of mescal stalks. The present-day tribe raises cattle and horses in the reservation's high meadows and lush valleys, and owns
and manages four recreational areas, including
the Inn of the Mountain Gods, a resort complex.

MUSEUMS AND EXHIBIT SPACES

Mescalero Apache Cultural Center
US 70, in Mescalero
PO Box 176, 88340
505-671-4494

COMMUNITY EVENTS

Coming of Age Ceremonial
505-671-4494
A four-day event featuring traditional
Indian dances, a rodeo, the nighttime
Apache Maidens' Puberty Rites, Dance of
the Apache Maidens, and Dance of the
Mountain Gods. Held near the Fourth of
July.

Tepees stand along the riverbank on the Mescalero Apache Reservation. Photograph by Mark Nohl

Displays traditional clothing of the Mescalero, Chiricahua, and Lipan subtribes; exhibits photographs of such Indian leaders as Chato, Cochise, Noiche, and Chihuahua; and presents a historical and descriptive video show.

HISTORIC BUILDINGS AND SITES
St. Joseph's Mission
US 70, in Mescalero
Completed in 1936, the church was built entirely by hand, using stones quarried from nearby mountains. A memorial to the dead of World War I.

LIBRARIES
Mescalero Community Center Library
US 70, in Mescalero
PO Box 176, 88340
505-671-4494

PORTALES

US 70 at NM 206
Initially a camping ground for cowboys on northbound cattle drives, the region was dotted with springs issuing from a series of porchlike caves. They called it Portales (Porches) Springs. When the Pecos Valley and Northern Railroad came through in 1898, the railroad workers, too, camped near the springs. A settlement quickly grew, and within a few years,

Portales was incorporated as the county seat of Roosevelt County. The irrigated valley plains soon began producing bountiful crops of Valencia peanuts, grains, sweet potatoes, corn, and cotton. In 1934, the town became home to what is now Eastern New Mexico University. Today's city is a dairy, agricultural, and educational center.

MUSEUMS AND EXHIBIT SPACES

Blackwater Draw Museum
US 70, 7 miles north of Portales
Station 9, Quay Hall
Eastern New Mexico University, 88130
505-562-2202
On display are artifacts, stratigraphy, and bones unearthed at nearby Blackwater Draw Site (see Historic Buildings and Sites). The museum also provides cultural information about the ancient Paleo-Indians and presents films to groups of schoolchildren. Fee (includes site entrance).

Dalley's Windmill Collection
Kilgore Street, 88130
505-356-8541
Exhibits more than 60 restored windmills.

Miles Mineral Museum
Roosevelt Hall
Eastern New Mexico University
Station 33, 88130
505-562-2651
Educational displays of geologic fossils and minerals found locally and throughout the world.

Natural History Museum
Roosevelt Hall
Eastern New Mexico University
PO Box 2289, 88130
505-562-2723

COMMUNITY EVENTS

Cultural Kaleidoscope
Eastern New Mexico University
505-562-2227
An award-winning multicultural celebration featuring entertainment and educational programs from countries around the world. Held in March and April.

Heritage Days
Roosevelt County Fairgrounds
505-356-8541
A rodeo, parade, barbecue, dance, arts and crafts fair, and entertainment in late April.

Peanut Valley Festival
Campus Union Building
Eastern New Mexico University
505-562-2631
Arts and crafts, a peanut food fair, and entertainment in October.

Features wildlife of the Llano Estacado as well as the aquatic and terrestrial ecology of the region. The museum's collection includes 10,000 specimens of mammals; 5,000 specimens of reptiles and amphibians; 1,000 specimens of birds; and 10,000 specimens of fish.

Roosevelt County Museum
Eastern New Mexico University
Station 30, 88130
505-562-2592
Exhibits late-19th- and early-20th-century firearms, kitchen utensils, art, costumes, photographs, and more depicting the ethnology and folklore of early settlers.

HISTORIC BUILDINGS AND SITES
Bank of Portales
123 Main Street
Constructed from 1902 to 1903, this is
Portales's least altered turn-of-the-century com-
mercial building. It exemplifies the brick-style,
railroad-town look typical of southeastern New
Mexico communities of the time. ◎□

**Blackwater Draw National Archaeological
Site**
NM 467, 5 miles north of Portales
508A NM 467, 88130
505-356-5235
Officially discovered by a highway crew in
1932, Blackwater Draw, a one-time pond fed by
the Río Brazos, was a camping and kill site for
the Paleo-Indians—earliest known inhabitants
of North America. This 11,300-year-old Clovis
culture left behind its arrowheads, scrapers,
bone tools, and the remains of its Pleistocene
prey: huge mammoths, camels, horses, bison,
sloths, sabertooth tigers, and dire wolves.
Although the pond dried up about 7,000 years
ago, human occupation of the area continued
until about the first century AD. Fee (includes
museum entrance). ◎□△

CULTURAL ORGANIZATIONS
High Plains Arts Council
508 East 17th Lane, 88130
505-356-5995

Paleo-Indian Institute
Eastern New Mexico University
PO Box 2154, 88130
505-562-2303
Maintains archaeological and anthropological
collections housed in branch museums. The
institute's library contains more than 1,000 vol-
umes on Paleo-Indians and paleontology.

LIBRARIES
Golden Library
South Avenue K
Eastern New Mexico University, 88130
505-562-2624
The Runnels Room contains a visual arts
gallery.

Portales Public Library
218 South Avenue B, 88130
505-356-3940

PUBLIC ART
**Eastern New Mexico University
Administration Building**
University Drive and South Avenue K
Lloyd Moylan
"The 12th Chapter of Ecclesiastes"—mural
New Deal Art

**Eastern New Mexico University Golden
Library**
University Drive and South Avenue K
Raymond Jonson
"Art" and "Science"—murals
New Deal Art

Eastern New Mexico University Theater
South Avenue N
Gary Mauro
Fabric relief mural

Portales Post Office
116 West First Street
Theodore Van Solen
"Buffalo Range"—mural
New Deal Art

ROSWELL

US 285 at US 380

An oasis of water and grass, the Roswell area was inhabited by ancient Indians long before conquistadores passed through on their northward march. In the 1870s and 1880s, the area was a popular watering place for the Pecos Valley cattle drives, and the site of a growing settlement. Known originally as Río Hondo, the small community underwent expansion and a name change with the 1872 arrival of professional gambler Van C. Smith, who changed its name to honor his father, Roswell Smith. In 1890, the year the town was incorporated with a population of 343, artesian water was discovered beneath its pastures. Roswell is now the most populated city in southeastern New Mexico and is situated in the world's most important artesian basin. Among those who

Roswell Museum and Art Center. Photograph by Mark Nohl

COMMUNITY EVENTS

Eastern New Mexico State Fair
Eastern New Mexico State Fairgrounds
Southeast Main Street
505-623-9411
A week-long event featuring livestock and agricultural displays, a rodeo, parade, carnival, and dances. Held in October.

Festival in the Park
Cahoon Park
505-623-5695
Arts and crafts plus food booths in early July.

Piñatafest
Courthouse lawn
Fourth and Main Streets
505-625-1564
A September celebration of Roswell's Hispanic heritage.

Roswell Artfaire
Eastern New Mexico State Fairgrounds
Southeast Main Street
505-623-5695
Arts and crafts in late April.

have lived and worked in the town are rancher Captain Joseph C. Lea; cattleman John Chisum; sheriff Pat Garrett; Dr. Robert H. Goddard, father of the space age; painter Peter Hurd; and author Paul Horgan. Renowned as well for its dairy cattle and agricultural pursuits, Roswell produces one of the world's largest pecan crops.

Gothic Revival-style architecture characterizes the New Mexico Military Institute. Photograph by Mark Nohl

MUSEUMS AND EXHIBIT SPACES

Historical Center for Southeast New Mexico Museum
200 North Lea Avenue, 88201
505-622-8333
Located in the 80-year-old home of former cattleman J. P. White, the museum chronicles the history of southeastern New Mexico, with emphasis on the Pecos Valley from 1865 to 1940. The facility houses a library, archives. and an extensive photography collection. Fee.

General Douglas L. McBride Museum
New Mexico Military Institute
101 West College Boulevard
PO Box J, 88201
505-624-8221
Dedicated to the preservation of US military history, the museum features firearms, static displays, uniforms, insignia, and decorations.

Additional offerings include a research library, photographic archives, Howard Cook's Guadalcanal paintings, and Peter Hurd paintings.

Roswell Museum and Art Center
100 West 11th Street, 88201
505-624-6744
Devoted to the arts and culture of the Southwest, with emphasis on New Mexico, the museum exhibits historical and contemporary Indian, Hispanic, and Western arts and artifacts. Features the work of Peter Hurd, Henriette Wyeth, and Taos and Santa Fe artists; the Rogers Aston collection of Native American and Western art; the Dr. Robert H. Goddard collection of experimental rocketry; and the Goddard Planetarium. Tours, classes, and special events are available.

HISTORIC BUILDINGS AND SITES

Castaño de Sosa's Route
US 70, through the vicinity of Roswell and Artesia
Between 1590 and 1591, Portuguese explorer
Gaspar Castaño de Sosa took a Mexican expedi-
tion up the Pecos River to establish a colony in
New Mexico, passing through this area in the
winter of 1590. Although his venture failed, it
led to the permanent settlement north of Santa
Fe initiated by Don Juan de Oñate in 1598.

Chisum Trail
US 70-380, 20 miles west of Roswell
Sometimes confused with the Chisholm Trail
from Texas to Kansas, the Chisum Trail was used
by New Mexico rancher John S. Chisum to supply cattle to Indian agencies in Arizona. In 1875,
Chisum sent 11,000 head of cattle over this
route—from Roswell to Las Cruces, then west to
Arizona, roughly paralleling present-day I-10.

Chisum's South Spring Ranch
NM 2, 6 miles south of Roswell
The ranch established in 1875 by John S. Chisum,
"Cattle King of the Pecos," to serve as headquar-
ters of his cattle-ranching empire, which extend-
ed 150 miles along the Pecos River. ◉

Downtown Roswell Historic District
West of the downtown business district
Developed as Roswell's premier residential area
in the late 19th and early 20th centuries, the
community attracted upper- and middle-class
people, including numerous prominent figures
in the city and state. ◉□

New Mexico Military Institute Historic District
West College Boulevard
Built from about 1909 through 1936, the cam-
pus illustrates a rare coherence of quality

architecture and planning: modified Gothic
Revival-style structures amid symmetrical quad-
rangles and formal axes. ◉□

PERFORMING ARTS

Roswell Community Little Theater
1101 North Virginia Avenue
505-622-1982
An amateur company that produces five plays
each September-through-early June season.

Roswell Symphony Orchestra
PO Box 2425, 88202
505-623-5882
Offers subscription concerts plus a chamber
series at Pearson Auditorium in a season running September through April. The orchestra
puts on a free Labor Day concert in the Spring
River Park and Zoo.

CULTURAL ORGANIZATIONS

Historical Society for Southeast New Mexico
200 North Lea Avenue, 88201
505-622-8333
Operates the Historical Center Museum.

LIBRARIES

Roswell Public Library
301 North Pennsylvania Avenue, 88201
505-622-3400

PUBLIC ART

Roswell Armory
Earl Cummins Loop
Joseph Wheeler
"Crossroad"—steel sculpture

Yucca Recreation Center
500 South Richardson Street
Stuart Ashman
"Sand Dragons"—wood sculptures

RUIDOSO

US 70 at NM 48
Originally known as Dowlin's Mill, the town was located on the Chisum Trial. The grounds of the mill formed the backdrop for such Lincoln County incidents as the murder of miller Paul Dowlin in April 1877. By 1885, the community had sprouted a store, a blacksmith shop, a post office, and a new name—after the fast-flowing stream called Ruidoso (Noisy) that ran into town out of the nearby mountains. Today, this ponderosa pine country is a year-round resort with special appeal to skiing and horse racing aficionados.

MUSEUMS AND EXHIBIT SPACES
Museum of the Horse
Ruidoso Downs Racetrack
PO Box 40, 88346
505-378-4142
Featuring Anne C. Stradling's collection of more than 10,000 carriages, saddles, and other horse-related artifacts, plus fine art by Charlie Russell and Frederic Remington. Fee.

HISTORIC BUILDINGS AND SITES
Dowlin's Old Mill
641 Sudderth Drive
505-257-2811
The grist mill built in 1853 by Paul Dowlin included a post office and a roadhouse. Among its notorious guests were Black Jack Pershing and Billy the Kid who, seeking refuge from gunmen, hid in one of the mill's flour barrels at the prelude to the Lincoln County War.

COMMUNITY EVENTS
Aspenfest
Downtown Ruidoso
800-253-2255
A chile cook-off, parade, antique car show, and arts and crafts fair on the first full weekend in October.

Christmas Jubilee
Ruidoso Civic Center
800-253-2255
An arts and crafts fair held in November.

Lincoln County Cowboy Symposium
Lincoln County Rural Events Center
US 70, 15 miles east of Ruidoso
PO Box 1679, Glencoe, 88346
505-378-4142
Cowboy poets, musicians, chuckwagon cooks, artisans, and storytellers in October. Fee.

Oktoberfest
Civic Events Center
800-253-2255
German food, folk dancing, and entertainment in late October. Fee.

Ruidoso Art Festival
Civic Events Center
505-257-7395
More than 125 professional artists exhibiting paintings, drawings, photography, glass work, porcelain work, woodwork, metalwork, jewelry, batik designs, pottery, weaving, fabric arts, leather work, and sculpture in late July.

LIBRARIES
Ruidoso Public Library
501 Junction Road
PO Box 3539, 88345
505-257-4335

TATUM

US 380 at NM 206
This agricultural town on the Llano Estacado
was established in 1909 when homesteader
James Tatum built a post office and general
store at the crossroads of a north-south cattle
trail and the route between Roswell and
Brownfield, Texas. The region's oil boom made
its last appearance at Tatum, resulting in the
drilling of a sizable well in the 1940s.

LIBRARIES
Tatum Community Library
216 East Broadway
PO Box 156, 88267
505-398-4822

TEXICO

US 70-84 at US 60
Soon after the Pecos Valley Railroad built a siding here in 1902, a small trading center for
ranchers evolved.

COMMUNITY EVENTS
Border Town Days
806-481-3681
A three-night event featuring a rodeo,
parade, barbecue, arts and crafts, and
water polo in late July.

HISTORIC BUILDINGS AND SITES
**Atchison, Topeka & Santa Fe Railway
Depot**
This Spanish-style depot with its red-tile roof
looks much as it did in 1908, when it was built.
It stands as one of the few visible reminders of
the railroad's Belén Cutoff. ☉

PUBLIC ART
Texico Welcome Center
US 70-84, on the Texas border
Dorothy Franklin
"Tres Ritos Fall"—oil painting
Peggy Jackson
"Heritage"—watercolor painting
Teresa Naggs
"Beaver Creek in the Gila Wilderness"—oil painting
Ginnie Seifert
"American Heritage"—watercolor painting

THREE RIVERS

US 54, 17 miles north of Tularosa
This Tularosa Basin country east of the great
lava flow known as El Malpais (The Badlands)
was part of a migratory route used by prehistoric Indians. In the late 1800s, it became a rail
station for the Three Rivers Ranch, where
owner Patrick Coghlan, "King of Tularosa,"
fenced cattle rustled by William Bonney (alias
Billy the Kid). Over the decades, the ranch land
played a prominent role in the cattle empires of
John S. Chisum; Susie McSween Barber, "Cattle
Queen of New Mexico"; and Senator Albert
Bacon Fall. In 1921, its mansion was the scene
of discussions erupting in the Teapot Dome
Scandal regarding oil-drilling contracts in
Wyoming. Over the past 100 years, Three Rivers
has been permeated by murder, suicide, and
financial ruin.

HISTORIC BUILDINGS AND SITES
Three Rivers Petroglyphs
County Road B-30, 3 miles east of Three Rivers
A mile-long array of thousands of pictures
pecked into the solid rock walls of a volcanic
ridge. The animal, human, and geometric forms
were most likely carved between AD 1000 and
AD 1400 by the Jornada branch of the prehistoric Mogollón Indians, whose partially
restored pueblo and pithouse dwellings are visible nearby. ◎

TULAROSA

US 54 at US 70
The first successful European settlement in the
lush, green Tularosa Basin dates back to 1862,
when 50 or 60 Hispanic farmers moved east
from the Río Grande Valley. Anglo settlement
began about 20 years later, as settlers and cattlemen from Texas began moving into New
Mexico. The town, also known as the City of
Roses, took its name from the Tularosa River
and the reddish-brown reeds growing in the
marshy lands along its banks. Tularosa's
farmlands and orchards form the landscape of
"Oasis" in the novels of Western writer Eugene
Manlove Rhodes.

MUSEUMS AND EXHIBIT SPACES
Tularosa Village Historical Museum
608 Central Avenue, 88352
505-585-2057
Displays prehistoric and historic pioneering
artifacts of the region.

HISTORIC BUILDINGS AND SITES
Round Mountain
US 70, 10 miles east of Tularosa
This cone-shaped landmark, once known as

COMMUNITY EVENTS
St. Francis de Paula Fiesta
St. Francis de Paula Church
303 Encino
505-585-2793
Festivities in commemoration of the settlers' 1868 battle against invading
Apaches include the crowning of the
queen, traditional street dancing,
games, food, and entertainment. Held in
mid-May.

Tularosa Rose Festival
505-585-2855
A four-day celebration of the blooming
of the roses, featuring a parade, concessions, crowning of the Rose Queen, and
a barbecue. Held in early May.

Dead Man's Hill, has been a backdrop for several military encounters. The most well-known
battle occurred in April 1868, when a small
group of soldiers and Tularosa settlers fought
off an attack by about 200 Mescalero Apache
Indians—a victory that protected the villagers
from further raids.

Tularosa Original Townsite Historic District
A 49-block area in the center of town
The village of Tularosa has come full circle
back to the peaceful farming town it was more
than 130 years ago. Many of its early homes are
still standing—small, simple, flat-roofed
adobes so well fortified that they have only tiny
"rifle holes" for windows. And St. Francis de
Paula Catholic Church, built in 1869 and
recently topped with a California-style tile roof,
remains the pride and joy of its parishioners.
◎□

WHITE OAKS

NM 349, 12 miles northeast of Carrizozo
Named in 1879 for the trees around its two springs, White Oaks was catapulted into prosperity with the discovery of gold and silver in its lithosphere. Within 25 years, the town had a population of more than 4,000—the largest in Lincoln County—as well as a school, churches, banks, four weekly newspapers, hotels, saloons, a casino, an opera house, and several bawdy houses. As the population began to dwindle in the early 20th century, the log-and-frame houses were torn down and used for fuel. Today, White Oaks is a ghost town. The old brick-and-stone structures are all that remain of the place that produced not only $3 million worth of gold and silver, but also the state's first governor, W. C. McDonald, and its first US marshal, Judge Andrew Hudspeth. ◉▢

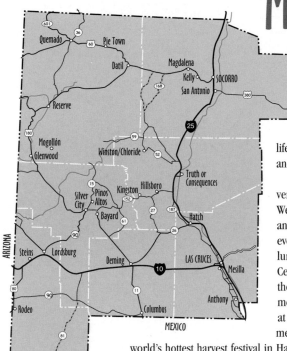

Much of southwestern New Mexico is undeveloped. In fact, the Gila Wilderness and adjoining Aldo Leopold Wilderness form the largest roadless area in the lower 48 states. Here, we find the hidden cliff dwellings of the ancient Mimbres people, who decorated pottery with strange astronomical symbols more than 1,000 years ago. Not far away are such historic buildings as the Pinos Altos Opera House, reminding us that life in the Old West had more to offer than horses and big hats.

Today, although many of the region's conventional cultural events take place around Western New Mexico State University in Silver City and New Mexico State University in Las Cruces, every town has its own special event designed to lure big-time crowds at least one weekend a year. Celebrations range from the graceful Festival of the Cranes at Bosque del Apache to the monumentally silly and fun Great American Duck Race at Deming. Who can resist the annual reenactment of Pancho Villa's invasion of Columbus, the world's hottest harvest festival in Hatch, the gathering of cowboy poets in Billy the Kid's boyhood home of Silver City, or the spectacle of a hungry mob devouring the world's largest enchilada in downtown Las Cruces?

ANTHONY

I-10 at NM 185, 25 miles south of Las Cruces
The Mesilla Valley site that was to become Anthony lay three miles east of the Camino Real (Royal Road), the 16th-century connecting link between Mexico and Santa Fe. Centuries of Apache raids kept the area free from settlement and, until the Gadsden Purchase of 1853, part of Mexico. The town was established about 20 miles north of El Paso just after the 1881 arrival of the Santa Fe Railway and the subsequent con-

struction of a small chapel dedicated to St. Anthony. Today, the cotton-growing and -processing center of Anthony serves as a southern gateway into New Mexico.

LIBRARIES
Valley Public Library
136 North Main Street
PO Box 1476, 88021
505-886-2439

BAYARD

US 180, 9 miles east of Silver City
Mogollón Indians lived in the area before departing in the 12th century. In the late 19th

A pilgrimage to Tortugas Mountain highlights the Our Lady of Guadalupe Festival in Las Cruces. Photograph by Charles Mann

century, the region was an Apache stronghold defended by Victorio and Gerónimo. Resettled in the 1880s as a residential community for miners working in nearby Santa Rita, Bayard today lies in a still active commercial mining region.

HISTORIC BUILDINGS AND SITES
Fort Bayard
US 180 at NM 152, 7 miles east of Silver City
Fort Bayard, established on the frontier in 1863 to protect settlers and miners from Apache attacks, was a base of operations for Company B of the Black 125th Infantry and for Lieutenant John J. Pershing. The fort became a military hospital in 1900, and today serves as Fort Bayard Medical Center.

Fort Bayard National Cemetery
US 180 at NM 152, 7 miles east of Silver City
Established in 1866 as the military cemetery for Fort Bayard, the graveyard became a burial ground for troopers, veterans, and civilians. It was designated one of New Mexico's two national cemeteries in 1973; the other is in Santa Fe.

LIBRARIES
Bayard Public Library
525 Central
Drawer T, 88023
505-537-6244

Rural Bookmobile Southwest
PO Box 36669, 88036
505-537-5121

PUBLIC ART
Fort Bayard Medical Center
Greg Whipple
"Buffalo Soldier"—bronze sculpture

CHLORIDE

NM 52, 42 miles northwest of Truth or Consequences
Chloride, founded in 1879, when mule skinner Henry Pye struck a silver lode here, was named for the character of the ore he unearthed. Soon, gold and copper were discovered as well. The ranching and mining settlers held horse and burro races, tangled with bears, even tarred and feathered a fellow villager. In the early 1900s, amid the waning silver supply, the declining price of silver, and a persistent range war between sheep and cattle ranchers, the town faded into near oblivion. Although present-day Chloride is considered a ghost town, it harbors a few residents.

COLUMBUS

NM 11, 32 miles south of Deming
Scene of the only attack on the United States mainland by a foreign power. On the moonless night of March 9, 1916, Mexican revolutionary Francisco "Pancho" Villa crossed the international border with about 1,000 guerrilla fighters, attacking and looting the railroad town of Columbus. The invasion—reputedly timed to ambush a trainload of gold, which turned out to be coal—resulted in the death of 18 United States soldiers and civilians and approximately 100 Villistas. Following the guerrillas' retreat, General John J. "Black Jack" Pershing led expeditionary forces into Mexico in pursuit of Villa, which, although unsuccessful, constituted the world's first military use of air power and motorized equipment.

Pancho Villa's 1916 raid left Columbus in smoking ruins. Photograph by W. H. Horne Co., courtesy Museum of New Mexico, neg. 5805

MUSEUMS AND EXHIBIT SPACES
Columbus Historical Museum (formerly Southern Pacific Railroad Depot)
PO Box 562, 88029
505-531-2620
The old depot, built in 1902, houses artifacts associated with the Pancho Villa raid, old railroad days, and other aspects of local history.

Pancho Villa State Park
NM 11, 35 miles south of Deming
505-531-2711
New Mexico's southernmost park—established in 1959 to commemorate the promise of cooperation between the United States and Mexico. The park encompasses a campground and a botanical garden filled with varieties of Chihuahuan Desert cactus.

HISTORIC BUILDINGS AND SITES
Camp Furlong
Site of the shattering attack by Pancho Villa and his horsemen in March 1916, Camp Furlong went on to serve as a base of operations for the United States retaliatory raids into Mexico. The tent fort, containing a few adobe buildings and a cement ditch, was the first military airfield in the country and home to the 1st Aero Squadron, which provided support for Pershing's ground troops of 6,000 men. ◑▢

LIBRARIES
Columbus Village Library
Main Street
PO Box 350, 88029
505-531-2612

DEMING

I-70 at US 180
In the 1770s, Governor Juan Bautista de Anza passed by this area while searching for a trade route to Santa Fe from the mines of Sonora, Mexico. Deming was founded more than a century later in 1881, when the Santa Fe and Southern Pacific rail lines were connected, giving New Mexico its first railway access to both the Atlantic and Pacific coasts. Immediately, the rip-roaring railroad town was dominated by desperadoes. Cattle ranching and irrigated farming took hold soon afterward, cultivated by the Mimbres River that coursed underground through the region. One of two towns in Luna County, Deming boasts desert fields of lettuce, cotton, and grains, and one of the world's largest crops of chile.

MUSEUMS AND EXHIBIT SPACES
Deming/Luna Mimbres Museum
301 South Silver Avenue
PO Box 1617, 88030
505-546-2382

A historical museum with more than 22,000 square feet dedicated to toys and dolls from 1850 through the present; Mimbres pottery and other Indian artifacts; minerals and rocks; objects left by early settlers; military memorabilia; a special Hispanic display; collections of antique glass, china, silver, quilts, lace, and old vehicles; and a reconstructed street scene.

HISTORIC BUILDINGS AND SITES
Cooke's Wagon Road
I-10, between Deming and Lordsburg
In 1846, while leading the Mormon Battalion to California to support the Mexican War troops, Lieutenant Colonel Philip St. George Cooke blazed the first wagon road from New Mexico to the West Coast, entering Arizona through the Guadalupe Pass. The route's potential for railroad construction helped inspire the Gadsden Purchase of 1854.

Deming Armory
Silver Avenue and Hemlock Street
A structure built from 1915 to 1916 in response to the Mexican Revolution across the

COMMUNITY EVENTS
Arts in the Park
Courthouse Park
505-546-3663
Free music, dance, and art materials for children. The program, sponsored by the Deming Arts Council, is held on Sunday afternoons in July.

Deming Arts and Crafts Fair
Courthouse Park
800-848-4955
A large show of work by local and out-of-town

participants, plus refreshment booths and entertainment. Held in early June.

Fiddlers' Contest
Hospitality House, 1.5 miles east of Country Club Road
505-546-9729
A two-day competition in early May.

Great American Duck Race
State Fairgrounds
800-848-4955
The world's richest duck races, combined with

nearby border and the growing war in Europe. The armory is now home to the Deming/Luna Mimbres Museum. ☺☐

Deming Coaling Tower
First Street, 75 yards east of the Southern Pacific Railroad Depot
The tower, built in 1926 by the Southern Pacific Railroad, is a vestigial reminder of the peak years of coal-fired steam locomotives. ☺

Fort Cummings
NM 26, 20 miles north of Deming
Established in 1862, the fort protected the Butterfield stage route between San Diego, California, and San Antonio, Texas. In the 1860s and again in the early 1880s, the military post was used as a base of operations in the Apache Wars against Cochise, Victorio, and Gerónimo. ☺

Seaman Field House
304 Silver Avenue
The home of Judge Seaman Field, constructed in the late 1800s, became what is today considered the oldest customs house in New Mexico. ☺☐

Silver Avenue Historic District
Silver Avenue, between Pine and Spruce Streets
The district, composed primarily of red brick buildings, was under construction between 1886 and 1917. Silver Avenue was the most important thoroughfare in the early history of this railroading town. ☺

PERFORMING ARTS
Deming Center for the Arts
100 South Gold Street
PO Box 1845, 88031
505-546-3663
Hosts chamber music concerts, small dance company performances, and poetry and fiction readings by local writers.

Deming Theatre Company
100 South Gold Street
PO Box 1845, 88031
505-546-3663

entertainment, flea market booths, hot-air balloon races, dances, and a tortilla toss. Held in late August.

Klobase Festival
Courthouse Park
505-546-9074
An October feast featuring Bohemian smoked sausage, barbecued beef, salads, beans, cakes, and pies. Sponsored by the local Czech community.

Rockhound Roundup
State Fairgrounds
505-546-8411
More than 500 rockhounds from 41 states participate in mid-March rock trips, auctions, and judging seminars. A snack bar and free camping are available.

Southwestern New Mexico State Fair
State Fairgrounds
800-848-4955
A livestock competition, rodeo, parade, and carnival. Held in late September or early October.

CULTURAL ORGANIZATIONS

Deming Arts Council
100 South Gold Street
PO Box 1845, 88031
505-546-3663
This nonprofit organization sponsors exhibitions, performances, workshops, and literary events by locally and nationally known people in the arts.

Luna County Historical Society
301 South Silver Avenue, 88031
505-546-2382
Operates the Deming/Luna Mimbres Museum.

LIBRARIES

Deming Public Library
301 South Tin Avenue, 88030
505-546-9202

PUBLIC ART

Deming Post Office
209 West Spruce Street
Kenneth M. Adams
"Mountains and Yucca"—mural
New Deal Art

Deming State Police Building
3000 East Highway 80
Gary Yazzie
"Colors of the Dance"—watercolor painting

GLENWOOD

US 180, 50 miles north of Silver City
Glenwood, on the west side of the Gila Wilderness—home to the Mogollón culture from 300 BC to AD 1500—was revitalized as a mining camp in the 1870s, when gold and silver were discovered in the Mogollón Mountains. The small town is now populated by ranchers, farmers, and vacationers.

LIBRARIES

Glenwood Community Center Library
PO Box 144, 88039
505-539-2686

HATCH

I-25 at NM 26, 35 miles north of Las Cruces
Originally established as Santa Barbara in 1851, the community was evacuated until 1853, when Fort Thorne was built to protect settlers from Apache raids. Abandoned again in 1860, after the fort closed, the town was reoccupied in 1875 and renamed for General Edward Hatch, commander of the New Mexico Military District. "Hatch's Station" later became a stop on the Santa Fe Railway's Rincon to Deming run. Today, the farming community on the Río Grande is considered the chile capital of the world.

LIBRARIES

Hatch Public Library
503 East Hall Street
PO Box 289, 87937
505-267-5132

COMMUNITY EVENTS

Hatch Chile Festival
Hatch Airport
NM 26, 2 miles west of Hatch
505-267-5050
Arts and crafts, food booths, a sidewalk sale, carnival, dancing, and music on Labor Day weekend.

PUBLIC ART
Hatch Public Library
503 East Hall Street
Samson Chavez
"Whirling Logs No. 5"—Navajo sandpainting
Robert E. Marshall
"Florida Mountains" and "Southern Río
Grande"—watercolor paintings
Jo Roduin
"La Familia"—acrylic painting

HILLSBORO

NM 152, 17 miles west of I-25
This small town set in the Percha Creek Valley
was the center of a productive gold and silver
mining district in the late 1800s. At the time, a
colorful hotel-brothel was run on Shady Lane by
Madame Sadie Orchard, who had moved here
from London. The community continued as a
small commercial center for cattle ranching and
eventually a haven for artists and craftmakers.

MUSEUMS AND EXHIBIT SPACES
Black Range Museum
NM 152
PO Box 454, 88042
505-895-5233
A privately owned history museum with mining
artifacts and other pre-19th-century area relics.

COMMUNITY EVENTS
Hillsboro Apple Festival
Downtown area
PO Box 155, 88042
505-895-5328
An arts and crafts show, food, and enter-
tainment on Labor Day weekend.

The building was originally the Ocean Grove
Hotel, owned by Madame Sadie Orchard, and
later the Chinaman's Cafe.

KELLY

US 60, 29 miles west of Socorro
A long-lived mining town, Kelly—named for
sawmill owner and miner Andy Kelly—yielded
more than $28.4 million worth of lead, zinc,
silver, copper, and gold between 1866 and
1945. Situated just south of the ranch town of
Magdalena, Kelly was frequently attacked by
Apaches staking claim to their territory and by
Magdalena cowboys keen on shootouts. Today,
the town lies abandoned—bearing few
reminders of its seven saloons, two hotels, two
dance halls, two churches, and countless ore
wagons used to haul the lodes' yields to the
Magdalena depot for smelting at Socorro.

KINGSTON

NM 152, 26 miles west of I-25
Within three months of the discovery of a rich
lode of silver in August 1882, Kingston expanded from a tent city to a townsite of 1,800 residents. Despite flying bullets and raids led by
Apache war chief Victorio, the town flourished.
By the mid-1880s, the population numbered
about 7,000 and the streets were bustling with
22 saloons, several dance halls, a popular theater, and the Victorio Hotel—a landmark in the
territory of New Mexico. Although more than
$10 million in silver and other minerals were
removed from its mines, Kingston now lies
silent in the foothills of the rugged Black
Range.

MUSEUMS AND EXHIBIT SPACES
Percha Valley Bank Museum
Displays mining artifacts and antiques in one of the ghost town's finest old stone structures. ◉

LAS CRUCES

I-25 at I-10

From the 1500s until the mid-1800s, the land sheltered between two mountain ranges in the heart of the Mesilla Valley was a camping and resting place for Camino Real travelers: explorers such as Don Juan de Oñate, colonists, foot soldiers, padres, conquistadores, and oxcart caravan drivers. In 1849, after the Mexican War, the fertile valley land—newly designated as United States territory—was surveyed, and a townsite was established near a large cluster of weathered crosses marking the graves of 40 travelers from Taos who had been killed by Apaches while camping in the area the year before. The town was named Las Cruces (The Crosses). With the arrival of the Santa Fe Railway in 1881, Las Cruces burst into life as a leading agricultural and ranching center. Over time, vestiges of the Camino Real gave way to extensive pecan orchards and fields of cotton, onions, alfalfa, chile, and other fruits and vegetables. County seat and headquarters of New Mexico State University, Las Cruces is today the largest city in southern New Mexico.

MUSEUMS AND EXHIBIT SPACES
Bicentennial Log Cabin Museum
Downtown Mall
106 West Hadley Avenue, 88001
505-524-1422
This 1850 log cabin, relocated from nearby Grafton, houses local history exhibits.

Branigan Cultural Center
Downtown Mall
106 West Hadley Avenue, 88001
505-524-1422
Hosts visual arts exhibitions, recitals and performances, classes for children and adults, and outreach art classes for public school students. Permanent collections focus on regional history, textiles, and Victorian artifacts.

Farm/Ranch Heritage Museum
PO Drawer BB, 88004
505-524-6081
Still in the planning stages, the museum will celebrate the role of agriculture in the development of New Mexico. The facility will inventory significant historical farms and ranches and will exhibit important artifacts. Presentation themes will include the history of agriculture in New Mexico, cultural adaptations to agriculture, and the science and technology of agriculture. A part of the New Mexico Office of Cultural Affairs.

Fort Selden State Monument
Radium Springs
I-25, 16 miles north of Las Cruces
505-526-8911
This frontier fort—now reduced to crumbling adobe walls—was the boyhood home of General Douglas MacArthur, whose father commanded the Army post from 1884 to 1886. The base was used between 1865 and 1891 to protect wagon and rail traffic in the Mesilla Valley. A museum beside the old corrals portrays the territorial life of the troops stationed here and presents a living-history program demonstrating the arms and equipage of the period. Leasburg State Park campground adjoins the monument. A part of the Museum of New Mexico. ◉☐

A chef flattens the tortilla for the world's largest enchilada at Las Cruces's Whole Enchilada Fiesta. Photograph by Mark Nohl

Las Cruces Museum of Natural History
Mesilla Valley Mall
700 Telshor Boulevard, 88011
505-522-3120
A city-funded facility depicting the natural science and history of southwestern New Mexico. The museum offers exhibits, field trips, family nights, and a children's natural history newspaper.

New Mexico State University Art Gallery
Williams Hall
New Mexico State University
PO Box 30001, 88003
505-646-2545
Features changing exhibitions of contemporary and folk art as well as a permanent collection of Mexican *retablos* (altar screens), contemporary prints, and photography. Programs include visiting artists and critics, films, and workshops.

New Mexico State University Museum
Kent Hall
New Mexico State University
PO Box 3564, 88003
505-646-3739
Displays prehistoric and historic American Indian artifacts primarily from the Southwest, including pottery, basketry, beadwork, rugs, and chipped and ground stone. Programs include guided tours, field trips, a lecture series, workshops, and educational outreach to schools.

HISTORIC BUILDINGS AND SITES

Alameda Depot Historic District
Las Cruces Avenue, west of the Downtown Mall
Portrays the architectural fashions brought into
town with the coming of the railroad around
1881. The district retains its historical character as well as its early gardens, trees, and
broad, grassy lawns. ◎▢

Amador Hotel
Amador and Water Streets
Built in 1850 by Don Martín Amador, the hotel
provided lodging to such luminaries as Mexico's
president Benito Juárez, sheriff Pat Garrett, and
Billy the Kid. Now home to the Doña Ana county
manager's complex, the old house has had several of its rooms restored and equipped with
period furniture and artifacts. ◎

Brazito Battlefield
I-10, 20 miles south of Las Cruces
One of the few battles of the Mexican War
fought in New Mexico occurred near here on
Christmas Day, 1846. United States troops
under Colonel Alexander W. Doniphan defeated
a Mexican army commanded by General
Antonio Ponce de León. Two days later,
Doniphan entered El Paso without opposition.

The Camino Real
Extending north-south through Las Cruces
A portion of the Royal Road that once spanned
more than 2,000 miles from Mexico City to Taos.
Although segments of the Camino Real were tra-
versed by Spanish explorers in the 1580s, it was
formally established in 1598 by Don Juan de
Oñate, New Mexico's first colonizer and governor.
Traveling north with his caravan of 129 men, many
of whom had brought along their families and servants, Oñate designated official *parajes* (campsites) along the trail, most of which were used by

subsequent expeditions. Oñate's colonizing expedition entered the Las Cruces area in May 1598.

Jornada del Muerto on the Camino Real
I-25, north of Las Cruces
This stretch of the Camino Real left the Río
Grande and cut north and south across 90
miles of desert. Despite its lack of water and
shelter, the dreaded Journey of the Dead Man
was heavily used by Spanish, Mexican, and
Anglo caravans traveling between El Paso and
settlements in northern New Mexico.

Mesquite Street Original Townsite
Historic District
Mesquite Street area
These remnants of the original townsite of Las
Cruces reveal the Spanish-Mexican-American
architectural styles that emerged with the influx
of early settlers. The low, flat-roofed adobes,
built between 1870 and 1930, represent the
largest surviving group of historic structures in
Las Cruces. ◎▢

Mormon Battalion Route
I-25, north of Las Cruces
The Mormon Battalion, composed of 500 volunteers, left Council Bluffs, Iowa, in June 1846
to join Brigadier General Kearny's expeditionary
force in the Mexican War. The battalion followed the Santa Fe Trail to Santa Fe, then the
Río Grande to this point, where the troops
turned west. The 2,000-mile march ended in
San Diego, California, in January 1847.

Nestor Armijo House
Lohman Avenue at Church Street
This pitched-roof adobe with rich Victorian trim-
mings was the first two-story home in Las Cruces.
Built during the 1870s by affluent rancher and
merchant Nestor Armijo, the virtually unmodified

building epitomizes the Victorian adobe tastes of a 19th-century *rico* (wealthy man). ⊙☐

Old Armijo Gallagher House
Lohman Avenue
A restored 1874 home, with many of its original furnishings on view on the second floor. The house, now serving as a savings and loan bank, is open to the public during business hours. ⊙☐

Our Lady at the Foot of the Cross Shrine
Water Street at Lohman Avenue
This reproduction of Michelangelo's Pietà was dedicated to the Sisters of Loretto, who established Santa Fe's Loretto Academy in 1875.

Tortugas
South Main Street at Tortugas Drive
According to local legend, the people who settled the village of Tortugas (Turtle) were Tiwa-speaking members of Isleta Pueblo who, taken from their home near Albuquerque during the Pueblo Revolt of 1680, were transplanted to this southwestern region. Present-day Tortugas is predominantly Hispanic, although the villagers' Tiwa chants and ceremonies reflect their Indian ancestry.

PERFORMING ARTS

American Southwest Honor Band
New Mexico State University Music Recital Hall
505-646-2421
A gathering of New Mexico's best high school band members for workshops and performances in early February.

American Southwest Theater Company
New Mexico State University
PO Box 3072, 88003
505-646-4517
A semiprofessional theater company initiated by Tony Award-winner Mark Medoff.

Ballet Folklorico de la Tierra del Encanto
Branigan Cultural Center
106 West Hadley Avenue, 88001
505-524-1422
The group, directed by José Tena, preserves regional Mexican dances through workshops and performances.

Big Band on the Río Grande
725 South Solano Drive, 88001
505-524-7176
Features big band and dance music of the thirties, forties, and fifties.

Chamber Players de Las Cruces
New Mexico State University Music Recital Hall
PO Box 3F, 88003
505-646-3709
This small professional organization offers a chamber music series in the spring and fall.

Doña Ana Lyric Opera
New Mexico State University Music Recital Hall
505-646-1986
Presents a spring and fall season performance series.

Doña Ana Youth Choir
3135 Executive Hills Road, 88005
505-522-6219
This choir for children ages 7 to 13 presents annual Christmas and spring performances.

Las Cruces Chamber Ballet
New Mexico State University Music Recital Hall
PO Box 2107, 88004
505-522-6219
Stages winter and spring performances, as well as ballet demonstrations in the elementary schools.

Las Cruces Community Theater
313 North Downtown Mall
PO Box 1281, 88004
505-523-1200
Produces six or seven musicals, comedies, and
dramas in a season running September to June.
The group also organizes an Ides of March
Festival featuring one-act plays by school and
community theater groups.

Las Cruces Symphony
New Mexico State University
PO Box 3F, 88003
505-646-3709
A local orchestra offering a subscription series.

Mesilla Valley Chorale
2713 Claude Dove Drive, 88001
505-522-4362
This community choir presents spring and winter
holiday concerts of classical and light-classical
music at the Northminster Presbyterian Church.

Mesilla Valley Community Band
New Mexico State University Music Recital Hall
505-646-2421
Performs classical, traditional, and march
music.

Mesilla Valley Saxophone Quartet
725 South Solano Drive, 88001
505-524-7176
Presents performances of classical and contemporary music for saxophone; lectures; and
recitals.

New Mexico State University Jazz Festival
New Mexico State University Music Recital Hall
505-646-2304
An April event featuring high school jazz bands
from throughout the state.

Tournament of Bands
New Mexico State University Music Recital Hall
505-646-2421
An awards competition among more than 30 high
school marching bands from the southwestern United
States. Held in late October or early November.

COMMUNITY EVENTS

ACT Children's Theatre of the Mesilla Valley
3398 Paradise Lane
PO Box 3416, 88003
505-527-1515
A nonprofit group offering Halloween and
spring performances; bilingual productions;
dance, acting, and voice classes for children;
plus a video for classroom viewing.

Arte Picante Feria
Young Park , PO Box 1721, 88004
505-523-6403

An open-air fair featuring arts and crafts,
entertainment, a *mercado* (market), and family activities on the last weekend in April.

Our Lady of Guadalupe Festival
South Main Street at Tortugas Drive
505-526-8171
A pilgrimage to Tortugas Mountain, followed by
a Mass by firelight and torchlight descent, a
Matachines Dance, and other entertainment.
The festival commemorates three appearances
of Mexico's patron saint, Our Lady of
Guadalupe, to Aztec Indian Juan Diego on a hill

University Singers and Concert Choir
New Mexico State University Music Recital Hall
505-646-2421
The university student and faculty choir presents spring and fall concerts.

Voz Vaqueros: The Singing Men of Las Cruces
PO Box 1688, 88004
505-525-8333
Founded in 1971, this community-based men's chorus performs show tunes, plus classical, country-western, and sacred music for the Christmas and Easter holidays at St. Paul's United Methodist Church and Young Park.

CULTURAL ORGANIZATIONS

Doña Ana Arts Council
132 West Las Cruces Street
PO Box 1721, 88004
505-523-6403
Sponsors children's programs, the Renaissance Craftfaire, Arte Picante Feria, seminars and workshops for artists, concerts, and outreach programs for Hispanic artists as well as adults with developmental disabilities. The Council also pro-

vides assistance to nonprofit groups and advocacy information to arts-based organizations.

Las Cruces Arts and Crafts Association
PO Box 1132, 88004
505-523-7024
Promotes fine arts and crafts through workshops, a major show in May, and supportive outreach to public schools.

Las Cruces Community Concert Association
PO Box 118, 88004
505-524-7568
Offers a subscription series of three to five classical music productions.

Potter's Guild of Las Cruces
PO Box 2334, 88004
505-522-3765
Programs include education workshops; an all-clay ceramic juried exhibition; a mid-December Christmas sale; and Empty Bowls, an international effort to help diminish world hunger.

outside Mexico City in 1531. Held December 10th through 12th.

Renaissance Craftfaire
Young Park
PO Box 1721, 88004
505-523-6403
One of the largest cultural events in southern New Mexico, showcasing 160 artisans in a Renaissance-style arts and crafts fair, Society for Creative Anachronism exhibition tournaments, and other entertainment the first full weekend in November. Fee.

Southern New Mexico State Fair
State Fairgrounds, 13 miles west of Las Cruces
505-524-1968
Livestock and agricultural displays, a rodeo, food booths, and contests in late September.

Whole Enchilada Fiesta
Downtown Mall
505-524-1968
The world's largest enchilada, a parade, arts and crafts, food, dances, and entertainment. Held the first weekend in October.

Río Grande Recorder Society
4460 Falcon Drive, 88011
505-522-4178
The local chapter of the American Recorder
Society presents workshops, performances, and
preclassical music concerts.

LIBRARIES
Thomas Branigan Memorial Library
200 East Picacho Avenue, 88001
505-526-1047

New Mexico State University Library
Breland Drive and McFie Circle
PO Box 30006, 88003
505-646-1508

PUBLIC ART
Branigan Cultural Center
106 West Hadley Avenue
Tom Lea
"The First Book about New Mexico: 1610"—
mural
New Deal Art
Danny Morales
Evolution mural
Beverly Penn
Steel piece

Thomas Branigan Memorial Library
200 East Picacho Avenue
Glenn Schweiger
Mirrored piece

Downtown Mall
Main and Water Streets
Tony Pennock
New Mexico Boys Ranch mural

First National Bank Building
500 South Main Street
Manuel Acosta
Historical mural

Mesilla Park
South Main Street
Glenn Schweiger
Interactive sculpture

**Mesilla Valley Hospital, Missouri Avenue
Fire Station**
3751 Del Ray Boulevard
Felix Carrion
Sculpture and mural

New Mexico State University Biology Building
Olive Rush
Dome fresco
New Deal Art

New Mexico State University Branson Hall Library
Grant Kinser
"The Joy of Learning"—bronze sculpture

New Mexico State University Business College
Duke Sundt
"Conquistador, Cowboy, and Indian"—bronze
sculpture

**New Mexico State University Corbett
Center—Jacobs and Hadley Halls**
Ken Barrick
Murals

New Mexico State University Library
Federico Armijo
"A Quest for Knowledge"—sculpture

New Mexico State University Speech and English Building
Sol Lewitt
"A square within which are horizontal parallel lines . . ."—concrete sculpture

Young Park
Walnut Street
Clifford Flint
Sculpture

LORDSBURG

I-10 at NM 90
In 1850, California-bound gold-seekers followed an Apache trail leading to a rare water hole about two miles south of the present site of Lordsburg. The Butterfield Overland Mail Company followed the same trail between 1858 and 1861. Soon the "oasis" known as Mexican Springs, and later Shakespeare, gave rise to a small settlement. The 1880 laying of tracks for the Southern Pacific Railroad along the often used route sparked the founding of Lordsburg, which eventually absorbed most of Shakespeare's population. The town's airport was officially dedicated by Charles Lindbergh during his 1932 cross-country flight in the *Spirit of Saint Louis.* County seat of Hidalgo County and port-of-entry into the state's sparsely populated "bootheel" region, Lordsburg has become an active mining and agricultural arena.

HISTORIC BUILDINGS AND SITES
Clanton Gang Hideout
NM 338, south of I-10
The site of two crude dugouts used by the infamous Clanton gang in the 1880s. The hideout served as a base for wide-ranging outlaw activities, including depredations along nearby Smugglers Trail.

Hidalgo Hotel
328 East Motel Drive
This 1928 hotel was designed by El Paso architect Henry Trost, who had studied with Frank Lloyd Wright. The Mission Revival-style building was the town's commercial and social hub for more than 40 years, until its closing in the 1970s. ☉

Lordsburg Coaling Tower
100 yards east of the Southern Pacific Railroad Depot
The thick-walled tower—one of the few remaining railroad coaling facilities in the West—served the Southern Pacific Railway from 1926 until 1951. ☉

Smugglers Trail
NM 338, 40 miles south of I-10
A late-19th-century trade route used by mule trains of contraband headed from Mexico to Arizona. In the summer of 1881, a group of Mexican smugglers was killed in nearby Skeleton Canyon by members of the Clanton gang, including Old Man Clanton, Ike and Billy Clanton, and Curly Bill Brocius. Old Man Clanton was ambushed south of the border in revenge for the massacre.

CULTURAL ORGANIZATIONS
Chiricahua Guild in Rodeo
PO Box 162, Rodeo, 88056
505-557-2291
Sponsors workshops and other development programs for local artists, and operates a cooperative art gallery featuring members' work.

LIBRARIES
Lordsburg-Hidalgo Public Library
208 East Third Street, 88045
505-542-9646

MAGDALENA

US 60, 27 miles west of Socorro
Mineral-rich Magdalena, at the base of a peak topped with a shale formation resembling Mary Magdalen, teemed with silver mining in the 1860s. In 1884, when a railroad was built from town to a smelter in Socorro, Magdalena became a railhead not only for ore but for cattle and sheep as well. Each year, hundreds of thousands of cattle trod the wooden windmill-dotted Magdalena Cattle Drive Trail across the San Agustín Plains from St. Johns, Arizona. In time, the town at the eastern end of the plains became one of the rowdiest and largest cattle-shipping centers in the Southwest. Today it is a retreat for tourists, hunters, hikers, and rockhounds. ◉☐

HISTORIC BUILDINGS AND SITES
Atchison, Topeka & Santa Fe Railway Depot
108 North Main Street
PO Box 86, 87825
505-854-2719
Terminus of an Atchison, Topeka & Santa Fe Railway spur constructed in 1884 to tap the lucrative freight business from western New Mexico's growing mine and livestock interests. The long, narrow, one-story frame depot now houses municipal offices and a community library. A nearby boxcar displays historic artifacts from Magdalena and the deserted mining town of Kelly. ◉☐

Council Rock Ruins
US 60 to State Road 176 to Forest Road 10, 12 miles west of Magdalena
Anasazi Indian ruins dating back to the 17th century.

COMMUNITY EVENTS
Alamo Indian Day
Alamo Navajo Indian Reservation
NM 169, 32 miles northwest of Magdalena
505-854-2686
A parade, arts and crafts exhibits, native food, dancers, and singers in early October.

Magdalena Old-Timers' Reunion
Salome Store
505-854-2341
A rodeo, parade, flower show, dance, and arts and crafts on the weekend following the Fourth of July.

CULTURAL ORGANIZATIONS
Magdalena Mountain Mail
PO Box 86, 87825
505-854-2719
Publishes a monthly historical newspaper with reprints from old papers and articles by and about old-timers in the area.

LIBRARIES
Magdalena Community Library
108 North Main Street
PO Box 86, 87825
505-854-2261

PUBLIC ART
Rodeo Grounds
Holly Hughes and *Pat Beck*
Rodeo gate—adobe and found objects

MESILLA

NM 28, 1.5 miles southwest of Las Cruces
Settled by members of Don Juan de Oñate's
1598 colonizing expedition, Mesilla has had a
colorful and variegated history. In 1854—after
the village had experienced more than 250
years of Spanish, then Mexican, rule—the
Gadsden Purchase was signed on the Mesilla
Plaza, turning the southern strip of the New
Mexico Territory over to the United States. For a
period of time in 1861, the crossroads community connecting the Camino Real with the
Butterfield Overland Stagecoach route served as
western headquarters of the Confederacy. Then,
in 1881, Billy the Kid was convicted of murder
here and sentenced to hang in Lincoln. The
charm and slow-paced ambiance of Old Mesilla
endure, as does its mission church, dedicated
to San Albino in 1851, among the longest-
standing missions in the region. ☺□△

MUSEUMS AND EXHIBIT SPACES
Gadsden Museum
Barker Road at NM 28
PO Box 147, 88046
505-526-6293
A privately owned history museum focusing on
local Indian and Spanish-Mexican artifacts. Fee.

HISTORIC BUILDINGS AND SITES
Butterfield Trail
Parallels I-10 to Deming
Stagecoaches of the Butterfield Overland Mail
Company began carrying passengers and mail
across this portion of southern New Mexico in
1858. The 2,795-mile journey from St. Louis to
San Francisco took between 21 and 22 days. In
1861, service was rerouted through Salt Lake City.
☺

Fountain Theater
1 block south of Mesilla Plaza
Originally a vaudeville house built in 1905 by
the Fountain family. According to legend, the
old theater is haunted by the ghost of a frustrat-
ed actress.

San Albino Church
Mesilla Plaza
One of the oldest missions in the Mesilla Valley,
San Albino was established by order of the
Mexican government in 1851. In 1906, after the
old adobe church had crumbled, the present
building was constructed on its foundations. The
bells of San Albino date back to the early 1870s.

CULTURAL ORGANIZATIONS
Mesilla Valley Film Society
PO Box 1139, 88046
505-524-8287
Sponsors daily showings of alternative art and
documentary films in the historic Fountain
Theater. The society also hosts a speakers
series and monthly audience discussion nights.

MOGOLLÓN

NM 159, 9 miles east of US 180
For 60 years beginning in the late 1870s,
Mogollón was known far and near as one of the
most wide-open towns in the West. Situated on the
banks of Silver Creek, it counted among its 2,000
residents Butch Cassidy and his crowd, gunmen,
claim jumpers, and gamblers. Neither Apache war
chiefs Victorio and Gerónimo nor troops sent in
by the governor could tame the lawlessness. An
estimated $19.5 million in gold, silver, and copper
came from Mogollón's mines which now, like the
town, lie largely abandoned. ☺□

MUSEUMS AND EXHIBIT SPACES
Mogollón Museum
NM 159
Offers a local history exhibit with mining arti-facts.

PIE TOWN

US 60, 83 miles west of Socorro
Named for its famous pies, this homesteading highway town was built during the 1930s by refugees from the dust bowls of Kansas and Oklahoma. Although the town's log and adobe buildings are crumbling, pies are still available from time to time.

PINOS ALTOS

NM 15, 7 miles north of Silver City
Pinos Altos (Tall Pines) was Apache country until the 1860s, when Anglos invaded and began mining gold—guardedly—in its moun-tains. By 1868, the town's 3,000 inhabitants had witnessed scores of attacks by Apache patrol forces; a major sweep of the area by 500 war-riors led by Mangas Coloradas and Cochise; the death of Mangas Coloradas at nearby Fort West; and a series of Navajo-assisted raids. In time, the Indian threat diminished, whereupon the mining enterprise expanded to include silver, copper, lead, and zinc. The ores played out in the 1920s, as did the life of the town on the southern edge of the Gila Wilderness. ◑□

MUSEUMS AND EXHIBIT SPACES
Grant County Art Guild (formerly Hearst Church)
Gold Avenue
The adobe Methodist-Episcopal church, built in 1898, was dedicated to the memory of William Randolph Hearst's father, who struck

it rich in the Pinos Altos gold mines. The funeral hearse of Billy the Kid's slayer Pat Garrett and other horse-drawn vehicles are on display.

Pinos Altos Museum
33 Main Street
PO Box 53083, 88053
505-388-1882
A history museum specializing in local artifacts.

HISTORIC BUILDINGS AND SITES
McDonald Cabin
Spring Street
Indian fighter John McDonald was in this area as early as 1851, before the discovery of gold or the founding of the town. His log cabin is considered the oldest in Grant County.

Pinos Altos Opera House
34 Main Street
Built in 1969 and styled after an Old West opera house, the facility is composed of ele-ments from local historic buildings, includ-ing those that once dominated the Hudson Street red-light district of Silver City. On dis-play are a collection of Mimbres pottery, many excellent artifacts, and old mining photographs.

Santa Rita del Cobre Fort & Trading Post
25 Main Street
Completed in 1980, this is a three-quarter scale reproduction of the fort built at Santa Rita cop-per mine in 1804 to protect the area from Apaches. The stronghold was renamed Fort Webster in 1851.

RESERVE

NM 12, 7 miles east of US 180 intersection
Ancient Mogollón country spawned this
Mormon cattle town in 1860. In 1884, it
became the site of a two-day encounter between
a gang of cowboys and folk hero Elfego Baca,
"invincible" sheriff of Socorro County. The town
was originally composed of three villages—
Upper, Middle, and Lower San Francisco
Plaza—and was renamed after the US Forest
Service designated the surrounding land as a
forest reserve. Only at Lower Plaza does any-
thing remain of the old Mormon settlement.
Upper Plaza has survived as a haven for hunting, fishing, and backpacking.

LIBRARIES
Reserve Village Library
PO Box 587, 87830
505-533-6276

SAN ANTONIO

I-25, 10 miles south of Socorro
In the mid-1800s, San Antonio was the last outpost on the Camino Real before southbound
travelers entered the Jornada del Muerto.
Today, the town is known as the birthplace of
Conrad Hilton and site of the first Hilton Hotel,
located in his family's adobe house near the
train station.

HISTORIC BUILDINGS AND SITES
Carthage, Tokay, and Farley
US 380, between San Antonio and Bingham
These coal mines were in full swing from the
1880s until 1925, when they closed. Although
the mines were originally developed by the
Santa Fe Railway, they were taken over by the

COMMUNITY EVENTS
Festival of the Cranes
Bosque del Apache National Wildlife
Refuge
NM 1, 8 miles south of San Antonio
PO Box 743, 87801
505-835-0424
In celebration of the return of 20,000
sandhill cranes, 50,000 snow geese,
bald eagles, wild turkeys, the endan-
gered whooping crane, and hundreds of
other feathered species that winter over
at the refuge. Activities include tours of
the bosque, fine arts and crafts shows,
workshops, children's events, and guest
speakers. Held in November.

San Antonio Fiesta
Downtown area
505-835-0470
A feast day celebration in mid-June.

Carthage Fuel Company, primarily to fire the
Kinney brick kilns in Albuquerque. Hotelier
Conrad Hilton's father Gus owned a mine in the
area.

Fort Craig National Historic Site
I-25, 15 miles south of San Antonio
505-835-0412
Fort Craig, the largest Civil War fort in the West,
was built in 1854 to protect the Jornada del
Muerto and the Río Grande Valley, ensuring safe
travel between El Paso and Albuquerque. The
largest Civil War battle in New Mexico took
place at Valverde, a few miles north of the fort,
on February 21, 1862, when the Confederate
army of New Mexico, led by Henry Hopkins
Sibley, clashed with Union troops under the

command of Edward Canby. This battle, together with the one at Glorieta five weeks later, decisively squelched Confederate aspirations in the Southwest. ◉☐

Hilton Bar at the Owl Bar & Cafe
US 380 at Main Street

The front bar at New Mexico's favorite green-chile hamburger joint dates back to the early 1900s, when it was situated in the Hilton Mercantile Store owned by Conrad Hilton's father. When the store burned to the ground in 1945, devoted citizens of San Antonio saved the bar and moved it to its present location. ◉

SANTA RITA

NM 152, 15 miles east of Silver City

An enterprise launched here in 1804 by Don Francisco Manuel Elguea, a wealthy banker from Chihuahua, resulted in the annual mule train transport of about 6 million pounds of copper to Mexico City, where it was used in the royal mint. Subsequent periods of activity were halted by Apache opposition until the coming of the railroad in the 1880s, when Santa Rita—site of the oldest copper mine in the Southwest—became a major copper producer. ◉

MUSEUMS AND EXHIBIT SPACES

Chino Mines Company Copper Mining Museum
Santa Rita townsite, 15 miles east of Silver City
PO Box 7, Hurley, 88043
505-537-3381

Displays mining exhibits overlooking an open-pit copper mine worked first by Indians, then by Mexicans, and in the 1850s, by Anglos. Open Memorial Day through Labor Day.

HISTORIC BUILDINGS AND SITES

Kneeling Nun
3 miles south of NM 152

The most time-honored historic landmark in the Black Range country is this monolith resembling a nun kneeling in prayer before a great altar. Numerous legends have grown up around the giant stone resting near the summit of the Santa Rita Range.

SHAKESPEARE

I-10, 2 miles south of Lordsburg

After a silver strike in 1869, a townsite was laid out at the Butterfield Overland stage stop known as Mexican Springs. Renamed Ralston City—after Bank of California founder William C. Ralston—it collapsed in 1874, following a diamond swindle. The town was revived in 1879 as Shakespeare which, after a brief spell of prosperity, succumbed to the depression of 1893. As soon as the mines closed, Shakespeare, like its predecessor, became a ghost town. Now located on the Frank Hill ranch, the specter of Shakespeare is open to visitors at specified times. ◉☐

SILVER CITY

US 180, at NM 90 and NM 152

Rich mineral deposits were no secret in this 6,000-foot-high part of the state: prehistoric Mimbres Indians had used the ores for trade, Spanish copper mines were operating by 1800, and gold was discovered in 1859. Then silver was struck in a valley marsh in 1870, and within days, a townsite was laid out and newly formed Silver City was swarming with miners. Apache chiefs Victorio, Gerónimo, and Mangas Coloradas were familiar figures about town, as was young Billy the Kid, who attended school

This view of Silver City was taken from the summit of Chihuahua Hill in 1940. Photograph by Dr. Bert O. Myra, courtesy Museum of New Mexico, neg. 56367

here for a while. Large cattle ranches soon dotted the landscape, and before long, the town emerged into a shipping point for mining camps in the area. Silver City survived the boom-and-bust cycles—a permanence attributed to the type of clay used to bind its brick-and-adobe structures. The Wild West boomtown is now a classic Victorian village still dependent on commercial mining and ranching, and an active center for the retail industry and medical services.

MUSEUMS AND EXHIBIT SPACES
Gila Cliff Dwellings National Monument
NM 15, 45 miles north of Silver City
Route 11, Box 100, 88061
505-536-9461
About 700 years ago, members of the Mogollón culture built homes in this series of five natural caves tucked into a narrow canyon along the west fork of the Gila River. About 600 years ago, they vanished, leaving 42 rooms fashioned of adobe bricks and logs, painted bowls and other

art objects, tools, and obsidian arrowheads. The mysteriously disappearing weavers and potters, while living in caves 200 feet above the creek, had grown corn, beans, and squash, supplementing their diet with game and nuts. ☉☐

Francis McCray Gallery
Western New Mexico University
PO Box 680, 88062
505-538-6517
Presents changing exhibitions of contemporary regional art, student-juried work, and private collections on short-term loan. The gallery also organizes traveling exhibits and maintains a permanent collection showcasing American and Japanese printmaking.

Silver City Museum
312 West Broadway, 88061
505-538-5921
This history museum displays articles from the early-20th-century model mining town of

Tyrone, 10 miles south of Silver City; Southwest Indian artifacts; historical documents; and photographs depicting frontier Victoriana. Located in the 1881 H. B. Ailman House, the museum hosts workshops, lectures, school tours, and such special events as the New Mexico Cowboy Poetry Gathering.

Western New Mexico University Museum
Fleming Hall
PO Box 680, 88061
505-538-6386
Features the Eisele collection of 700- to 1,000-year-old Mimbres pottery and artifacts; the Harlan historic photograph collection; the largest permanent exhibit of Mimbres pottery and artifacts in the United States; the Western New Mexico University collection of photos, yearbooks, and memorabilia from 1893 to the present; mining and ranching exhibits; and Casas Grandes pottery.

HISTORIC BUILDINGS AND SITES
H. B. Ailman House
312 West Broadway
This grand old Victorian mansion was constructed in 1881. Beginning in the 1930s, it became the firehouse for the Silver City Volunteer Fire Department; a bell by the front door sounded fire alarms and tolled curfew for the city's youngsters. The Ailman house now serves as the Silver City Museum. ⊚□

Billy the Kid's Cabin Site
1 block north of Broadway Bridge
Billy the Kid spent part of his childhood here in a log cabin with his mother, brother, and stepfather William Antrim.

Billy the Kid's Jail Site
304 North Hudson
Parking lots currently cover the site of the jail in which Billy the Kid was imprisoned in 1875 for stealing from a Chinese laundry. A slender boy of 15, Billy escaped by climbing out the jail's chimney.

Billy the Kid's Mother's Grave
Memory Lane in Silver City Cemetery
Catherine McCarty, Billy's mother, came to Silver City with her second husband, William Antrim, in 1873. She died of tuberculosis in September 1874 and was buried here in the town cemetery.

Black's Addition Historic District
College, Black, and Market Streets area
The first subdivision of Silver City, featuring architectural styles ranging from Queen Anne to Territorial. This handsome, cohesive neighborhood was established between the 1870s and 1920s. ⊚

Chihuahua Hill Historic District
Copper, Spring, and Chihuahua Streets area
The small Spanish-speaking community living here in the 1870s combined Spanish and Indian building styles in their dugouts—stacking houses into a hillside by terracing. The original "Mexican Village" of Silver City. ⊚□

Silver City Historic District
Between Black and Bullard Streets and College and Spring Streets
The original townsite of Silver City, featuring prestigious Victorian homes and commercial buildings constructed of locally made red brick. ⊚□

Silver City North Addition Historic District
College Avenue area
Beautiful mansions on these wide, tree-lined
streets reflect the outstanding architecture
prevalent during the mining boom of the early
1880s. ⊚□

Western New Mexico University Historic District
Pope Street and College Avenue
Western New Mexico University, established in
the early 1900s, was one of the first territorial
institutions of higher education. The campus
features the work of prominent regional archi-
tects John Gaw Meem, Henry Trost, and Charles
Whittlesey, chief architect of the Santa Fe
Railway Company. ⊚□

PERFORMING ARTS
Expressive Arts Department
Western New Mexico University
PO Box 680, 88062
505-538-6616
Sponsors a madrigal program in November and
theater productions in April and late October to
early November.

CULTURAL ORGANIZATIONS
Mimbres Region Arts Council
PO Box 1830, 88062
505-538-2505
A multidisciplinary organization dedicated to
bringing the performing and visual arts to the
Silver City area.

Pinhole Resource
Route 15, Box 1355, San Lorenzo, 88041
505-536-9942
Collects pinhole photographs from artists
throughout the world. The group also publishes
Pinhole Journal and offers workshops.

COMMUNITY EVENTS
Frontier Days
Gough Park
800-548-9378
A Fourth of July celebration featuring
an ice cream social at the Silver City
Museum plus entertainment, food
booths, a gem and mineral show, hot-
air balloons, and arts and crafts.

Mining Days
Gough Park
505-538-3785
Old-time storefronts, mining contests,
food, entertainment, and arts and crafts
on Labor Day weekend.

**New Mexico Cowboy Poetry
Gathering**
Silver City Museum
312 West Broadway, 88061
505-538-5921
Literary entertainment celebrating cowboy history and folklore. Held in August.

San Vicente Artists of Silver City
PO Box 1911, 88062
505-538-2535
A group of area artists committed to promoting
Silver City as an art market and to supporting
arts education in the schools.

LIBRARIES
Silver City Public Library
515 West College Avenue, 88061
505-538-3672

Western New Mexico University Miller Library
PO Box 680, 88062
505-538-6350

PUBLIC ART
Big Ditch Park
Hudson and Broadway
Western New Mexico University art students
Southwest Indian motifs—mural

Grant County Courthouse
West end of Broadway
Theodore Van Soelen
"Chino Mines" and "The Round Up"—murals
New Deal Art
Greg Whipple
"Our Legacy"—oil painting

San Lorenzo Senior Center
NM 152, 21 miles east of Silver City
Dianne Anderson
"Pajaro de Fierro"—welded steel

**Western New Mexico University
Fine Arts Auditorium**
College Avenue
John Davidson
"Mousa"—cast concrete mural
Cecil Howard
"Heritage"—mural

**Western New Mexico University
McCray Art Building**
College Avenue
José Barraza
"El Bailador"—sculpture

**Western New Mexico University
Miller Library**
College Avenue
John Battenberg
"Peace Warrior"—sculpture

SOCORRO

I-25 at US 60
The area populated by Piro-speaking Pueblo Indians was first seen by the Spanish in 1581. Visited by Juan de Oñate in 1598, the Indians supplied his expedition with much needed corn and supplies, whereupon Oñate named the place Socorro (Help). Around 1615, Franciscan friars began building a mission at the settlement. The Church of Nuestra Señora de Pilabo del Socorro, completed in about 1628, was destroyed in the Pueblo Revolt of 1680, and the village itself, abandoned. Indians who fled south with the retreating Spaniards founded a new village near El Paso and called it Socorro del Sur. Not until 1816 was the original village resettled. Intense mining activity, rail transport, and the construction of a smelter for ore excavated throughout the region contributed to prosperity in Socorro.

MUSEUMS AND EXHIBIT SPACES
Hammel Museum
Neal Avenue at Sixth Street
PO Box 923, 87801
505-835-0424
Originally a beer garden in the 1880s, the building became, successively, a brewery, ice plant, soda bottling plant, and base for a still active ice-making industry. Now a history museum, the structure's authentic period rooms reflect its past.

Mineralogical Museum
Workman Center
New Mexico Institute of Mining and Technology, 87801
505-835-5420
Displays more than 12,000 mineral specimens as well as mining artifacts and historic photographs.

The museum houses one of the most complete mineral collections in the United States.

Very Large Array
US 60, 50 miles west of Socorro
PO Box O, 87801
505-772-4011
Called the National Radio Astronomy Observatory, these 27 dish-shaped antennae together form the most powerful radio telescope in the world. Using VLA, astronomers study such celestial phenomena as the sun and planets of our solar system, distant galaxies, and quasars at the edge of the universe. The facility offers a visitor center and walking tours.

HISTORIC BUILDINGS AND SITES
Atchison, Topeka & Santa Fe Railway Depot
706 Manzanares Avenue
The depot was built in 1880, upon the arrival of the railroad. The last passenger run through Socorro was in 1968. ◎

Chihuahua Historic District
Nicholas Avenue
Established in the 1880s, this district is composed of adobes with mud plaster walls and pitched roofs. ◎

East Abeytia Avenue Historic District
A late-19th-century area noted for its bungalow-style houses. ◎

Espejo's Expedition on the Camino Real
I-25, 25 miles south of Socorro
Part of the route taken between 1582 and 1583 by Antonio de Espejo's party as they paralleled the Río Grande north to the Bernalillo area. Their purpose was to learn the fate of two Franciscan friars who had stayed with the Pueblo Indians after the Rodríguez-Sánchez Chamuscado expedition had returned to Mexico in 1581.

Snow geese take flight at Bosque del Apache National Wildlife Refuge, 18 miles south of Socorro near the village of San Antonio.
Photograph by Mark Nohl

Juan Nepomuceño García Opera House
Abeyta Avenue at California Street
The long, pitched-roof adobe was constructed
in 1886 to provide facilities for traveling
operatic troupes, which offered entertainment
in boomtowns across the West. Neo-Greek
architecture of this sort flourished in
Midwestern towns before finding its way to
the frontier. ◉▢

Kittrel Park (formerly Socorro Plaza)
The center of old Socorro—dating back to
1816. Socorro Plaza was an important stopping
place on the Chihuahua Trail as well as a significant outpost for Spanish and Mexican authorities during the Civil War. ◉

Mesa del Contadero
I-25, 25 miles south of Socorro
A large volcanic mesa on the Chihuahua Trail,
marking the northern end of the Jornada del
Muerto (Journey of the Dead Man). The
Contadero (Counting Place) was a narrow path-
way through which people and animals had to
pass one by one.

Old San Miguel Mission
403 El Camino Real
505-835-1620
This mission church, built in 1821 on the
foundations of the early-17th-century mission,
has five-foot-thick walls, carved beams, corbels, two-tiered bell towers, and red trim. The
south wall of the structure was part of the
original 1628 mission; the remainder was
reconstructed after the resettlement of
Socorro. A new wing was added in 1853.
Artifacts from the mission are on display in the
nearby church office, open during business
hours. ◉

Val Verde Hotel
203 Manzanares Street
One of the few remaining Spanish Mission-style
structures designed by Henry Trost, student of
Frank Lloyd Wright. The *Albuquerque Morning
Journal* said of the hotel, when it was built in
1919, "From the standpoint of beauty and con-
venience, it stands without a peer." The Val
Verde is now a restaurant. ◉▢

Valverde Battlefield
I-25, south of Socorro
The first major battle of the Civil War on New
Mexico soil occurred here in February 1862,
when a Confederate force of Texas volunteers
under General H. H. Sibley defeated Colonel E. R.
S. Canby's Union forces stationed at Fort Craig.
Following his victory, Sibley marched north and
was defeated at Glorieta Pass near Santa Fe.

CULTURAL ORGANIZATIONS
Socorro County Historical Society
PO Box 923, 87801
505-825-5242
Owns and operates the Hammel Museum.

LIBRARIES
**New Mexico Institute of Mining and
Technology Library**
Campus Station, 87801
505-835-5615

Socorro Public Library
401 Park Street, 87801
505-835-1114

PUBLIC ART
Main Avenue Median
Holly Hughes
"Bike and Crane"—sculpture

COMMUNITY EVENTS

Enchanted Skies Star Party
New Mexico Institute of Mining and
Technology
PO Box 743, 87801
505-835-0424
A gathering of amateur astronomers
from around the nation. Held in late
September or early October.

Oktoberfest
Hammel Museum
Neal Avenue and Sixth Street
505-835-0424
Arts and crafts, German food, beer, and
music in early October.

San Miguel Fiesta
Old San Miguel Mission
505-835-0424
Arts and crafts, food booths, and outdoor dances on Saturday, followed by a
fiesta mass and procession on Sunday.
Held in early August.

State Science Fair
New Mexico Institute of Mining and
Technology
505-835-5678
A statewide junior high and high school
science competition held in April.

**New Mexico Institute of Mining and
Technology Library**
Donna Deckard and *Patrick Phillips*
"Crystal Zia" and "Woven Glass"—stained glass
Holly Hughes
"The Miner's Friend"—sculpture
Evelyn Rosenberg
"In the Beginning Was the Word"—sculpture

Eugenie Shonnard
"Desert Maiden"—stone carving

Quemado
US 60, 140 miles west of Socorro
Walter DeMaria
"The Lightning Field"—steel sculpture

Very Large Array
NM 60, 50 miles west of Socorro
Jon Barlow Hudson
"Shiva/Shiwana"—stainless steel

STEINS

I-10, 17 miles west of Lordsburg
Steins (pronounced steens) was founded in
1858, when the Butterfield Overland Mail
Company built a stage station at the point where
the Butterfield Trail crossed the Peloncillo
Mountains. Steins Peak Station it was called—
after US Dragoon major Enoch Stein, who had
died while defending the stop from hostile
Indians. Steins served east- and westbound
wagon trains for decades before its 1888 conversion to a stop on the Southern Pacific
Railroad. The rail stop became turf to Black
Jack Ketchum and his gang who, in December
1897, killed a trainman in a failed attempt at
robbery. The busy railroad station boasted
1,000 residents during its peak of prosperity,
from 1905 until 1945; then it faded into a ghost
town. Restoration of Steins began in 1977.

HISTORIC BUILDINGS AND SITES
Doubtful Canyon
I-10, 3 miles east of the Arizona border
The site of frequent Apache massacres in the
1850s.

TRUTH OR CONSEQUENCES

I-25 at NM 51
In 1581, Captain Francisco Sánchez Chamuscado took possession of this region of New
Mexico for the King of Spain, and named it the
Province of San Felipe. Significant European
settlement, however, did not occur until the
mid-1800s, when the town came to be known
as Hot Springs because of the curative mineral
water bubbling up from underground. People
from nearby mining communities flocked to
town to drink and bathe in the healing waters.
Truth or Consequences—often called T or C—
took its present name from Ralph Edwards's
1950 radio program.

MUSEUMS AND EXHIBIT SPACES
Callahan's Auto Museum
410 Cedar Street, 87901
505-894-6900
Features vintage automobiles from the 1920s
through the 1960s, including Steve McQueen's
1951 Chrysler convertible and Governor
Meechan's 1950 Chrysler limosine. Toys, maps,
and books are also on display.

Gerónimo Springs Museum
211 Main Street, 87901
505-894-6600
A history museum with local artifacts,
Mimbres pottery and other Indian relics, a
Ralph Edwards Room, a historic log cabin, a
mineral and rock collection, and fine art
exhibits. Fee.

HISTORIC BUILDINGS AND SITES
Elephant Butte Dam
NM 51, 5 miles east of Truth or Consequences
At the time of its completion in 1916, Elephant

COMMUNITY EVENTS
Gerónimo Days Peace Gathering
211 Main Street, 87901
505-894-6600
A multicultural event with music and storytellers, games and rides, Apache spirit
dancers, arts and crafts, living history
and films, food, and a street dance on
the second weekend in October. Fee.

**Old-Time Fiddlers' State
Championship**
Convention Center
505-894-2847
A statewide competition held in mid-
October.

Truth or Consequences Fiesta
Downtown area
PO Box 249, 87901
505-894-3536
An international fiddlers' contest,
dances, sports tournaments, a carnival,
special museum exhibits, and other
activities. Held the first weekend in May.

Butte Dam's 600,000 yards of concrete formed
the largest irrigation reservoir in the world.
Ever since, the dam has provided a dependable
water supply for irrigation along the Río
Grande. ☉☐

CULTURAL ORGANIZATIONS
Sierra County Historical Society
211 Main Street, 87901
505-894-6600
Operates the Gerónimo Springs Museum.

An abandoned school house evokes bygone days in Winston. Photograph by Mark Nohl

LIBRARIES
Truth or Consequences Public Library
325 Library Lane, 87901
505-894-3027

PUBLIC ART
Truth or Consequences Post Office
400 Main Street
Boris Deutsch
"Indian Bear Dance"—mural
New Deal Art

Veterans Center
992 South Broadway
Ernesto Martínez
Acrylic painting
Eugenie Shonnard
"Children's Fountain"—stone

WINSTON

NM 52, 38 miles northwest of Truth or Consequences
Originally called Fairview, the town was estab-lished in 1881, during the peak of the silver boom. The following year marked the arrival of Frank Winston—miner and owner of a mercantile store, a cattle company, and by 1915, a garage. Horseraces and literary society theatrical productions turned the community into a cultural, event-filled oasis on the frontier. When the silver failed, Winston attempted to keep the town alive on his credit, whereupon the villagers changed its name to honor him. Soon afterward, his credit, too, ran out, and the town toppled.

COMMUNITY EVENTS
Winston Spring and Fall Fiestas
505-894-3536
Old-fashioned country festivals with games, food, and entertainment in mid-April and mid-September.

JANUARY

NORTHWESTERN NEW MEXICO
Laguna Pueblo—New Year's Day Celebration, Three Kings Day

NORTH-CENTRAL NEW MEXICO
Nambé Pueblo—Three Kings Day; **Picurís Pueblo**—New Year's Day Celebration, Three Kings Day; **San Ildefonso Pueblo**—New Year's Day Celebration, San Ildefonso Pueblo Feast Day, Three Kings Day; **San Juan Pueblo**—Three Kings Day; **Santa Clara Pueblo**—Three Kings Day; **Taos Pueblo**—New Year's Day Celebration, Three Kings Day; **Tesuque Pueblo**—Three Kings Day

CENTRAL NEW MEXICO
Cochití Pueblo—New Year's Day Celebration, Three Kings Day; **Jémez Pueblo**—New Year's Day Celebration, Three Kings Day; **San Felipe Pueblo**—Three Kings Day; **Santa Ana Pueblo**—New Year's Day Celebration, Three Kings Day; **Santo Domingo Pueblo**—New Year's Day Celebration, Three Kings Day; **Zia Pueblo**—Three Kings Day

The Most Elegantly Dressed Duck contest adds a touch of fowl finery to the festivities at Deming's Great American Duck Race. Photograph by Mark Nohl

FEBRUARY

NORTHWESTERN NEW MEXICO
Acoma Pueblo—Governor's Feast Day; **Chama**—Chama Winter Carnival; **Jicarilla Apache Reservation**—Jicarilla Apache Day; **Picurís Pueblo**—Candlemas Day

NORTH-CENTRAL NEW MEXICO
Red River—Mardi Gras in the Mountains

CENTRAL NEW MEXICO
San Felipe Pueblo—Candlemas Day

MARCH

NORTHWESTERN NEW MEXICO
Laguna Pueblo—San José Feast Day

NORTH-CENTRAL NEW MEXICO
Nambé Pueblo—Easter Celebration; **Picurís Pueblo**—Easter Celebration; **Red River**—Mardi Gras in the Mountains; **San Ildefonso Pueblo**—Easter Celebration

CENTRAL NEW MEXICO
Cochití Pueblo—Easter Celebration; **San Felipe Pueblo**—Easter Celebration; **Santa Ana Pueblo**—Easter Celebration; **Santo Domingo Pueblo**—Easter Celebration;

Tomé—Easter Procession; **Zia Pueblo**—
Easter Celebration

SOUTHEASTERN NEW MEXICO
Melrose—Easter Pageant; **Portales**—Cultural
Kaleidoscope

SOUTHWESTERN NEW MEXICO
Deming—Rockhound Roundup

APRIL

NORTHWESTERN NEW MEXICO
Farmington—San Juan College Apple Blossom
Festival; **Gallup**—Square Dance Fest-i-gal

NORTHEASTERN NEW MEXICO
Clayton—Dinosaur Days

CENTRAL NEW MEXICO
Albuquerque—American Indian Week,
Founder's Day Weekend, Gathering of Nations
Powwow

SOUTHEASTERN NEW MEXICO
Portales—Cultural Kaleidoscope, Heritage
Days; **Roswell**—Roswell Artfaire

SOUTHWESTERN NEW MEXICO
Las Cruces—Arte Picante Feria, New Mexico
State University Jazz Festival; **Socorro**—State
Science Fair; **Winston**—Winston Spring Fiesta

MAY

NORTHWESTERN NEW MEXICO
Acoma Pueblo—Santa María Feast Day;

Farmington—Farmington International
Balloon Festival, Riverfest

NORTH-CENTRAL NEW MEXICO
Angel Fire—Memorial Day Activities; **Los
Alamos**—Los Alamos Arts and Crafts Fair;
Madrid—Madrid Blues Festival; **Santa Fe**—Civil
War Weekend at El Rancho de las Golondrinas,
Santa Fe Powwow, Taste of Santa Fe; **Taos**—Meet
the Artist Series, Taos Spring Arts Celebration;
Taos Pueblo—Santa Cruz Feast Day; **Tesuque
Pueblo**—Blessing of the Fields

NORTHEASTERN NEW MEXICO
Santa Rosa—Santa Rosa Days; **Watrous**—
Living History Portrayal of Frontier Garrison Life

CENTRAL NEW MEXICO
Albuquerque—Arts in the Park, Fiesta
Artistica: Gathering of Native American Art,
Magnífico! Albuquerque Festival of the Arts,
Mother's Day Concert at the Río Grande Zoo,
Visions of Excellence; **Cochití Pueblo**—Santa
Cruz Feast Day; **Corrales**—San Ysidro Fiesta;
Rio Rancho—Springfest; **San Felipe
Pueblo**—San Felipe Pueblo Feast Day

SOUTHEASTERN NEW MEXICO
Alamogordo—Saturday in the Park;
Carlsbad—Mescal Roast; **Cloudcroft**—
Mayfair; **Clovis**—Cinco de Mayo Fiesta;
Hobbs—Cinco de Mayo Celebration;
Tularosa—St. Francis de Paula Fiesta,
Tularosa Rose Festival

SOUTHWESTERN NEW MEXICO
Deming—Fiddlers' Contest; **Truth or
Consequences**—Truth or Consequences
Fiesta

JUNE

NORTHWESTERN NEW MEXICO

Acoma Pueblo—San Juan Feast Day; San Pedro and San Pablo Feast Days; **Aztec**—Aztec Fiesta Days; **Farmington**—Anasazi: The Ancient Ones Pageant, Farmington Trade Days/SummerFun Showcase; **Laguna Pueblo**—San Juan Feast Day, San Pedro and San Pablo Feast Days; **Zuni Pueblo**—Zuni Rain Dance

NORTH-CENTRAL NEW MEXICO

San Ildefonso Pueblo—San Antonio Feast Day; **San Juan Pueblo**—San Juan Pueblo Feast Day; **Santa Clara Pueblo**—San Antonio Feast Day; **Santa Fe**—Santa Fe Chamber Music Festival, Santa Fe Summerscene, Spring Festival at El Rancho de las Golondrinas; **Taos**—Meet the Artist Series, Taos Poetry Circus, Taos School of Music Summer Chamber Music Festival; **Taos Pueblo**—San Antonio Feast Day; San Juan Feast Day

NORTHEASTERN NEW MEXICO

Las Vegas—Las Vegas Rails 'n' Trails Days; **Ratón**—Santa Fe Trail Rendezvous; **Tucumcari**—Billy the Kid Pageant, Piñata Festival, Tucumcari Arts and Crafts Fair; **Watrous**—Living History Portrayal of Frontier Garrison Life

CENTRAL NEW MEXICO

Albuquerque—Arts in the Park, June Music Festival of Albuquerque, New Mexico Arts and Crafts Fair: Summer Festival of the Arts, San Felipe de Neri Fiesta, Summerfest; **Belén**—Río Valley Festival; **Sandía Pueblo**—Sandía Pueblo Feast Day; **Santa Ana Pueblo**—San

Juan Feast Day, San Pedro and San Pablo Feast Days; **Santo Domingo Pueblo**—San Juan Feast Day, San Pedro and San Pablo Feast Days

SOUTHEASTERN NEW MEXICO

Alamogordo—Flight Fest; **Clovis**—Pioneer Days; **Dexter**—New Mexico Dairy Day; **Fort Sumner**—Old Fort Days Celebration; **High Rolls**—Cherry Festival; **Hobbs**—June Teenth Celebration

SOUTHWESTERN NEW MEXICO

Deming—Deming Arts and Crafts Fair; **San Antonio**—San Antonio Fiesta

JULY

NORTHWESTERN NEW MEXICO

Acoma Pueblo—Arts and Crafts Festivities, Santiago Feast Day; **Bloomfield**—Bloomfield Days Celebration; **Farmington**—Anasazi: The Ancient Ones Pageant, Farmington Freedom Days; **Laguna Pueblo**—Santa Ana Feast Day, Santiago Feast Day

NORTH-CENTRAL NEW MEXICO

Angel Fire—Balloons over Angel Fire; **Eagle Nest**—High Country Arts Festival; **Española**—Oñate Fiesta; **Jicarilla Apache Reservation**—Little Beaver Roundup; **Los Ojos**—Fiesta de Santiago; **Nambé Pueblo**—Nambé Pueblo Waterfall Ceremony; **Picurís Pueblo**—High Country Arts and Crafts Festival; **San Ildefonso Pueblo**—Eight Northern Indian Pueblos Artist and Craftsman Show; **Santa Fe**—Contemporary Spanish Market, Santa Fe Chamber Music Festival, Santa Fe Summerscene, Santa Fe Wine Festival at El Rancho de las Golondrinas, Traditional Spanish

A gazebo is the centerpiece of Mesilla's historic plaza. Photograph by Mark Nohl

Market; **Taos**—Taos School of Music Summer Chamber Music Festival; **Taos Pueblo**—Santa Ana Feast Day, Santiago Feast Day, Taos Pueblo Feast Powwow

NORTHEASTERN NEW MEXICO
Clayton—Clayton Independence Day Celebration; **Folsom**—Folsom July Jam; **Las Vegas**—July Fiesta, Southwest Culture Festival; **Tucumcari**—Billy the Kid Pageant, Mesa Redondo Cowboy Camp Meeting; **Watrous**—Living History Portrayal of Frontier Garrison Life

CENTRAL NEW MEXICO
Albuquerque—Arts in the Park, Native American Arts and Crafts Fair, Summerfest; **Cochití Pueblo**—Cochití Pueblo Feast Day; **Santa Ana Pueblo**—Santa Ana Pueblo Feast Day; **Santo Domingo Pueblo**—Santiago Feast Day

SOUTHEASTERN NEW MEXICO
Capitán—Smokey Bear Stampede; **Carlsbad**—Carlsbad Western Week Celebration; **Cloudcroft**—July Jamboree; **Clovis**—Clovis Music Festival; **Eunice**—Old-Time Fiddlers' Contest; **Fort Sumner**—Billy

the Kid–Pat Garrett Historical Days; **Mescalero Apache Reservation**—Coming of Age Ceremonial; **Roswell**—Festival in the Park; **Texico**—Border Town Days

SOUTHWESTERN NEW MEXICO
Deming—Arts in the Park; **Magdalena**—Magdalena Old-Timers' Reunion; **Silver City**—Frontier Days

AUGUST

NORTHWESTERN NEW MEXICO
Acoma Pueblo—San Lorenzo Feast Day; **Farmington**—Anasazi: The Ancient Ones Pageant, San Juan County Fair; **Gallup**—Inter-Tribal Indian Ceremonial; **Laguna Pueblo**—Feast Day at Mesita, San Lorenzo Feast Day

NORTH-CENTRAL NEW MEXICO
Angel Fire—Music from Angel Fire; **Chama**—Chama Days; **Picurís**—San Lorenzo Feast Day; **Santa Clara Pueblo**—Santa Clara Pueblo Feast Day; **Santa Fe**—Mountain Man Rendezvous and Buffalo Roast, Santa Fe Chamber Music Festival, Santa Fe Indian Market, Santa Fe Summerscene, Summer Festival & Frontier Market at El Rancho de las Golondrinas; **Taos**—Taos School of Music Summer Chamber Music Festival

NORTHEASTERN NEW MEXICO
Cleveland—Cleveland Roller Millfest; **Las Vegas**—People's Fair and Places with a Past; **Ratón**—Ratón International Arts Show and Crafts Fair; **Santa Rosa**—La Fiesta de Santa Rosa de Lima; **Tucumcari**—Billy the Kid Pageant; **Watrous**—Living History Portrayal of Frontier Garrison Life

CENTRAL NEW MEXICO
Albuquerque—Arts in the Park, East Mountain Rendezvous, Summerfest; **Belén**—Our Lady of Belén Fiesta; **Bernalillo**—Fiesta de San Lorenzo; **Isleta Pueblo**—San Agustine Celebration; **Jémez Pueblo**—Old Pecos Bull Dance; **Santo Domingo Pueblo**—Santo Domingo Pueblo Feast Day; **Zia Pueblo**—Zia Pueblo Feast Day

SOUTHEASTERN NEW MEXICO
Carlsbad—Bat Flight Breakfast; **Hobbs**—Hobbs Arts and Crafts Festival; **Lincoln**—Lincoln County Fair, Old Lincoln Days; **Melrose**—Melrose Old-Timers' Days

SOUTHWESTERN NEW MEXICO
Deming—Great American Duck Race; **Silver City**—New Mexico Cowboy Poetry Gathering; **Socorro**—San Miguel Fiesta

SEPTEMBER

NORTHWESTERN NEW MEXICO
Acoma Pueblo—San Estévan Feast Day; **Aztec**—Aztec Founders' Day; **Farmington**—Native American Days, Totah Festival; **Laguna Pueblo**—Feast Day at Encinal, Feast Day at Paguate; **Zuni Pueblo**—Zuni Fair

NORTH-CENTRAL NEW MEXICO
Angel Fire—Labor Day in the Pines, Music from Angel Fire; **Jicarilla Apache Reservation**—Gojiiya Feast Day; **Red River**—Aspencade Celebration; **Santa Fe**—La Fiesta de Santa Fe; **Taos**—Old Taos Trade Fair, Taos Fall Arts Festival; **Taos Pueblo**—Taos Pueblo Feast Day; **Tierra Amarilla**—Fiesta de Santa Niño

NORTHEASTERN NEW MEXICO
Cimarrón—Cimarrón Days; **Watrous**—Living History Portrayal of Frontier Garrison Life

CENTRAL NEW MEXICO
Albuquerque—Arts in the Park, New Mexico State Fair, Río Grande Arts and Crafts Festival; **Bernalillo**—New Mexico Wine & Vine Festival; **Isleta Pueblo**—Isleta Pueblo Feast Day; **Santa Domingo Pueblo**—Santo Domingo Pueblo Indian Arts and Crafts Market

SOUTHEASTERN NEW MEXICO
Alamogordo—Cottonwood Festival, International Space Hall of Fame Induction; **Carlsbad**—September 16th Celebration; **Hobbs**—Hobbs Hoedown Days, Staked Plains Roundup; **Roswell**—Piñatafest

SOUTHWESTERN NEW MEXICO
Hatch—Hatch Chile Festival; **Hillsboro**—Hillsboro Apple Festival; **Las Cruces**—Southern New Mexico State Fair; **Silver City**—Mining Days; **Winston**—Winston Fall Fiesta

OCTOBER

NORTHWESTERN NEW MEXICO
Gallup—Gallup Film Festival; **Laguna Pueblo**—Feast Day at Paraje; **Shiprock**—Northern Navajo Fair

NORTH-CENTRAL NEW MEXICO
Angel Fire—Angel Fire Artsfest; **Española**—Española Valley Arts Festival; **Los Alamos**—Early Christmas Arts and Crafts Fair; **Nambé Pueblo**—Nambé Pueblo Feast Day; **Santa Fe**—Harvest Festival at El Rancho de las Golondrinas; **Taos**—Meet the Artist Series,

Taos Fall Arts Festival, Taos Mountain Balloon Rally, Taste of Taos, Wool Festival

NORTHEASTERN NEW MEXICO
Clayton—Clayton Arts Festival; **Santa Rosa**—Billy the Kid Fiesta

CENTRAL NEW MEXICO
Albuquerque—Albuquerque International Balloon Fiesta, Grecian Festival, Weekend Indian Dances and Craft Demonstrations; **Corrales**—Harvest Festival

SOUTHEASTERN NEW MEXICO
Artesia—Art in the Park; **Cloudcroft**—Cloudcroft Oktoberfest; **High Rolls**—Apple Festival; **Hobbs**—Llano Estacado Party and Cowboy Hall of Fame Induction; **Portales**—Peanut Valley Festival; **Roswell**—Eastern New Mexico State Fair; **Ruidoso**—Aspenfest, Lincoln County Cowboy Symposium, Oktoberfest

SOUTHWESTERN NEW MEXICO
Deming—Klobase Festival, Southwestern New Mexico State Fair; **Las Cruces**—Whole Enchilada Fiesta; **Magdalena**—Alamo Indian Day; **Socorro**—Enchanted Skies Star Party, Oktoberfest; **Truth or Consequences**—Gerónimo Days Peace Gathering, Old-Time Fiddlers' State Championship

NOVEMBER

NORTHWESTERN NEW MEXICO
Farmington—Holiday Arts and Crafts Fair

NORTH-CENTRAL NEW MEXICO
Dixon—Open Studio Tours; **Los Alamos**—Los Alamos Arts and Crafts Fair; **Taos**—Meet

the Artist Series; **Tesuque Pueblo**—Tesuque Pueblo Feast Day

CENTRAL NEW MEXICO
Albuquerque—Indian National Finals Rodeo, Southwest Arts and Crafts Festival, Weems Artfest; **Jémez Pueblo**—Jémez Pueblo Feast Day

SOUTHEASTERN NEW MEXICO
Clovis—Clovis Arts and Crafts Show; **Lovington**—Southeastern New Mexico Arts and Crafts Festival; **Ruidoso**—Christmas Jubilee

SOUTHWESTERN NEW MEXICO
Las Cruces—Renaissance Craftfaire; **San Antonio**—Festival of the Cranes

DECEMBER

NORTHWESTERN NEW MEXICO
Acoma Pueblo—Acoma Pueblo Christmas Festivals; **Aztec**—Festival de los Farolitos; **Gallup**—Winter Market; **Zuni Pueblo**—Shalako Ceremony and Dance

NORTH-CENTRAL NEW MEXICO
Madrid—Christmas in Madrid; **Nambé Pueblo**—Dances to Commemorate the Christmas Season; **Picurís Pueblo**—Dances to Commemorate the Christmas Season; **Pojoaque Pueblo**—Our Lady of Guadalupe

Feast Day; **San Ildefonso Pueblo**—Dances to Commemorate the Christmas Season; **San Juan Pueblo**—Dances to Commemorate the Christmas Season; **Santa Clara Pueblo**—Holy Innocents Day; **Santa Fe**—Christmas at the Palace, Guadalupe Feast Day at the Santuario, Las Posadas, Santa Fe Community College Arts and Crafts Show, Winter Market; **Taos**—Meet the Artist Series, Yuletide in Taos; **Taos Pueblo**—Dances to Commemorate the Christmas Season; **Tesuque Pueblo**—Dances to Commemorate the Christmas Season

NORTHEASTERN NEW MEXICO
Tucumcari—C.R.A.F.T. Fair

CENTRAL NEW MEXICO
Albuquerque—Las Posadas de Barelas; **Cochití Pueblo**—Dances to Commemorate the Christmas Season; **Isleta Pueblo**—Dances to Commemorate the Christmas Season; **Jémez Pueblo**—Dances to Commemorate the Christmas Season, Our Lady of Guadalupe Feast Day; **Santa Ana Pueblo**—Dances to Commemorate the Christmas Season; **Santo Domingo Pueblo**—Dances to Commemorate the Christmas Season; **Zia Pueblo**—Dances to Commemorate the Christmas Season

SOUTHEASTERN NEW MEXICO
Cloudcroft—Christmas in Cloudcroft

SOUTHWESTERN NEW MEXICO
Las Cruces—Our Lady of Guadalupe Festival

INDEX